LONDON TO LOWESWATER

LONDON
TO
LOWESWATER

A journey through England
at the end of the
TWENTIETH
CENTURY

HUNTER DAVIES

MAINSTREAM
PUBLISHING

EDINBURGH AND LONDON

First published in Great Britain in 1999 by
MAINSTREAM PUBLISHING COMPANY (EDINBURGH) LTD
7 Albany Street
Edinburgh EH1 3UG

ISBN 1 84018 205 9

A catalogue record for this book is available from the British Library

Typeset in Bembo
Printed and bound in Great Britain by Butler & Tanner Ltd, Frome

For my sister, Annabelle,
who loves both

CONTENTS

Chapter One

LONDON

I was about to leave London when the invitation came from Number Ten. New Labour, New Excitement. When we get to Loweswater, this sort of excitement will not happen. There will be shows and displays up there in Cumbria, people in their best, doing their best, and other people looking at them, but on a humbler, gentler, more modest scale.

One of the things both Londoners and non-Londoners like to believe is that London is full of famous people. You can spot them in the street, observe them in shops and restaurants. It does happen surprisingly often, even if their fame rests on little more than reading the weather forecast. London has them. It's where they live. Not much chance of seeing them in Main Street, Cockermouth.

The embossed invitations came with our names in beautiful calligraphy, including my first Christian name, 'Edward' which I hate and never use. I think the last time was during a health inspection at primary school. There was also a note saying you must not bring a camera or mobile phone to Downing Street and you should carry identification, such as a passport. I'm not doing that, I said. My Visa card will have to do, but my wife dutifully took her passport.

They still have big security gates at the entrance to Downing Street, one of Mrs Thatcher's many legacies to the nation. Three policemen were on duty. None of them asked for our identification, just our admission cards.

Once through the front door of Number Ten you are into a wide hall which leads down a wide corridor. The women in charge of the coats were jolly and cockney, calling everyone 'love' or 'darlin''. Down a far corridor I spotted John Prescott carrying a bundle of papers, walking very fast and chewing, as if to say, 'Oh, I am far too busy to be going to cocktail parties.'

I joined a long queue of other guests, winding its way slowly up a staircase. My wife was behind me, talking to her old Cumbrian chum Melvyn Bragg, who of course gets invited everywhere. I found myself standing beside Mick Hucknall of Simply Red. As we chatted, going up the stairs, I examined the photographs of past Prime Ministers which line the staircase. One of my collections is of Prime Ministers. I have all their autographs, back to Walpole. At the top of the staircase was a blank – no photograph of John Major. A deliberate snub? Oh no, said an attendant. They were waiting for a suitable photograph. Each one has to be black and white and a certain shape.

We progressed slowly into a large reception room. Tony and Cherie Blair were standing in the middle, greeting each guest personally. Names were given to an official and announced in turn. We had our two-minute chat, during which Cherie talked to my wife about her novels, naming one she had just finished. She appeared to have read it, or had at least done her homework.

We then moved into a larger reception room, holding about 200 guests, where I recognised some recognisable faces: Lord Callaghan, Ben Elton, Richard Branson, Harry Enfield. My wife spotted Cindy from *EastEnders*, so she said, and I believed her.

What surprised me was the wide range of people from a variety of professions. I had thought it might be dominated by luvvies, Labour-loving supporters from the arts, but they were in the minority. I noticed a bishop, a QC, the editor of the *Guardian*, Jimmy Knapp, the trade union leader, and the rabbi Lionel Blue. I talked for some time to Sir George Martin and his wife, whom I had last met in Montserrat, where they had a house and recording studio, before all the disasters. My wife talked to Helene Heyman, the life peeress, who happens to be one of our neighbours. The tallest person in the room, with the most people around him, was Greg Rusedski, the tennis player. In John Major's day, so someone told me, you got a lot of cricketers.

I enjoyed it, of course, enjoyed the experience, but no more than I enjoy all shows and displays. But it made me look forward all the more to Cumbria. At the Loweswater Show, we have the added attraction of animals.

* * *

For the last few years we have divided our life equally between our home in London and our home in Loweswater, at the far distant corner of England, tucked away in one of Lakeland's most beautiful valleys.

Each time we are ready to move north we can't wait, counting the days, eager to be there, and once we arrive we feel instantly and totally settled, as if we had never left, as if this is our true home. Each time we move back south, it seems to hang over us. London looms rather than beckons. And once we get there, it takes weeks to be settled. I feel disorientated, out of step, as if I no longer belong.

When a man is tired of London, he is tired of London. That's all Dr Johnson should really have said. It's London life that eventually tires, not life itself. Life goes on, everywhere, and most people today consider that it goes on better, cleaner, healthier and generally much nicer outside of London than inside.

At one time, 30 years or so ago, when provincials sneered at London – which, of course, they have always done, making nasty remarks about the Smoke, how can you stand it, is it true you don't know any of your neighbours? – Londoners would smile, indulgent, totally unfazed, knowing that, deep down, it was being said out of jealousy, out of a feeling of inferiority. All Londoners believed this, in their smug, self-satisfied way, convinced they were the heart of the matter. After all, did not London swing? *Time* magazine had said so. Everyone else was on the fringes, stuck in the sticks, poor things. Today, Londoners are the first to run themselves down, wondering how much longer they can stand it.

Greater London's population used to be around ten million. Now it's down to six million. Depends how you hold the measuring tape, of course – boundaries have moved, definitions changed – but there is no doubt that Londoners have been fleeing London. Being relocated by their firms and businesses, or just grabbing their bags, taking the loot from their inflated house and scarpering.

In 1996, a study produced by the Economic and Social Research Council revealed that 628,000 people had left London between the 1991 census and 1994. Throughout the 1980s there had been a steady decline, but this indicated an avalanche, an urban retreat which is being mirrored in all our great urban centres. During those four years, 220,000 left Birmingham, 120,000 left Manchester, 115,000 left Merseyside.

Where have they all gone? Not to the suburbs. The suburbs were once longed for by all white-collared, city-working Mr Pooters, where they could have their own bit of lawn and a pleasant journey to their place of work. Commuting is now purgatory, expensive and unreliable. The new, younger generation consider the suburbs as places for the dead.

The retreat has been towards the countryside, to small towns and villages, near real open spaces, real green fields, where one is able to commune with nature, not commuters. People have gone back to where we all began, to our rural roots, our sylvan past, from whence we had to flee or were transported once that nasty horrid Industrial Revolution had got under way and transformed us into urbanites.

The only group not moving in large numbers from the urban centres, so that 1996 report noticed, was the 16–29-year-olds. The young, employed or otherwise, still love the city, if only as an escape from the confines of small-time communities or small-minded families. Once they are over 30, the pattern immediately changes. Those aged 30–44 show a particularly marked desire to get away. The self-employed, so we are told, can do it easily these days if they are part of the electric village, or hamlet, if not very soon just one computerised, internetted little box. This exodus also includes the retired, whose ranks grow all the time with recruits coming from those still in their forties, hardly out of nappies.

The flow was completely the other way when I was a lad. I couldn't wait to come to London, longed for it, dreamt about it. My first ambition in life had been not to live in Carlisle. My next ambition had been to live in London. I managed it, aged 23, when in 1959 I came to London and joined a paper called the *Sunday Graphic*. The following year, the year I got married, I joined the *Sunday Times*. Oh, bliss it was to be young and alive and in Fleet Street. Okay then, Gray's Inn Road, but near enough.

The first smells, sights, sounds and accents seemed so different, so foreign. Sitting on a London bus, sitting in a London pub, I would literally breathe it in, my eyes closed, knowing I could be nowhere else except London.

I didn't mind the London smog, for that was part of London, what we provincials all knew about, had read about since Dickens. There were evenings in the winter, driving home from Gray's Inn Road to Kentish Town in my Mini, brand new, cost only £500, when I would get completely lost, finding myself driving onto pavements, into gates, with no idea where I was. The smog was so thick, such a deep grey-yellowy snot-like substance, that it was impossible to breathe through, far less see through. At its worst, you could have whole days without daylight, the streetlights on all day – and a fat lot of good they did. I tell my three children this, all Londoners born and bred, and they have no idea what I'm talking about.

It's one of the minor miracles of my life and times in London. We are now smokeless and smogless. The Thames has also been cleaned up; fish are swimming in its waters, salmon can be seen a'leaping from the House of Commons, so they say, which I don't personally believe. Must ask Tony, if I ever see him again.

But as for other forms of pollution, there has not been the hint of any miracle, no trace of any improvement. We are being choked to death by traffic, which we have caused ourselves, by our own laziness, by our own wealth, ruining our health and our lives, creating more poisons, more constant dangers, than were ever caused by the dreaded smog.

I gave up travelling on the Northern Line ten years ago. One of my ambitions in life is never to travel on a tube again. I use the bus, if it's wet, but normally I walk, which is often quicker. I can get to Broadcasting House in 55 minutes, cutting across the edge of Hampstead Heath, through Primrose Hill and Regents Park. By bus, on the C2, if it's anywhere near rush hour I have to allow at least an hour. I do still have a car, but a car in London is now a nonsense. You can't park in your own street. You are stationary for most of your journey. You can't park when you get there.

When I arrived in London 40 years ago, gents and the better sort of foremen and craftsmen walked down the street wearing bowler hats, all buses and telephone booths came in one colour, which was red, taxis were black, national newspapers were produced in Fleet Street, chirpy cockney newspaper vendors shouted out the latest editions of London's three evening papers, the *News*, the *Star* and the *Standard*, and in every pub stood a mysterious jar on the bar, left over from the war, filled with ancient pickled eggs. In my lunch hours, I ate greasy British food in greasy caffs with lots of HP sauce. On Saturdays I queued for hours to get into White Hart Lane, where crowds of 60,000, as at all of London's main football grounds, stood to watch, guarding their pockets in case anyone peed into them. There were no adverts in the ground, or in the programme, and at half-time scores were fixed manually onto boards. Real men drank hot Bovril; rattles were still being rattled by kids in school caps wearing National Health specs. Just look at all the photos, if you don't believe me. In central London, fruit and veg were sold in Covent Garden. Fish was bought in Billingsgate. In Hampstead High Street there was a little old-fashioned shop called Gazes where for one and sixpence you could buy a reel of cotton, a ball of wool and a packet of Woodbines.

Okay, I made up that last bit. Gazes didn't sell fags. But I clearly remember all the rest, culled at random from the back of my brain. The black cab is the only thing left. Though even that can come in other colours, with nasty, sick-making patterns, but on the whole the London taxi is still roughly the same shape, the same colour, the same design. You can't say that about the buses or the telephone boxes. You now need sunglasses to identify any of them. Fleet Street has gone, along with the old Covent Garden and Billingsgate. We all now sit at football matches, pay ten times as much, watching players earning a hundred times as much. Electronic wizardry tells us the scores, shows us replays of what we have seen, but mainly tries to sell us stuff we don't want. At half-time, real men have smoked salmon bagels.

Eating and drinking, in pubs and restaurants, has been perhaps the most welcome change in the last 40 years. You could, in 1960, eat Italian or Indian, but you'd have to make a special expedition to Soho. Now, such restaurants are in every High Street. In ordinary homes everywhere it is now commonplace to have Chinese or Thai takeaways, heat up a frozen pizza, eat naan bread or pitta bread and consider pasta, in all its forms, as part of the staple British diet. In 1960, spaghetti still came in tins, often in hoops, and any raw, uncooked pasta was looked upon as terribly exotic. In the normal working-class home, wine was never seen, except for a bottle of VP sweet wine at Christmas. Rice only came in one form, as pudding.

These changes in our eating and drinking habits might have started first in London, but they soon spread. Even Carlisle has outdoor French-style caffs selling cappuccino and fancy foreign breads. You can buy aubergine in Cockermouth, something I'd never heard of as a boy. Mushrooms were funny and exotic enough.

Going back to Cumberland in the early 1960s, with my first wages, wanting to drive out into the Lake District, show off and treat the folks, there was nowhere to do it. The hotels had ancient waiters in ancient shining evening suits, the dining-rooms smelled of boiled cabbage and if you were later than 1.30, hard cheese, the boiled cabbage was over.

London no longer has the monopoly on the good life, the exotic food, the fancy lifestyles. In fact, it's hard to think of anything good where London has the monopoly, except perhaps a spurious sense of excitement, a feeling of self-importance and a chance to ogle some famous faces. I don't expect in Loweswater to see much of Richard Branson or Ben Elton.

What London now has is a monopoly on the drawbacks of modern life, the grime and the crime, the overcrowding and the pollution, the stresses and the strains. No wonder they are all leaving. Jonathan Dimbleby, in something called the Country Life Centenary Debate, predicted that by the year 2097 we will all have moved to the countryside, leaving the cities behind. I think he's being conservative. If you consider the figure for those who have recently left London, which works out at around 200,000 a year, then London could be totally empty as early as the year 2030. I might come back then. It will be brilliant for parking.

It won't, of course. The future rarely does what present figures suggest it will. The future goes its own way, making twists and turns, going into reverse or entering new avenues we had never thought of, making a nonsense of most Orwellian predictions.

But sitting here now, in the middle of urban London, just four miles from Piccadilly, unable to get my car out into our street, knowing my lungs will be choked if I walk even a hundred yards down Kentish Town High Road, I do wonder how much longer I can stand it. Do the excitements make up for the aggravations? Is it worth hanging on, just in case Tony and Cherie invite us back and I can kid myself I am near the seat of power? What in fact we did discuss was football.

Last night, while we were in our beds, a burglar came through the window in my office, which is on the first floor, walked past our bedroom door, which was open but we were asleep, went down the stairs and proceeded to remove the television and video and various other items of our modern life, such as my credit cards. Yes, it can happen anywhere, but it's never happened in 20 years in our Lakeland homes, touch wood, whereas this is now our fourth burglary in London over the same period. What a drag having to ring round and cancel the credit cards and order new ones. What a bore having to find a locksmith, because in London these days you can never get any workman to do anything. And what a cheek that bloody burglar had – or 'youth', as the Kentish Town policewoman immediately suspected. They don't miss a thing. He calmly walked out of the front door with our gear, taking all of our keys and leaving the front door open all night. Anyone could have got in.

★ ★ ★

So tomorrow I am off out of London, taking it slowly, progressing roughly due north at first, up towards the Great North Road, then left hand down, aiming across for Lancashire and the north-west, then up again to Lakeland. A traditional route, one which many travellers and writers have taken, starting off from London, exploring England and themselves. Writers and travellers do like to think they can take the pulse, get a feeling of the nation, report on what's happening out there. Celia Fiennes did it in 1697. So did Daniel Defoe in 1724 and J.B.

15

Priestley in 1933. The dates of their travels were not in themselves significant, though the social conditions were. We happen to be at the end of a millennium, perhaps the end of my London life. A timely time just to see, just to observe, what's going on out there. A journey through England, and through my life.

Chapter Two

TRING

J.B. Priestley was living in The Grove, Highgate, just up the hill from me, when he set off on his 1933 journey through England. I drove past the front door of his old house, one of the most desirable in all London, a Georgian gem with a stunning garden looking over Hampstead Heath, worth around £2 million. Sting lives in that row today, in the house where Yehudi Menuhin used to live. I didn't spot him at the window, but I gave him a wave.

I'd better mention that Sting is a singing person of our times, dead famous, just in case no one can remember him in years to come, or even in hours to come. Priestley didn't name any of the persons he waved at, caught sight of or even talked to on his journey, not even old friends he stayed with or commercial travellers he met in provincial hotels along the way. He met a lot of them. England seemed to be awash with travelling reps and salesmen in those days, eating warm cabbage and drinking warm beer. I suspect a great many of their thoughts he recorded, overheard at the bar late at night, were his own thoughts.

In his first chapter he boasts about going by public coach, giving him a chance to meet real people and travel cheaply and effortlessly. 'I doubt if even the most expensive private motor – those gigantic, three-thousand-pound machines – are as determinedly and ruthlessly comfortable as these new motor coaches.' Three thousand pounds for a car? What sort of person paid such prices in 1933?

Priestley made his first forays to Southampton and to Bristol, returning to London each time. Nothing wrong with that. I propose to do much the same, taking a year over the whole journey, splitting it into stages. But once he's done his early trips to the West Country and has begun heading north, he lets slip that he is no longer taking coaches. In fact, he is in his own car, with his own chauffeur. He doesn't reveal how

17

much the car cost him, but admits it is a Daimler. This comes out when he decides to pop into the Daimler factory in Coventry. He obviously feels a bit guilty about the chauffeur, but manages to explain it away: 'I used to drive myself, but have given it up these last few years, not because I think myself too important to change my own gears but simply because I am a very bad driver.'

For my trips, I often did go by car. But just as often I took the train and then walked. When I drove, I was in my, er, okay, I'll admit it, I was in my Jaguar. Oh, come on, a very old one, *circa* 1993. I bought it third-hand in 1997 for only £10,000. I've gone through life hating cars, hating driving, but I woke up one day in 1997 and thought, hmm, I'd like to have had a Jaguar in my life. Then I thought, in order to have had one, I'll need to buy one soon, so I found one through an advert in the *Evening Standard*. And I love it, just as Priestley loved his Daimler. I'm sure he would be interested to know that Daimlers and Jaguars are still going strong, but they are no longer British-owned, having been taken over by Ford. Naturally, I drove it myself. Automatic, of course, so no need to change any of those annoying gears.

Once through Highgate, round a bit of the North Circular, I went straight up the M1, as I wanted to be away from London as soon as possible and into the Home Counties.

Home Counties? I used that phrase without thinking because we all know where the Home Counties are, Herts and Bucks and that lot. We accept that it really means London's Home Counties, though we don't have to say so. Yet hasn't Manchester got any home counties, or Newcastle, or Glasgow? Just a few miles out of London and I am already feeling not of London, objecting to London's assumption that England, life and the universe means London.

I drove on till I caught the first hint of hills, which means the Chilterns, turned off and stopped at the first place which sounded vaguely interesting and, more importantly, I'd never been to before. That was going to be one of the elements of my journey, taking the chance to see places I'd never seen, as well as those I hadn't seen for many years. Thus I arrived in downtown Tring.

I also liked the name. Tring tring, I said to myself as I drove in. I am easily amused. They like the ring of the name as well. On a notice in the main car park, the Tring and District Chamber of Commerce had a poster which announced THINK TRING.

I studied another notice about opening times in the public lavatory because I always need to find the lavatory in any new place. The notice was headed 'Dacorum Borough Council'. Yet I thought I was in Tring.

Must be a newly made-up name, the sort new councils in the 1980s created for themselves during all that reorganisation, ignoring or killing off names we had been familiar with for centuries. I find it hard to remember that Loweswater is now in an authority called Allerdale, or that Bristol is in Avon. At least it was. I think. Allerdale and Avon are geographical names. Dacorum sounded fictional. Or could it be a joke name, so that you think it reads 'Decorum', part of a THINK TRING campaign dreamt up by some whiz kid in the council's marketing department?

An old battered Escort came into the car park with a large poster stuck on the side window. I couldn't make out the words, so I went over to examine it. In new places, as with new people, your eyes are on the lookout for mannerisms and messages, signs and symbols. Tring's public body language might provide clues to the private worlds beneath. Unlikely, of course. The public face of every town is much the same, now we have the same cars, same clothes, same shops, same displays.

'IT'S A NICE DAY — NOW WATCH SOME BASTARD COME ALONG AND SPOIL IT!'

It was a printed notice, stuck on a rearside window. Someone somewhere must be turning them out, probably supplying them to motorway service stations, where they are bought by young blokes to put in their cars when they go to football matches. Out of the Escort stepped an old man, which was a surprise. 'I like your notice,' I said, 'in your car window.' I didn't have to say that as he knew exactly what I meant. Strangers must say it to him all the time. It is his identity. Everyone knows him. He is the man with the stupid bloody poster in his car window.

'And it's true,' he grunted. 'They try to do it all the time. Now out of the way . . .'

Near the car park, I could see what was obviously the parish church, large and imposing, made of flint and stone, impressive enough to be a small abbey, set back behind a large grassy space. Unusual, I thought, for a church in the middle of a town to have such a large garden. All was explained inside. The church of St Peter and St Paul used to have another building in front but this had been demolished in 1901. The open bit in front they call Church Square. I would have called it a Green.

There was an old man sitting inside the main door, doing nothing, just sitting, putting in the day, so I said hello, being a friendly soul, and then wandered round the church. Very nice, as churches go. Back at the entrance I noticed a cardboard box which said 'Supermarket Receipts', picked up the box, shook it, and it was empty. Why would a church want supermarket bills? To destroy symbols of Mammon? I asked the old man if he could explain.

'Yeeeesss,' he said. 'Just a few minutes afore you come in, I was a-thinking that myself . . .'

Well, then, what conclusion did you come to?

'Hmm, I can't work it out either.'

Are you here every day?

'Where?'

Here, sitting dozing, I mean, sitting here in the church.

'Oh, us takes turns. I get relieved in an hour. There's always someone on duty, when the church is open. You won't believe what can disappear. Last month, some furniture was taken out. Never seen again! In broad daylight! Shocking. I don't know what the world is coming to . . .'

I was going to tell him about our burglary, share the experience, but I think he was dozing off again.

Tring High Street was most attractive, cobbled pavements, olde worlde shops, handsome buildings, attractive frontages. I particularly admired the National Westminster Bank and, next door, the Midland, both early nineteenth-century buildings, presumably lived in at one time by notable Tringian merchants. Tringly? Or Tringy? I bet there's a prettily drawn Tring town trail, little numbers done in a nice hand, neat notes written by a retired schoolteacher, with references to Jane Austen or Dickens, who allegedly based characters on allegedly real merchants who lived in Tring, at number 21 or, other records suggest, 29; no visitor to Tring should miss the Tudor Inn where Queen Victoria once stayed, and tradition has it that the Russian Czar also slept there, though not at the same time.

On the way into Tring I had noticed a muddy building site which announced TESCO IS COMING, a battle cry of our times, notifying another victory for the giants and a terrible defeat for the little people – which is what conservationists usually maintain, but in Tring High Street there was no evidence of any malls or chain stores. The modern world had been kept at bay, so far.

Walking down the right-hand side, I counted three estate agents, almost next to each other, a sure sign of local affluence. I wrote down their names: Brown and Merry, Cole Flatt, Cesare Nash. Which would I choose to sell my house? Mr Merry could be too jolly. Mr Cesare might prove too tough. Selling a flat, I'd obviously ask for Mr Flatt. Har har. I bet someone goes in every day and makes that remark.

Now why did I presume there would be a Mr Jolly and a Mr Flatt? Sexist thinking. I would not expect local solicitors or local doctors to be all men, not today. In fact, I would expect them to be mainly women. Yet in my mind, estate agents are still men. True or false? I'll never get to Loweswater at this rate.

I noticed a charity shop and that immediately focused my mind. I never miss them, though in every street, in every town, they are always the same – same smell, same clothes, same books, same pointless objects and run by the same middle-aged, lower-middle-classish women. One is always bossy and self-important. But for the way life has panned out, she could have been very big in shops, possibly Anita Roddick, even Laura Ashley. She is very keen on labels and displays, forever rearranging pointless piles of tat which no one is ever going to buy. The other is quiet and distracted, looks vaguely artistic, or possibly might be about to fall asleep. Often they take it in turns, but on this occasion both were on duty. Mrs Bossy was calling everyone My Dear, very loudly, and rushing round talking to herself, even more loudly, wondering where to display the tickets for some piffling raffle.

Mrs Sleepy was attending to an enormous woman who was struggling to try on a torn plastic mac, but not attending to her very well. In fact, she appeared to have dozed off while still standing. Mrs Bossy caught sight of her and poked her in the ribs, commanding her to go and arrange the jewellery on the counter while she would attend to Madam. It was a designer plastic mac, actually, they'd just got it in, and Madam looked wonderful in it; lots of people had admired it for a long time, er, since we'd just got it in, Madam.

I was studying the second-hand books. I always hope a charity shop might have interesting books on the local area, but they never have. Real second-hand book shops must grab them first, or local people must hang on to them. Instead you always get national, not local, junk, whether you search in Cornwall or Cromarty. Jeffrey Archer in hardback, Mills and Boon or Doctors and Nurses in paperback. The non-fiction is always pre-war or encyclopaedias on gardening, health or popular science, the sort the *Daily Express* did as special offers.

I also look out for pop music books and annuals, which they often have, hoping for something from the '60s containing bits on the Beatles, or any pre-1950s football annuals. Anything pre-war on football is now impossible to find. Not a sausage. So I glanced at the gents' jackets, out of academic interest. I have enough clothes to get me through life. After that, I won't need any. I haven't bought a new jacket for, oh, it must be ten years now, ever since my sister in Leighton Buzzard, who is a world expert on charity shops, bought me a rather natty cream one, practically new, for £2.

As I left the shop, Mrs Bossy had turned on Mrs Sleepy for being so silly. The jewellery, all of it clearly made of nasty plastic, was not, repeat not, to go on top of the counter but underneath it, inside the glass cabinet. 'We've had enough stuff pinched this week already. No need to cause temptation.'

I stood outside a hardware shop called Grace which boasted 'Established Over 200 Years'. All the best hardware shops are ancient. We have one in Cockermouth which is probably prehistoric, judging by the displays – which, of course, you can hardly see unless the oil lamps are on. Hardware stores do seem to stand still while chemists, food shops, clothes shops and newsagents are forever changing their style and frontage. Desperate to be modern, yet only ever succeeding in looking cheap and tawdry. Is this because hardware stores don't come in chains but tend to be owned by the same family for generations?

Inside it was rather disappointing. It didn't feel at all old, and I wondered if I might complain under the Trade Descriptions Act. I asked a woman behind the counter how old it really was. She thought 1890, this particular shop, but they had been elsewhere in the town for over 100 years before that. And is Mr Grace still with us? 'Oh yes. He used to race motor cars in the 1950s with Stirling Moss.' She pulled out some wooden drawers, stacked high to the ceiling, made out of First World War gun carriages, so she said. More proof of ancientness.

'We used to do our own tinning,' she said.

You mean tin cans?

'No, screws and nails, that sort of thing. Come out the back and you'll see the old pump which we used for our water. And if you like I'll call Mr George. He'll give you the whole history. Oh, he knows so much about the Graces . . .'

She was picking up the phone, so I said, er, no thanks, regretting I'd doubted their ancient history. Another time, perhaps. I've got a lot to do, such as, well, wandering around.

I wandered into a café called Tringfellows and ordered a cappuccino. Good joke, I said to the waitress, it must bring in a lot of customers. She stared at me as if I was barmy. Perhaps she was from the Far North, such as Milton Keynes. Tring is in London commuter country, so many locals will have heard of Stringfellows night club. It would be totally meaningless in Loweswater.

At the table beside me were two elderly women and a very thin man. The man ate his lunch in total silence, while the two women talked loudly all the way through about where to put their new fridge freezer. After 30 minutes I was practically screaming, wanting to tell them to stick it in the bloody garden, when two girls came in and took the table on my other side. They were well dressed, confident, middle class. probably sixth-formers from a local school. They spoke in whispers, with lots of giggles, but as I left I heard one say to the other, 'My problem is that I'm crap at stealing.'

Stealing, in cosy, comfy Tring? Should I warn Mrs Bossy?

Out in the street again I noticed a sign saying 'Zoological Museum', pointing up a side street. Can't say I'm interested in animals, stuffed or otherwise, but it was a very nice sign, prettily lettered, so I followed it down Akeman Street and came to what appeared from the front to be an ordinary house. There was a little kiosk saying 'Entry £2.50', which seemed a bit steep, especially if it turned out to be a couple of scraggy squirrels in a glass cage. 'And here's a sticker for you,' said the woman on the till. 'You can come and go all day long if you like.'

She'll be lucky. Ten minutes is usually enough for me, even in a London museum – but it proved to be astonishing. The size, for a start. There were endless galleries, leading on and on, and yes, they were filled with stuffed animals of every conceivable species, from massive elephants to tiny insects, all so well displayed, so clean, so warm. I could easily have spent a good part of the day there. Well, at least two hours.

It took me straight back to my childhood in Carlisle, going round Tullie House, our local museum, the sort of museum you never see today. At the time I found the stuffed birds and animals dank and depressing. As schoolchildren, on school visits, you were not allowed to touch anything or even talk, so we dragged ourselves through, bored stiff.

Tullie House is now a modern museum, touchy and feely, with state-of-the-art displays full of sounds and furies, exciting visual and oral displays, very good compared with some of the flashier museums I have been to recently. The worst fear for any modern museum curator is that any child or human being might be bored. So they do away with all the glass cases, all the dusty objects, and install games and flashing lights. The object is show, not content; entertainment rather than enlightenment.

But this was how it used to be, when genuinely interesting stuff – which, okay, I wasn't interested in at the time – was simply plonked down or crammed into cabinets, and it was up to you to do the inspecting, not for the objects to jump out and hit you over the head. So I found myself bending down to gaze in amazement at a long showcase full of stuffed dogs, over 80 of them, all in one case. A modern curator would have chucked out 79, and had a spotlight on one dog, with stereo barking, disco music, computer screens.

They were each identified, which was jolly useful. I've always wanted to tell one breed of dog from another. Football teams I can manage, and motor cars at a pinch, but stuff like birds, plants and trees, they all come in one type to me. With dogs, I might manage to spot a Dalmatian, and I can recognise a sheepdog when we are in Lakeland, but that's about it. Otherwise they are big or small, brown or not so brown. I did try to get clued up on birds once. I bought a *Bird Watching for Beginners* book and sat studying it in our garden in Loweswater. But the birds in the pictures never looked like those in real life. And they wouldn't sit still. Here I had 80 dead dogs, which were not going anywhere, all clearly labelled. No excuses now.

A party of schoolchildren arrived, all of them equally impressed. They rushed up and down, spotting the different dogs, ticking them off in their worksheets. An attendant was keeping a watchful eye on them, so I congratulated him on the exhibition, saying how surprised I was by the whole museum. It is the biggest in the whole country, he said proudly. The biggest? Yet I'd never heard of it.

It has 4,000 exhibits, so he explained, and was established by Walter Rothschild, who had handed it over to the nation when he died in 1937. Officially, they're part of the Natural History Museum in South Kensington, but they operate on their own, as a separate branch. 'Untouched, unadded to since 1937,' he said.

I can see that, I said. 'Yes, South Ken is not a museum any more,' he continued. 'They've been to Disneyland. We haven't. It's now a fairground, not a museum. That, of course, is my personal opinion, sir . . .'

He then corrected himself on his use of the words 'unadded to'. In the case of the dogs, he said, pointing to the case of the dogs, they are added to in that they get prize exhibits passed on to them from Crufts. After, of course, they have died, sir.

'That's Ballyregan Bob, a champion greyhound, who came here in 1995, or it might have been 1994. I'll just check . . .'

He was about to pick up a phone from the wall but I said no, don't bother. So, was the museum doing well, then, bringing in lots of punters?

This time he'd picked up the phone before I could stop him. I suppose in a totally traditional museum, with no modern gimmicks, no audio-visual amusements for the public, the attendants don't have a lot of fun either, hence they have to take any chance they can for diversion, even if it's only a bit of dialling on the internal phone.

'Visitor input per annum, could you elucidate?'

I wondered if he'd done his MBA or was still struggling with his

Open University degree. Clearly a mature student of the higher sort.

The answer was 60,000, for which I thanked him kindly. 'Used to be better. A couple of years ago it was 70,000. Now on a wet Sunday afternoon, you find local families take their kids to run up and down the Harlequin Shopping Centre in Watford, instead of coming here. But we still do very well. There's nowhere else to go in Tring, as you have probably noticed, sir . . .'

On the way back to the High Street, I passed a little Tourist Information shop which I hadn't noticed earlier, which, of course, I should have visited first, if I had known it existed, if I had done some proper advance research, which I will for my next stop. Tring was an attempt at just wandering round. Trial by Tring.

I asked the young woman running the tourist centre what it was like, living in Tring. 'Very good,' she said. What's good about it? She turned to an older woman and asked her opinion.

'No traffic lights,' said the woman. 'And free parking in the car park.'

'It is a nice community,' said the tourist woman, remembering her duty to trill for Tring. 'There are families and companies going back hundreds of years. The two big events are the Victorian Fiesta, when the High Street is closed and everyone wears Victorian clothes, or is supposed to, and the Canal Festival. You should come for both of those. They're very good.'

The older woman had a slightly rural accent whereas the younger woman seemed standard south of England. I hadn't actually noticed any accents while walking around.

'There is a Tring accent,' said the older woman. 'It's a definite Herts accent. If one passes the window, I'll call them in.'

'But we're not in Herts,' said the younger woman.

'Oh yes we are,' said the older.

'Technically we are in Bucks,' insisted the younger one.

'No we're not . . .'

I left them arguing about where they were, what they are, who they are, all too philosophical for me, and came out with a bundle of tourist literature.

I now know that Tring is a pretty big place with a population of some 11,000, that Dacorum is its Roman name, that the whole area should really be called Rothschildshire.

In the 1720s Daniel Defoe came to Tring, which he said was where the River Thames rose, so his geography was not all that reliable, but he reported how even then the local rich were building themselves fine homes. He told the story of a certain Mr Guy who had built himself 'a most delicious house, built *à la moderne*, as the French call it', but only after a lot of trouble with the locals. They had objected to him roping in common land and had torn up his fences and burned his timber, till he had to change the plans for his house. 'I mention this as an instance of the popular claim in England which we call right of commonage, which the poor take to be as much their property as a rich man's land is his own.'

The first Rothschilds came to England from Frankfurt in the early nineteenth century, quickly becoming rich bankers, powerful and famous, part of the English establishment, buying or building for themselves huge mansions all over the Home Counties – handy for London, not Manchester, of course. Across Herts and Bucks and Beds, these Rothschild establishments still exist, even if the Rothschild family members do not live in them.

The zoo, as that knowledgeable attendant told me, was the creation of Walter Rothschild, who was brought up in Tring Park and inherited the title Lord Rothschild in 1923. He refused to be a banker, much preferring insects and animals. As a child in Tring, he had his own museum, and when he went up to Cambridge, he took with him a flock of kiwis. He also had a collection of four million butterflies and moths.

Tring Park, their local stately home, is now a school, and most of the other Rothschild manors have also changed their uses or ownership, such as the ones at Ascot, Aston Clinton, Haltom, Waddesdon and Mentmore. Mentmore – now that struck a bell. Something funny happened at Mentmore. Now what was it . . .

Chapter Three

MENTMORE

In the summer of 1967 I caught a train from Euston to Bangor in North Wales, along with the Beatles, Mick Jagger and assorted friends and relations. I was working on the authorised biography of the Beatles and had been told the night before by Paul's brother that there was going to be some sort of happening which I shouldn't miss. Happening. I haven't used that noun for years.

In my compartment were Paul and John, Mick Jagger and Marianne Faithfull, all in their flower-power, multi-coloured, flowing, clothes. Throughout the journey I watched John and Mick carefully, to see how they would relate. At the time, the world was divided into Stones fans and Beatles fans. John and Mick hardly talked to each other, but seemed friendly enough. Afterwards, I asked John if he had felt in any way jealous at the arrival and success of the Stones. Not about the music, he said. Just their image. From the beginning, the Stones had been seen as threatening, rebels and rowdies, whereas the Beatles in their early years had been seen as nice and charming, put into neat suits by Brian Epstein. John had always hated that, so he said. He wished he could have stayed scruffy, and dangerous, like the Stones. I said it was thanks to the Beatles paving the way that the Stones had been allowed to be themselves.

The object of this mysterious train ride was to meet someone called Maharishi. I wanted to mock and scoff when I first heard about him and what he was doing, but the Beatles, normally so cynical and realistic, seemed to be taking him seriously.

In Bangor, we were shown into the presence of this funny-looking little Indian gentleman and each Beatle was given a mantra to recite when doing their meditations, all part of something called transcendental meditation. I suspected Maharishi was a publicity seeker, who had somehow been able to influence young multi-millionaires with some exotic spiritual codswallop, but I remember being impressed by the TM adherents themselves, the ones who were organising this weekend in Bangor. They did seem so sensible, intelligent, gentle, middle class, not at all mad or fanatical. Perhaps there was something in it.

The Beatles eventually gave up on Maharishi, without actually rubbishing him, and George at least remains very interested in Indian spiritualism, but the world at large in Britain came to look upon Maharishi as something of a joke figure, left over from the '60s. I thought his movement had petered out in Britain, apart from occasional satirical mentions of his followers levitating. Until I knocked at the door of Mentmore.

Mentmore is an enormous country house about 12 miles north of Aylesbury, so grand and stately it looks like a set from *Brideshead Revisited*. Kempt and well-cared for, with sweeping lawns and mani-cured gravel. Yet close up it seemed lifeless and dead. Had I got the right house? There had been no sign at the main gates saying either TM or Mentmore Towers.

Mentmore was once at the heart of Rothschildshire, the first of their grand estates, created by Baron Rothschild in 1855. The architect was Sir Joseph Paxton, formerly gardener at Chatsworth, a working-class boy who went on to be the architect of the Crystal Palace. I've often thought he was worth a biography, but every publisher I've mentioned it to has moaned and groaned. Doing George Stephenson, a friend and contemporary of Paxton, was hard enough. Keats or Shelley or Byron, you can do them on the hour, but horny-handed Victorians of an industrial bent who actually changed the nature of our lives, they don't appeal as much to the Eng Lit mafia who control publishing and the nation's literary pages.

Into the Rothschild family in 1878 came a young Scottish aristocrat, Archibald Primrose, 5th Earl of Rosebery. He had ambitions in politics and on the racecourse but not much money – until he married Hannah Rothschild, aged 26, mistress of Mentmore and the richest heiress in England. A smart move. At Mentmore, his wife entertained all the Victorian greats from Britain and Europe. Rosebery went on to become Prime Minister and to win the Derby three times.

By 1974, the Rosebery fortunes and power had declined somewhat. The latest Earl preferred to be based at the family's Scottish home, Dalmeny House, deciding to get rid of Mentmore to pay death duties. He offered it all to the government of the day in lieu of a sum said to be around £3 million. The government refused it. There was then a sale of contents only, organised by Sotheby's in May 1977, described as the sale of the century, there being so many precious paintings and furniture acquired by the Rothschilds and Roseberys over the centuries. It raised £6 million, thus showing how silly the government had been. That left the house. Which no one appeared to want, considering it too grand and too expensive to run. It had been empty for almost two years when the Maharishi Foundation came along in 1978. They got it for only £242,000, in theory a bargain for all those rooms, all that grandeur, but it was in need of several million pounds to renovate it.

I could see that money had been spent, but not on a bell or even a door knob. I shouted and banged on the massive front door, but succeeded only in hurting my knuckles, not in raising any human beings. They couldn't all be levitating.

An old Ford drew up behind me and an elderly woman got out, carrying a vacuum cleaner. She pressed some buttons, which I hadn't noticed, entering some secret code, the door opened and I followed her through. I went up some steps into a massive Grand Hall, more like an indoor courtyard, the height of the house, with arcades and balconies stretching above my head. At the top I could see an elaborate glass ceiling. Paxton did love glass.

In front of me was an enormous fireplace, the size of a house, and a carpet the size of a football pitch. Masses of carved cornices, alabaster and marble, ornate gilt work, fine panelling – but no furniture or paintings. Leading off the Grand Hall I could see equally ornate reception rooms, all with fancy finery – and all of them empty. No people, no things, like last year in Marienbad. Where was everybody?

I could hear the woman I'd followed in hoovering in a far room. I waited till she'd stopped and asked if there was a reception desk, some sort of office. I had spoken on the phone to a Mr Warburton, who had said he would see me at 2.30 p.m.

'Oh, if he said that, he'll turn up. They're very punctual, the people here. Just you wait, dear. Now I must get on.'

A gentleman did eventually appear, Mike Toomey, who said he was 'in charge of events'. Was I an event, or was he waiting for one? It didn't seem a place where events happened much, not since the Roseberys had left. He offered to show me the house until Mr Warburton was ready.

As we walked around, he explained that his job was to attract events, things like business meetings and conferences. They'd had an antiques fair at Easter, that's always very popular, and a fireworks concert. Then there's the film and TV people. Oh, Mentmore has been used in many films. The dining-room was used for an important scene in Terry

Gilliam's film *Brazil* and the house appeared in an episode of *Inspector Morse* as the setting for a rave party. Rave? Doesn't sound very TM. Mr Toomey smiled gently. They needed money for restoration and the upkeep of the house. It costs £150,000 a year just to heat it. So money had to be raised in any way they could. Well, almost any.

Every room and corridor we walked down was empty, yet he said there were 50 TM people living and working in the house. They must all be crouching, or hiding. In the kitchens we did come across one young man, head down, cleaning up. Mr Toomey opened some bedroom doors, revealing some bedroom suites, all empty. In the Napoleon Suite had once slept Napoleon III. Tsar Nicholas had once used the Russian Suite.

Mr Toomey said he had worked for TM for about 20 years, since leaving Newcastle University. He was a scientist by training and had worked in various TM laboratories, doing experiments. I didn't know TM had such things but he said they were very active in many branches of science and medicine, anything really to do with good health.

I asked about levitating. Could that really be true? He explained that its proper name is yogic flying. And, really, it's just sort of hopping or jumping in the air. Sounds fun, I said. 'More than fun,' replied Mike. 'There is a feeling of elation and bliss, a great increase in coherence. And the more people who do it, the better for them and for peace in the world.'

How does it help world peace, Mike?

'It just does. We did an experiment in Washington, DC, with teams of people doing yogic flying. During that time, crime in Washington fell by 24 per cent. I think it was 24 per cent. Anyway, it was an impressive number . . .'

I tried to look impressed, staring out of the window, over their 83 acres. Out there, said Mike, are buried three winners of the Derby, all owned by Lord Rosebery, with plaques to identify them – Blue Peter, Macaronic and Ocean Swell. Now that was impressive, remembering their names.

We walked through yet another empty room and came to a fireplace which he said was known as the Rubens fireplace. 'It came from Rubens' house in Amsterdam. Well, that's the story. I'm not sure if it's true.'

Suddenly he opened a dark door and led me into what he said was the library. It happened so quickly that I had to refocus my eyes. For the first time on the tour of the house we had come across human beings, presumably of the TM variety. There were four desks, close together, and people talking on phones or staring at screens, working very hard.

Goodness, what a lot of energy and concentration. Could this be the heart of TM in Britain, from whence their various enterprises are run? And what exactly are their current enterprises?

Ah, Peter Warburton would be the person to tell me that. He was sorry to have kept me. When he eventually appeared, he was equally pleasant and calm, clean and composed, quietly spoken, earnest and sincere, without appearing either dopey or fanatical. He had gone to Cambridge, picked up TM along the way and had become a TM teacher, moving around the globe, from India to the UK, working for the Maharishi.

The master himself was last here in 1982, but in the UK there are now some 200,000 people who have been on a TM course. That doesn't mean to say they are TM members. He explained they don't have members in the sense of a club or party, just people from all walks of life, all religions, who have studied TM at some time, such as William Hague, leader of the Tory Party. How do you know that, I asked.

'He learned TM at the age of sixteen. When he was at Oxford, as President of the Union, he invited me to come and give a lecture on TM, which I did. This was in 1979. I can give you cuttings on Mr Hague which confirm his interest in TM . . .' And he did, which will teach me not to be sceptical, plus a massive pile of literature and booklets and charts about the wonders of TM.

In the world as a whole, there are now four million TM people. So much for them having disappeared. In the UK, he said, they have a university and a political party. A university? How could I have missed it? I don't remember it on any UCCA lists my children got when they were doing A levels. Oh, it's real and official, he said, with their own vice-chancellor. They are authorised to give London University degrees in management and technology. So far, hmm, they only had six or so students.

And the political party? That's called the Natural Law Party. I had heard of them, but somehow missed the connection with Maharishi. Peter is the deputy leader. They first stood in the 1992 general election, putting up 310 candidates. In 1997 they had 195 candidates and received 30,000 votes. The party is active in 54 different countries with the aim of reviving the natural laws of the universe based on Vedic principles which cover architecture, health, the environment. Almost everything, really, according to the pamphlets. I couldn't quite work out all the scientific and ancient charts, but the main message was pretty clear: follow these paths, these wisdoms, and you will have health, happiness and good fortune.

At present, so he said, there are about a hundred people in the UK working for TM full time. Around 50 are based at Mentmore, plus another 50 around the country. Then there were several thousand working part time.

I said I was surprised to hear there were 50 working here. I'd only seen about ten people at most.

'Oh, they are here, but we hope to be moving soon. Mentmore is on the market.'

Why is that?

'Because it's too small. It's grade one listed, so we couldn't turn it into a university. We would need to divide up rooms, which we are not allowed to do. It looks very big, but there are only 50 rooms.

'We are looking to buy a new open site of some 300 acres where we will build a university for 1,000 students, plus a housing estate and an industrial estate, We already have a small complex at Skelmersdale in Lancashire with around 400 people.'

I said I'd be going through Lancashire on my journey, though I wasn't sure where Skelmersdale was. 'I'll give you a map. Do pop in. It will give you an idea of what we are aiming at.

'At our new site, TM people will live there, in the houses, but they will also bring their own businesses, their own factories or workshops. We have already been promised the money and have an eye on a place in the Midlands. It will happen. It doesn't necessarily depend on selling Mentmore . . .'

That was in the hands of Savills, the estate agents, and had been for some time, though he would not give me exact dates. Initially there had been talk of £15 million. People had flown in by helicopter from Japan and Hong Kong, interested in it for either personal or commercial purposes. But nothing had happened.

On paper, it might appear to have been a good investment – from a quarter of a million to £15 million in just 20 years. But they might only get half of that in the end, and the repairs and running costs have been enormous. Why on earth had Maharishi wanted it in the first place?

'The idea was to have a showplace, somewhere well known, where people could be entertained, where we could hold conferences in nice surroundings. It has been useful, but now, well, it's not useful enough. We will be sad to go. I have enjoyed living here.'

Did he live here alone, or with his wife and family – if, of course, he had any? No, he was single. So was Mike. There had been a TM programme to attract single men, and also one for single women. They had both been on these programmes at one time. Which, of course, had been a wonderful experience.

He then started talking about the even more wonderful experience of yogic flying, how it was a pure integration of mind and body. I found myself becoming glazed again, my attention drawn by the wallpaper. I am at fault, of course. When people become sincere and serious about their beliefs, I become embarrassed, and then confused. How can such highly intelligent, awfully nice people be so consumed by such things? 'It's a bubbling bliss,' I could hear him saying as my eyes traced a particularly fascinating pattern on the walls. 'The mind and the body is energised. You really should try . . .'

I bid him farewell, thanking him for his time, and, as I left, I found myself suddenly becoming desperate for the bubbling bliss of a strong drink. Now, which way is the nearest pub?

There is a small hamlet called Mentmore just outside the front gates, with a small square of houses, and, yes, it has a pub. It was now lunch time, so I'd have myself a meal as well. I parked outside and went up to the front door. It was locked. I tried other doors. All locked. I looked through a bar window and could see a television on, so I banged on the window. Eventually a man came and said they were closed. Oh no. Why hadn't I stayed in London? You don't get pubs closed at lunch time in London.

I could try the pub in the next village, he said, just a mile away. So I drove like mad to the Hare and Hounds in Ledburn, which looked equally dead and empty from the outside, but inside all was jolly and noisy, with groups of salesman-types sitting at large tables. Where had they come from? Ledburn seemed a village on the edge of nowhere. But I was more interested in grabbing the menu. I chose a toasted cheese and ham sandwich on ciabatta bread – very nice – and a glass of Beamish, which was new to me but also nice. Then I looked round the pub, which was large and open plan. It too was nice.

On a wall, I noticed some framed newspaper front pages. I love any collections and, of course, newspapers, so I went across to read them. They were all from 1963. A great year for news; I remember it well. There was the Philby affair, the Christine Keeler–Profumo scandal and Macmillan's resignation. I didn't actually cover any of those big stories. In 1963 I was the boy assistant on the Atticus column of the *Sunday Times*. People elsewhere in the room, the heavies from Insight who slept overnight at their desks and didn't shave, they were covering those big stories, bringing down governments, so they thought, while my job was writing little stories about boring bishops or who might be the next head of some Oxbridge college. Those were the sort of soft stories we did on the Atticus column in 1963.

Overnight, it all changed. About a year later, when I took over the column, the '60s proper had arrived at the *Sunday Times*. I was allowed to write about people who hadn't been to public school or Oxbridge, i.e. people like myself, with northern backgrounds, gritty, provincial novelists or loud-mouth working-class photographers.

I'd forgotten one of the other Big News Stories of 1963 – the Great Train Robbery. I don't think the Insight got as excited by this. Too low class, too tabloid. I'd followed it, of course, but never quite known where it had all happened. I knew they'd stopped the Glasgow–London train near some bridge which was, well, somewhere out there, you know, north of Watford. The whole nation had been amazed by the daring and skill of the men, who hardly harmed anyone, except some railwayman who had his head bashed. They got away with all those millions, making it the biggest train robbery of all time. There have been many books since, and a film, and the continuing saga of Ronnie Biggs in Brazil has turned it into one of the legendary stories of our times.

I studied the framed cuttings and saw that the total sum stolen was £2.6 million. I'd remembered it as being more like £10 million. Seems little today. A lottery winner wouldn't make the front pages for that amount, or a footballer being transferred.

When I paid the bill, I asked the barmaid, who was Irish, why the cuttings were here. 'Oh, this is where the robbers met to plan the robbery. That's what I've been told. A pity they didn't leave any of the money behind, eh?'

And that's probably what she says every time someone asks. I read the cuttings again and saw that the robbery had taken place at the nearby village of Cheddington. Would there be a commemorative plaque? Did the local tourist board offer conducted tours? Was there a Great Train Robbery Banquet held every 3 August – bring your own truncheon and beat up a railway guard? Few crimes are so gruesome that they don't eventually attract a tourist trade. After all, there are now Jack the Ripper walks in south London.

I found the bridge under the railway line, but no sign of any plaques. In the village of Cheddington, I asked a man if the robbery did attract any tourists. Now and again, he said, but they were not encouraged. Most local people didn't want their village to be known for that sort of thing.

I then asked him about Mentmore Towers and if the local community liked the Maharishi people. He looked a bit puzzled. I said they presumably brought in some useful extra trade. He still looked blank. He'd never actually seen any of them.

Perhaps when they move on, the TM people will be totally forgotten locally. They were only here by chance anyway. The Great Train Robbers didn't have a local connection either. Biggs at the time was a £35-a-week carpenter in Reigate, Surrey. He had a police record, which was how his fingerprints were identified on a bottle of ketchup in their abandoned hideout.

Two events, two arrivals, two happenings, each in the same small community, which for a time made national headlines. And absolutely no connection between them. Though you could say a Great Train Robbery was followed by a Great Brain Robbery.

Chapter Four

MILTON KEYNES

One of the things New Labour was looking for when it achieved power in 1997 was a 'big idea' which would galvanise Great Britain, which we would identify with them and bless them for, if not for ever, then at least until the next general election. Like all political parties, really.

As their term of office progressed and they had to spend a lot of time reacting to 'events' rather than 'ideas', there didn't seem to be all that many new creations, not in a specific sense, not like, well, say, the National Lottery, which was Mr Major's gift to a grateful nation. Then it slowly began to emerge that New Labour was thinking on a loftier, more grandiose plain, hoping to extend all our hopes and horizons, give us a new self-image, generally improve and redefine the nation. For a time it seemed that something called Cool Britannia was going to be created, making the '90s as exciting and fashionable as the swinging '60s, though not, of course, as superficial. This was largely ridiculed, so New Labour gently backed away, saying we had got it all wrong. What New Labour was really going to create was, well, New Britain.

What precisely did this mean? The spin doctors told us it would be a combination of private and government initiatives, more nationalisation but not quite total privatisation, sort of putting together the best of Labour and Conservative ideas, using private and state finance, which would make us dynamic and forward-looking.

Sounded good. But where and when would this take place? And would we recognise it when we saw it? Well, it would be very IT. Nothing to do with It as in It Girl but as in Information Technology, state-of-the-art, modern communication, with lots of computers and high-tech thingamabobs, new buildings, new ways of living and working.

Sounded very like Milton Keynes. Mentmore was clearly part of the past, a grandiose stately home no one quite wanted any more, which had lost its family and not found a new purpose in life. Milton Keynes is clearly part of the future which New Labour has promised us. Or similar.

Milton Keynes would have amazed Priestley. Such a place, such a concept, did not exist then, but it has been very much part of New Britain for the last 30 years – a New Town with New Industries. And still growing, still expanding, with a population of 200,000 and some white-heat, shit-hot modern enterprises. None of that old-fashioned hewing of coal, or building of ships, or hammering of metals. It's all New Labour – i.e. the labour is mainly engaged in new fields, which our grandfathers could never have imagined. There is for a start a lot of moving money around. Takes skill, to move money. They do it best in the City of London, but, as we know, London is shrinking and money-moving, in this modern age, can be done anywhere, thus banking and insurance and suchlike firms are moving out to new sites, with lower costs and cheaper wages. Then there are enterprises which shift around information, as opposed to money, though they often go together.

It is therefore not unexpected that amongst the biggest employers in Milton Keynes are the UK HQs of the Abbey National, Mercedes Benz and the Open University. Guess which of these three has most staff? Before I tell you, don't bother pointing out that Mercedes is a motor manufacturer, one of those so-called old-fashioned industries. Yes, it is, but Mercedes does not manufacture cars in Milton Keynes, or anywhere else in the UK. It's where they have their administrative base, supervising the import and sales of Mercedes cars.

I'd never been to Milton Keynes before so I gave a whoop of delight when I saw it ahead, staring at me on the map. Then I worried that it would turn out less new, less exciting than I had imagined. Usually, with a new person or a new place, they are smaller than expected. Robert Redford, so I'm told, is only four foot tall, though I've never actually met him. I have met Ben Elton, Jeffrey Archer and Martin Amis, all of them considerable personalities with large reputations, and all of surprisingly modest height.

Milton Keynes turned out the opposite – much bigger than I had ever imagined. Studying the map of central Milton Keynes, it all looked very simple and straightforward and I led myself to believe I could walk around it in ten minutes. So I parked and started to walk, and it went on for ever and ever. I had to get the car out of the car park again – and I'd paid – in order to drive around and work out where the hell I was.

I suppose I should have thought of America, with their new towns, new places. They start with all that wide open space, so the scale is totally different. On the drawing boards, they rule in a few grids, colour wash the plots, drop a splodge of greenery, and it all looks small and bijou, like someone's back garden – but one small dot of green turns out to be a tree-lined boulevard that goes on for miles. At Milton Keynes there were a few existing small, unconnected villages, but basically they began with a green-field site of some 4,000 acres in which they have plonked and planted out four million trees, and yes, they do have boulevards which stretch as far as the eye can see.

They have poncy names, like Midsummer Boulevard, and confusing numbers, like H6, which indicates a vertical street, and V7, a horizontal street. I couldn't understand them, or the intersections, so I drove around in a daze along immensely wide, tree-lined dual carriageways. Now and again there would be clusters of modern blocks, with lots of glass and concrete in strange designs and shapes, then a gap of greenery, followed by more blocks. There was no sign of any shops, not as I know them, with names on, or clues as to what businesses might be going on. Nor any sign of people. It wasn't the future after all. I had arrived too late. Milton Keynes had been evacuated.

When I eventually realised I had been going round in a circle, I found another car park and started exploring on foot. That's when I came across some human beings, of the walking-on-all-fours variety. I had, of course, seen masses of motor cars. You couldn't enter or get out of Milton Keynes otherwise. What I hadn't seen were the underpasses and pathways, hidden from the dual carriageways, where pedestrians of the more adventurous kind use their feet to get from glass and concrete block to glass and concrete block. Mostly the natives seem to drive between them, for they all have ample parking spaces.

I went first to the civic offices in Saxon Gate East. One of the rules of new towns is that street names must sound as ancient as possible. I picked up some literature and learned that every new house in Milton Keynes is connected to cable television. That's New Britain for you.

Milton Keynes, so one of the booklets said, is 'not named after those two eminent economists – John Maynard Keynes and Milton Shulman.' A bit confusing, this joke. Maynard Keynes was, of course an economist, but Milton Shulman was drama critic of the *Evening Standard*. I later found a corrected version, with the same joke, but changed to Milton Friedman. The truth is that there was a place called Milton Keynes, very small, a mere hamlet, in existence long before the new town was built.

All the leaflets boast that Milton Keynes is 'at the centre of England's greatest tourist attractions'. This is illustrated with photographs of Big

Ben, Stratford-upon-Avon and Warwick Castle. None of them is in Milton Keynes, or even very near, though if you were living in Texas and booking up a holiday, they all might look handy. They also boast that no town in England 'is more than four hours away from Milton Keynes'. Is this meant to be a warning or an attraction?

Milton Keynes is now a metropolitan complex, having swallowed up all the existing ancient villages, but it is not yet, alas, a city. It was deeply disappointing for them, the last time city status was handed out, that Sunderland got it and they didn't. Next time, perhaps, if New Labour has any sense.

In the nation at large, Milton Keynes is probably best known for its concrete cows which can be seen from the main north–south railway line as one whizzes past. 'Don't mention them,' said a woman official when I asked about them. 'We're trying to live them down.' But they're fun, they're distinctive. Better to be known for something than nothing at all. 'Yes, but they've been the butt of jokes by TV comedians for years. Everyone in Milton Keynes is fed up with the cows. It's sort of patronising, people going on about them.'

I studied the town guide and the literature she had given me and noticed two things lacking for a cutting-edge sort of town. No professional football team. 'Ah, well, we did hope Luton Town would move here and build a new stadium, but it didn't happen.' The other missing element is a newspaper, a real, professional, local newspaper. All the ones listed appeared to be free sheets. Not quite the same.

But what Milton Keynes does have, in abundance, in extravagance, is shops. The main shopping centre is one of the wonders of the late twentieth century, the biggest in Europe when it opened. Now there are others making similar claims, so Milton Keynes has changed its boast to 'the longest in Europe'. I don't know how I had missed it, as it's three-quarters of a mile long. I just didn't know what it was, and I hadn't been able to read any of the shop names while driving on the boulevards. It's all on one level, rectangular in shape, so you walk up one way for almost a mile, turn at right angles for a few hundred metres, than walk back for almost a mile. You could easily put in a day and still not visit all the shops, which is what five million shoppers do every year, coming from up to a hundred miles away, hoping to shop till they drop.

I made my base camp at Marks and Spencer's, at one end, and set off into the unknown, hoping that if I didn't return, search parties would be sent out. None of it, of course, was the slightest bit unknown. The atmosphere, the ambience, was exactly the same, with the same shops and logos, as in shopping precincts everywhere in the UK today, from

Brent Cross to Gatwick Airport, Gateshead to Carlisle. Yes, even Carlisle has got a wonderful, prize-winning shopping precinct called The Lanes. They are all incredibly clean and well scrubbed. No signs of beggars or, perish the thought, poorish persons.

The Milton Keynes version is so enormous, so long, laid out like an indoor dual carriageway, that they have roundabouts, junctions where you can slow down, stop and pause – and, of course, buy. At each junction I came to there was a pretend old-fashioned barrow stall, gaily decorated, nicely painted, devoted to selling just one single item. It made a change from being bombarded with a whole variety of goods. One was selling balloons, another cards, while one was devoted to waistcoats. Do they hope people in Milton Keynes will have a sudden impulse to buy waistcoats? Probably the same sort of people who on railway stations feel a sudden desire to buy knickers or socks. One stall was selling aromatherapy products, so I paused and breathed in the sweet smell of the oils and the lotions and wondered if this was the northern-most outpost of this passion of our age. I have seen such stalls all over Covent Garden, London, but not elsewhere. Something to look out for.

I had a cappuccino in a coffee bar, regular, not even large, priced £1.25, which is like Covent Garden prices. 'Will the parents of two-year-old Darren Skelton please return to the crèche AT ONCE,' said a voice on the loudspeaker system in a tone of desperation. I had an image of two-year-old Darren with a skinhead haircut, an earring and a beer belly, wreaking havoc on the bouncy castle while his parents had done a bunk, fleeing Milton Keynes to take refuge in Rio with Ronnie Biggs.

I came to a Shopping Information Desk, which is presumably to provide answers to questions on shopping, so I went inside and asked why I hadn't seen any hardware shops. 'We're all chain stores here, dear,' said the kindly middle-aged woman on the desk. 'You have to go further out for them.' Outer Milton Keynes or outer space? She didn't say.

My next question was to ask what sort of questions they get asked. Well, she was one of 14 staff who work shifts, and their job is like the social services, really. 'People pop in here to ask about family planning, pensions, social security, what they are entitled to. Oh, we help everyone we can. People treat us like we're Milton Keynes High Street, not a shopping centre.

'Yesterday I had a little man who staggered in and collapsed. Sat on that chair, over there, and all he could say was, "I've just lost my wife." I got him a cup of tea, said there there, poor you, don't bother about anything, just you rest and sit quiet as long as you like. I went back every so often to see how he was while I attended to other people. After 40 minutes, during which he kept on repeating the same thing, it dawned on me what he'd really meant by saying he'd lost his wife. I'd presumed he'd recently been widowed. What had actually happened was they'd arrived together by bus, one of the buses which go round and round central Milton Keynes. He'd got off at the front door of the shopping centre, thinking his wife was following him. When he got inside, she wasn't there. She'd disappeared. Once I got all this straight, I rang the buses. They all have radios, you see. His wife was still sitting on the bus, on her own, going round and round! The conductor himself brought her into the shopping centre. So it all ended happily.'

I could hear the sound of music further along the shopping centre and came upon two buskers playing accordions. I was surprised they were allowed, as the security presence was heavy and officious. They had the usual hat on the ground in front of them, containing a few odd pennies and a glimpse of silver, and a large handwritten note propped up which read: 'We are both full-time musicians and busking provides us with part of our income. Unlike some, we rely only on your generosity and our digital dexterity.'

I had to read this twice, and check the punctuation, before I worked out the message. It seemed to be saying 'We are not beggars'. When they finished their tune, I put a pound coin in their hat, being a big spender, and asked what their notice meant.

'Yes, we're certainly not begging. We are proper musicians. Between us we've done thirty-two albums.'

So there. I apologised if my expression had suggested otherwise. They came from Northampton, which is apparently full of beggars pretending to be musicians. 'Begging is prohibited in Northampton, so the beggars get a tin whistle, play one note on it, hold their dogs on a rope with the other hand, and the police turn a blind eye. But they're still beggars. Everyone knows it. It means when you do busk in Northampton, all you get is abuse, with people saying, "Why don't you go and get a proper job?"'

So they come busking in Milton Keynes – and have a licence to prove it. They showed it to me, Simon and Gareth, known professionally as Squeezbox.

'You're supposed to have an audition before you get this licence, but we sent them one of our tapes. That was enough. There are eight pitches in this shopping centre – four musical and four non-musical.' Non-musical mainly means jugglers.

As they are so highly qualified, with so many albums, wouldn't a pitch in Covent Garden be more lucrative?

'We did go down for the day, to look at their system. We found you had to have a proper audition, which meant going down another day. We couldn't afford the time or the money.'

How much, er, can they make?

They hesitated. I assured them I was not from the Inland Revenue or VAT.

'Well, today, we'll probably be lucky to make £10 each. We just look upon it as a practice session. When it gets nearer Christmas, though, that can go up to £100 each, if we're lucky.'

As I was speaking, a mobile phone rang. I thought at first it was a shopper or a security officer, but it was one of the buskers. I then noticed each had his own phone, fixed to the back of his waist. Business can't be all that bad. 'Oh, we need them. My wife's a teacher and out at work all day. If I get rung for some session work and I don't answer, then someone else gets the job. It's vital to have a mobile phone.'

Both had partners and children, plus mortgages, not something you usually associate with blokes playing accordions in the street. Diatonic button accordions, actually. But I could call them accordions if I wanted, or even melodeons. 'That's "eon" at the end, in case you can't spell it,' said Simon.

I put another coin in their hat and asked if they did requests. I'd like them to play 'The Bluebell Polka', in the style of Jimmy Shand and his Band. My mother used to be awfie fond of it.

I could still hear the tune as I left the shopping centre and crossed the road, heading towards a large domed church which looked a bit like St Paul's. It's the tallest building in central Milton Keynes. Not that there's any competition. Milton Keynes was laid out flat, not built up.

On the pavement outside the main entrance I read a plaque which said that the Church of Christ the Cornerstone had been opened by the Queen on 13 March 1992 in the presence of the Archbishop of Canterbury and Cardinal Hume. Seemed unusual, to have the big cheeses from two different denominations. But it was because the church is a totally ecumenical church, the first in any town centre in the UK. They have six resident clerics: a Church of England vicar, a Church of England canon, a Catholic priest, a Catholic sister, a Baptist minister and a Methodist minister.

Who's in charge, I asked at the reception desk. 'No one. It's a team ministry.' Yes, but someone must have the final say? 'Each person takes a turn at chairing the team for one year.'

The building cost over £4 million and has a central worship area for all services except for the Catholic sacraments, which take place in a smaller chapel. Under Roman Catholic rules, which could not be changed, only Catholics can participate in a Catholic mass. Apart from that, the clerics share all functions and duties. One cleric, for example, is responsible for the shopping centre. You mean he goes round blessing the shops at Christmas? 'Not quite. He's like an industrial chaplain, looking after the people who work in or use the shopping centre.' Shopping is, after all, one of Milton Keynes's major industries.

The church also has its own restaurant, which looked busy and very wholesome, but I had arranged to meet two young women for lunch. Which was nice. And rather fascinating.

★ ★ ★

Anna is aged 21 and is my niece, daughter of my sister who lives nearby in Bedfordshire. She had just graduated from university in Liverpool with an upper second in French and German. She was already working, which not all graduates can boast, in some modern-sounding firm in Milton Keynes, doing some modern-sounding job which I didn't quite understand. I promised her and her friend Claire lunch if they'd tell me about life and work in exciting Milton Keynes.

We met at a large pub called Wetherspoons which seemed to me incredibly noisy. 'This isn't noisy,' said Claire. 'That's why we chose it. It's a music-free pub. We don't usually use it because we prefer music, the noisier the better.'

After a bit of head clutching and asking for everything to be repeated on my part, they took pity on me and we moved on to a Pizza Express. I hadn't noticed one of these before. You have to be a native to find it, as it's hidden inside a large, anonymous glass building.

Claire had got the job first, then told Anna about it. For recruiting Anna, she got forty pounds in M & S tokens. Did you share it with Anna? 'Did I heck.'

All the same, Anna had to have an interview and language tests, produce references and her degree certificate, then sit a little exam, all for the honour of being on a telephone all day long, ringing people. Didn't sound much of a job, after the slog of getting a degree, but it's where the future lies. Without realising it, they had become a part of what is today one of the biggest growth areas of modern white-collar life. All over the country, a new factory system is springing up. Where once people were herded into industrial plants, textile works or shipyards, they are now herded into modern open-plan office blocks, treated nicely enough, given clean surroundings – but made to sit cheek by jowel and spend each day staring at a computer screen, talking to customers they will never meet.

These call centres, as the original versions were known, came from America and were at first mainly in the financial sector, selling insurance or banking services by phone. Now they cover many services and many products. With telephone charges getting cheaper and computers quicker and better, they can be set up anywhere, hundreds or thousands of miles from where you think you are ringing. Another of the reasons why firms are moving staff from London.

Work is often in shifts, so it suits women or those who want part-time work. Enhanced computer sophistication means that each task can be exactly timed and programmed, answers and questions learned off pat, so that productivity can be easily monitored. All that needs to be worked on is motivation. It has been estimated that 200,000 people now work in these call centres, more than in the steel, coal or car-manufacturing industries combined.

Anna and Claire were employed by a telephone research firm along with several hundred other telephone workers. The firm takes on projects, usually from big multinational businesses, and has to provide certain information over a certain period. Most people get hired for a limited period, for as long as the project lasts, but they can move to other projects if they are suitable.

Anna and Claire had been hired for their French language skills. From their glass and concrete open-plan office block in Milton Keynes, their job was to ring firms in France and go through a set list of questions about each firm's computer software. They were meant to find out how big the firm was, how many staff there were, the size of turnover and so on, going through a list of 25 set questions. On their heads they wore earphones, with a mouthpiece attached, leaving their hands free to type in the answers on to a keyboard in front of them.

'We have a target of 15 completed profiles a day,' said Anna. 'When you complete one, you shout out loud, "PROFILE!" It then goes up on the target board — and everyone else claps. Every hour, on the hour, one of the ops managers shouts out, "NEW HOUR!" All day long — at two o'clock, three o'clock, etc. Basically, it's bollocks, but he thinks he's encouraging us, making us all try harder.'

They weren't quite sure where the telephone numbers and names of the French firms come from in the first place. Presumably at some stage they have been customers of the company behind the project, or it's thought they might be, or they have been acquired by other means, such as purchasing lists of such numbers from firms which sell such numbers.

Anyway, they are just provided with a list, and have to work their way down.

'Getting someone in authority to speak to is the hardest part,' said Anna. 'You're supposed to ask for the marketing director, but of course you don't always get put through. They often suspect who you are, what the real object is, and ask your name and where exactly you are ringing from.

'Some people are rude and hang up. But some just love it and they start telling you all their computer and software problems, going on and on, which I don't understand, really. I don't know what some of the stuff means in English, never mind in French . . .'

Their firm is very big on bonding and group dynamics. Each morning they have a ten-minute session at 7.20, before work begins. 'The team leader starts by saying, "Hi, guys. How are you all feeling today, guys? Well, let's go for it! Let's get into them! And good luck, guys!" It is all bollocks, but they think it raises our energy level. At the end of the day, we also have a debriefing session, where the leader says well done. What really pisses me off is that we don't get paid extra for coming in early or staying late for these pep talks.'

In Claire's first week, she was told off for chewing, which really annoyed her. 'The woman who told me off was only two years older than me. It's like being back at school. There is no smoking, eating, drinking or chewing at work. Yes, I know it's to protect the computers. But it's very irritating.

'I'd been on the piss one night and came in feeling really wicked. I was dying for a Polo and I asked my team leader if it would be okay. Oh, come on, I said, just one Polo, but she wouldn't let me. It means when you do have a break, there's a smokers' corner, where all the smokers immediately congregate. It's all the cool people, of course. Just like school.'

'We also have to wear smart dress,' said Anna. 'It's sort of power dressing for the girls and the blokes have to wear suits, usually with big braces. The other day, in one of the debriefings, a bloke asked if goatee beards were okay. Fridays are a bit more casual. That's dressing-down day.'

So was the bloke allowed to wear a goatee beard? Neither could remember what the answer was, as neither had been listening. Which made both of them burst out laughing.

I couldn't, however, see the point of any sort of dress code when they are sitting at a desk all day, speaking on the telephone.

'Yeah, we used to think that. But there are visitors coming round all the time, prospective clients who want to see us at work. So we have to look impressive. When a client is due to come round, the ops manager says to us all, "Clean desks and lots of French!"'

Although they were slagging off the bosses, poking fun and taking the piss, I suspected that each of them did take their work pretty seriously. They did admit there was a certain feeling of excitement that they were in an expanding business, with new people arriving all the time, and that on the whole they had good employers.

'We have been promised a free booze-up as our Christmas treat,' said Anna. 'With champagne and a coach laid on. So that's good. I think I'll wait till then, before I leave . . .'

Their hours were 7.30 to 4.30, for which they were getting paid £7 an hour. Those speaking English only, ringing firms in Britain, get only £6 an hour. They felt quite well off, and lucky to have a job. With a bit of luck and careful massaging of the details, it could be made to look good on their CVs.

'We're technically TOs – telebusiness operatives. There's a lot of work in this field if you want it. It's growing all the time, but it's so tiring. When I get home, I'm knackered. I am thinking of leaving, but I've no energy to think about applying for any other job.'

Both live at home with their parents and so save on rent, which means they hoped to save about £1,000 each by Christmas. 'There are people working with us who can't save a penny. Their homes are in places in the north, like Warrington and Sunderland. They've had to find somewhere to stay down here, so they can't save. But they were prepared to move anywhere just to get a job, any sort of job.

'I suppose we're doing about average for people who left college with us this year. There is one boy getting £20,000 in IT, but he's been fluky. And I know a girl a year older who is getting £30,000 in the City. But she's had two promotions already.

'One boy in our year, after he'd graduated, decided he wanted to be a chef. He went off on this course in Wales which cost him a fortune. He then got a job in Mezzo in London, you know, the big new posh restaurant, feeling pretty excited. But it turned out he only got £3 an hour for doing a 14-hour shift. It was slave labour, he said. He hated it and gave it up. He's now travelling somewhere in Ireland.'

Anna wants to move, not just because of the work but because she doesn't like Milton Keynes. She finds it boring, with no character. 'I've been coming here shopping with my mother for twenty years. I've had enough.'

So where would she like to go to?

'London, of course. That's my ambition.'

I said that was very common, according to the national figures, which show that it's the 20–30 age group who love London the most. But Claire quite likes Milton Keynes, now she's got to know the local pubs and clubs.

'I'm not desperate to get to London like Anna. But I will probably leave here at Christmas as well. By then I hope I'll have paid off all the debts from college. Then, well, I dunno. I'd quite like to get into organising things, events or parties. Actually, my real fantasy is not having a job, just travelling . . .'

★ ★ ★

What neither of them fancied was further study. They'd had enough learning and examination-taking, thank you very much.

If they had fancied it, though, they would have been handily situated. The nation's biggest provider of further study, the Open University, is right on their doorstep. It has its HQ in Milton Keynes – and, yes, that is the town's biggest employer, after the council itself. It now has 3,700 full-time employees, 3,000 of them in Milton Keynes. There are also another 7,600 part-time tutors, spread throughout the country. As new ideas go, it's arguably one of the most successful creations of the century. The original idea goes back to the 1920s, when the BBC first began and the idea of a 'wireless university' was first suggested. But nothing happened at the time. Michael Young, in 1962, appears to have been the first to coin the term 'Open University'. Harold Wilson then took it up as one of his personal passions. In a speech in Glasgow in 1963, he launched a proposal for a University of the air. Wilson was leader of the opposition, so not much notice was taken, but when Labour got power in 1964, he handed the proposal over to Jennie Lee, telling her it was her responsibility. She is the one who therefore deserves the most credit for its creation.

It depended from the beginning on participation from the BBC. They were the means by which lectures and programmes would be broadcast to the nation. Because of this, it was felt that the HQ should be no further than one hour away from Alexandra Palace, the BBC's transmitting station in north London. Milton Keynes is exactly one hour up the M1, traffic and congestion willing. It was also felt that a new town was a good place for a new sort of university. It opened in 1971, with 2,400 students. Today it has 200,000 students, all studying in their own homes or their places of work, making it the biggest higher education centre in the country. Around 110,000 are doing first degree courses, with another 50,000 on postgraduate courses or continuing education. Since it began, it has had two million students.

There is no entry requirement. Anyone can join. The average age is 37. Around 5,500 students are disabled. There are tuition fees – in 1998 it was £288, plus around £200 for a summer course – but many courses are paid for by employers, especially for those doing a business degree of some sort.

It's on the edge of the town, and, of course, I got lost driving out to it, still confused by the dual carriageways and all the roundabouts which look alike. At first sight, it does seem like the sprawling campus of any modern university, with libraries, laboratories, all spread out on a green-field site. You then notice the BBC TV studios, which not many universities can boast. Then you realise the biggest difference of all – there are no students. Not on the site. The folk wandering around are lecturers, professors, administrators, plus TV producers.

The vice-chancellor's office is in the only period-looking building, a small, bijou, whitewashed villa, Walton Hall, which dates back to 1830. On the stairs are imposing oil paintings of the previous vice-chancellors – only two so far, but then the OU is very young.

Sir John Daniel is the third vice-chancellor. Aged 55, Welsh by background but brought up in Surrey, he went to school at Christ's Hospital, Horsham, then Oxford, where he read metallurgy. He spent the next 25 years in Canada as an academic and then as an administrator in various universities. In 1990 he applied for the OU job as a long shot, thinking it would be bound to go to someone in the UK, someone already part of the UK university network, so he was surprised and delighted to get the job. His wife, who is American, was pleased to move with him, but his three children, all now grown up, have remained in North America.

He was sitting in his office at his polished boardroom table, looking clean and lean, formal yet relaxed in his shirtsleeves. I admired a piece of stained glass hanging on a window which happened to catch the afternoon light. It looked like an astronaut walking on the moon. A good image for a scientist now running a high-tech university. But it wasn't the moon. It was somewhere in Canada, which I didn't catch, where some sort of space experiments were carried out. Still pretty apt.

So what's been happening today, Sir John? Tell me some of your problems and concerns, running the OU. He asked if I meant today's or long-term problems. So precise, these scientists. Let's start with today, then.

Well, first thing that morning he'd opened the latest issue of *The Times* Higher Education Supplement. He does that each week, to see if the OU has got a mention, favourable or otherwise. Today they had been mentioned – a report on some survey the OU had produced. He handed it to me. Looked a pretty boring story, but reasonable enough. Did that count as favourable or not? 'It's fine. We've got off lightly.'

Then he had various meetings, starting with one to promote a senior lecturer into a reader. He likes to be present at all senior appointments. Yes, the person had been duly promoted. The rest of the meetings sounded fairly routine, though he was willing to go through them, but I said okay, give us the future.

'One long-term problem is moving at the right pace with the new technology. Go too quickly and people have problems because we have to rely on students acquiring their own kit. But if we go too slowly, our image is harmed. So far we seem to have got it right. For a new science course, we've created a CD Rom, which has been well received.'

One area in which they have been rather late is languages. It was only in the last few years that you could take an OU diploma in French or German. Until then, it was accepted that a French course had to have a literary base, using the French classics. It was thought this would prove hard for an Open University student, with little previous higher education. Now they offer an OU degree in speaking and understanding the language, with no need to plough through the classic novels and plays. In fact, Sir John's wife is about to start a course in German. He himself is planning to do one in Spanish.

The OU has traditionally been for people who missed out on education first time round, the *Educating Rita* syndrome, where you suddenly realise late on what you have missed. Now, of course, not as many miss out first time round, with so many new universities, and so many different courses.

At the beginning of this century, only one in 2,000 went to university. Now, at the end of the century, the figure is around one in three. Surely, therefore, in future there will be fewer late starters for the OU to mop up?

'In theory that's what should happen, but we haven't noticed any such trend so far. Anyway, there will always be a desire and need for continuing education for people who want to learn new things, follow new courses, all from their own homes.'

Good point. And with modern technology, these homes can be anywhere, right across the globe. Some 25,000 of the OU's current students live overseas: 5,000 in Western Europe, 5,000 in Singapore,

6,000 in Hong Kong. And all of them are studying in English. Then there are 8,000 in the former Soviet bloc countries, mainly doing business courses, who have the courses translated into their own languages.

Sir John likes to think the British OU is the best in the world, the model for all the others – but it is not the oldest. Similar systems began much earlier in France and in South Africa. And it's not even the biggest. Eleven countries now have at least 100,000 students at some sort of open university. With 200,000 students, ours is currently third in size, the two biggest being Turkey, with 577,000 students, and China, with 530,000.

'But I know we are the best. We are the most developed, mainly because we have a network of personal tutors based in every major town in the UK. Wherever you live, you can get personal help from your local study centre. That's not possible in other countries. They don't have the money.

'The USA doesn't have an Open University, not on a national level. Their education is based on a state system, not federal. Their broadcasting system has also always been mainly commercial. They don't have anything like our public-funded BBC.

'The UK Open University is regarded as the intellectual leader all round the world. That's what I perceive as I go round the world. I'm looked upon as the sort of Archbishop of Canterbury of the Open Universities . . .'

Which he presumably enjoys, as he is very much a Christian gentleman. One of his claims to fame, according to his CV, a copy of which his office had given me in advance, is that he is a lay reader and has had the honour of being 'the first person to preach in Westminster Abbey from a laptop computer'.

Seemed rather a weird record. Does it mean there is someone on duty at Westminster Abbey checking all the preachers, making lists of the precise details of their sermonising technology?

'Well, that's just what I was told after I'd delivered mine. I always write my speeches in advance on my laptop. That particular day, I decided to read it straight from the machine. So it was a first for me as well.'

You must have pretty good eyes, I said, being able to stand up and read from such a small screen. 'Ah, but I can enhance the size of the words. Look, I'll show you.'

He got out his laptop and showed me. Most impressive. Science is wonderful. But then he is a scientist by training, and he is based in

Milton Keynes, at the cutting edge of modern technology and communications. All the same, I couldn't have done it.

'Well, there is another thing I haven't mentioned. I am wearing contact lenses . . .'

Chapter Five

THE GRAND UNION CANAL

I set off on a hike for my next stage. One foot in front of the other, or walking, as it's also called. Quite easy, once you get the hang of it. I hadn't realised, till I studied the maps, that Milton Keynes is on the Grand Union Canal. It flows right through the middle of the town, providing a sylvan retreat for boaters, walkers, fishermen and wildlife. So I decided to follow the canal due north out of Milton Keynes, heading from the present and future into the past.

In fact, I could have walked from London all the way to Lakeland along canal footpaths. An amazing thought, and doubtless a fascinating experience. You couldn't have done it 200 years ago, when our canals were first established. They were not built for walkers but for workers. Today you can wander at will along 2,000 miles of canals, through England, Scotland and Wales. The route to Lakeland would have been a bit complicated but perfectly possible, either by foot or by boat, starting right in the middle of London in Little Venice, a pretty place from whence to begin any journey. From there you can walk or boat all the way up the Grand Union Canal to Birmingham. There is then a choice of canals, taking you through the Potteries to Lancashire, where again there are lots of possible routes. Finally, you link up with Lancaster Canal near Preston. Then it's due north again, taking you not quite into Lakeland itself but right to the outskirts of Kendal.

That would have been fun, would have provided an interesting journey and definitely would have made me one up when I arrived in Loweswater. What was the traffic like on the M6? You what, I'd say. I didn't drive. I'm not one of your nasty polluters of the atmosphere. I came by boat. Yup. Almost all the way. Only took about a thousand times as long.

Alas, I didn't have quite that sort of time, and I doubt anyway I would have got a broad variety of people or places, or managed much of a cross-section of English life today. Going by canal boat has a certain romance but must be a bit like viewing England from the outside, as if from a train window. Only slower.

When I used to visit my sister, the one who lives in Leighton Buzzard, we often walked the canal when our children were young, looking at the locks and the boats, having a pub lunch or a picnic. That was the bit I really enjoyed. On one visit, a brilliant sunny day, I rashly promised my children that I would hire a boat and take them on a canal holiday. They kept on about it and I kept on putting it off, saying soon, my little ones, soon. The years went by, my excuses mounted up. Daddy's too busy, Daddy's got this book to finish, Daddy's got a poorly knee. Eventually they all grew up and left home. They haven't forgotten. Oh no. Once a year one of them still brings it up. 'You said. You promised.'

As I strode out of Milton Keynes, with the little canal boats chugging past me, I started thinking, yes, it would be nice to have a boat trip, but I kept this rash thought to myself. I now know, with age, that I hate being on a boat of any sort. Looking at them, that's fine. Being on them, not for me. One of the worst mistakes I ever made was sailing across the Atlantic on the *QE2* with all my family. Arriving in New York, going under the Narizana bridge at dawn and seeing the Manhattan skyline, yes, that was pretty exciting, glad to have seen it, but it still wasn't worth it. Not just because we all got seasick, but because for five days there was nothing to do, nowhere to walk, and I was totally, utterly, screamingly bored.

Walking a canal is easy on the foot and on the eye, as a canal is your map, your three-dimensional route plan, so you don't have to keep looking things up or looking around to work out where you are. You can go into a dream, soothed by the passing boats, so pretty and attractive, the peace and calm of it all. So unlike how it must have been when it all began. At the height of canal mania, I imagine the Grand Union was just as filthy and noisy and hellish as its modern replacement, the M1, with coal barges bashing along, trying to get to London as quickly as possible, and bargemen screaming and shouting at each other. Did they have canal rage? I bet they did.

Ancient Egyptians and Chinese had canals of sorts but then we are led to believe the ancients had everything, though I was surprised recently to learn that the Romans had television and that Leonardo da Vinci was on the Internet. Okay, I just made that up.

I know from my schooldays that canals began with the Duke of

Bridgewater in 1761. He got the engineer James Brindley to build one from his estates at Worsley, wherever that is – near Manchester, I think – so he could transport his coal to, er, wherever he was transporting his coal to, but I do remember that the result was he doubled the price of his coal. Or did he halve it? It was a jolly good thing anyway. I had it all off pat when I was doing A level history in 1954. Probably all changed by now. You know what historians are like. Never content with history.

But I do know that after the Bridgewater Canal opened, canal mania started. By 1800 the whole nation was going wild, with canals being built all over Britain. They were wonderful pieces of engineering and architecture, as we can see to this day. Millions were spent, fortunes were made, landscapes were carved apart, lives were lost – and then it all collapsed, just suddenly as it had begun. How rotten for the canal makers. Every other major form of transport in history had a good run for its money, but almost from the moment this one really took off, its death was being planned and plotted. George Stephenson was working on railways from as early as 1810, and by 1825 he had got most of the problems solved when he opened the Stockton to Darlington. And that was it, really. End of story for the canals. The real life span for most of them was barely 30 years.

How lucky motor cars have been, and undeservedly so, when you think of the damage in human terms and for the environment. The internal-combustion engine has been with us since 1886, when Mr Daimler and Mr Benz, who never met despite living only 60 miles apart, perfected their petrol-fuelled road carriages. Motor cars have now survived over three times as long as canal transport, yet the basic principle has not altered since 1886. Why hasn't something else come along to supersede the petrol-driven engine? Surely in the twenty-first century there will be a new form of mass transport, currently just waiting in the wings?

Meanwhile, canals have had a new lease of life. They may have been dead in the form for which they were intended, but they have reinvented themselves. Canals today are no longer utilitarian. More of an art form.

I went to Canada once to interview Marshall McLuhan, one of the gurus of this last half-century, big in his day for coining smart phrases such as 'the medium is the message' and 'the global village'. I didn't understand all the things he told me, as he did speak very quickly and confusingly and was always rushing off to consult various research documents. When I followed him, they turned out to be torn-out newspaper pages which he kept stored in old cardboard boxes.

One of his notions I do remember was that when a circle goes around another circle, the old circle becomes an art form. He illustrated this by saying that when colour movies appeared, black-and-white films became an art form. I suppose he was right in a sense. When life moves on, we start valuing bits of the old life. Collectors certainly do. The moment steam railways died, railwayana arrived. In this age of television, people collect old radios. Once the Beatles split up, everything to do with them became valuable.

With canals, there are two strands in their new existence. There is nostalgia for their history, for the way of life, the boats and the artefacts. But they have also been reborn with a new use. They are part of our leisure industry.

Today, the canals are run by British Waterways, a government organisation funded by the Department of the Environment. They are responsible for 2,000 miles of canals and inland waterways. In this portfolio, they are lumbered with – though they wouldn't necessarily use that phrase, not publicly – looking after 1,549 locks, 1,036 lock cottages and dwellings, 4,763 bridges, 397 aqueducts and 60 tunnels. Amongst this lot are 2,200 structures which are listed, meaning they have some sort of historic value and can't be destroyed or mucked around with. I could certainly feel lumbered having to care for that lot. New Labour, or Old Labour, or any government, doesn't quite see the canals as a sexy, vote-winning, headline-grabbing subject, or even as a low priority, so there is the constant problem of getting money and attention.

However, British Waterways have done a pretty good job in recent years. They estimate that they now attract ten million visitors a year. This figure includes around two and a half million who take some sort of canal boat trip and another two and a half million who are anglers. The rest are assorted visitors on foot, who walk the towpaths or come to gape at the locks and the boats. It costs around £100 million a year to run the canals. Half of that comes from the government and half British Waterways earn themselves in fees, licences and other incomes. Altogether, some 35,000 people earn their living through the canals.

I was surprised by the scale of British Waterways' operation, which does make them an important player in the leisure industry. I got these figures from their HQ at Watford, but had long passed Watford, not knowing they were there. So I had arranged to meet a British Waterways supervisor at a certain point on the route ahead of me, a few miles out of downtown Milton Keynes. When I got there, there was a message saying he had cancelled. Something had come up. Instead I was given the name of a British Waterways bricklayer, Graeme Haines, who would be working on that stretch. He might be available. I could talk to him if I wanted to, and if he wasn't too busy.

I was a bit disappointed at first. Not at the thought of talking to a humble brickie, for even J.B. Priestley talked now and again to real workers in real motor-car factories, but because I had been looking forward to meeting a British Waterways Top Official – no doubt a thrusting young man in a Paul Smith suit, with a university degree in engineering and media studies, an imposing civil service title and the latest flow charts on the Ethos of BW, Caring for our Community, Marketing our Heritage for the Twenty-First Century.

Graeme, the bricklayer, was in his green overalls and dirty boots and his hands had bits of cement stuck to them. He was in his late thirties, very tough and muscular, with a skinhead haircut and both arms totally covered in tattoos. He didn't say much at first, eyeing my little notebook suspiciously. He has his own boat, his work boat, where he has all his tools and stuff. He said it was tied up beside the lock where he was working, further along the canal.

We set off walking in that direction, with me asking him about his life so far and also about his boat – or his Beast, as he called it. Yes, he would let me visit it, so he said, but he didn't initially seem all that keen, not until later, when we discovered we had a mutual passion in life.

He was born in 1960 in the village of Fenny Stratford, now part of the modern Milton Keynes. His father was a farm labourer and his grandfather worked for British Waterways. It was he who helped Graeme get an interview on leaving school.

'I got taken on as an apprentice bricklayer. One of my first jobs was in Blisworth Tunnel, where there had been a small collapse in the middle. We had to take all our gear into the tunnel on a boat, put a dam in and drain the water out of a stretch about 150 yards long before we could start work. It was very cold and damp inside, and quite scary. This was the summer of 1977. I had just turned 17. All summer long two gangs of us worked there on 12-hour shifts, from six in the morning till six in the evening. I never saw that summer. In fact, I never saw any real daylight. We used our own generator, so that we could see to work.'

Sounds tough, not to say nasty.

'Oh no, I didn't think so. Never thought of packing it in. After five minutes, I knew it was a job for life. Still can't think of anything I'd rather do. It's never boring. Being a brickie on a housing estate, now that would be really boring.'

As a Waterways bricklayer, he gets to work on bridges, tunnels, locks, cottages, gates, pathways – something different almost every week. There were many gangs when he began, all doing this exciting work, but British Waterways, like most government businesses, now use a lot of contract firms. They tend to get called in for the big or urgent jobs. Graeme is now essentially on maintenance. He's their only staff bricklayer from Weedon down to London, a distance of around 100 miles, though he mainly works the upper section, from Weedon to Aylesbury.

He was working that day in a gang of three, with a one-armed labourer and a young trainee who was learning so-called multi-skills. 'This is the new thing, when they take young lads on. They do two weeks bricklaying, two weeks on some other skill. I mean, how can you learn bricklaying in two weeks? Bloody stupid. It took me four years, and I'm still learning.'

They are busiest in the winter, when most repair work gets done. Canals can then be closed, sections drained, locks emptied, and they can work below the water line. During the summer, from Easter onwards, they work above the water line.

'A canal is always leaking to some extent. We know from experience where the weak parts are, where things can go wrong. Local knowledge, you might say. I picked mine up from older blokes when I first started. They'd worked on this section for 25 years before me, doing the same sort of work.'

Why doesn't the water all just leak away? At locks and the properly built bits, you can see the brick retaining walls, so that must keep the water in, but out in the open, where we were now walking, the banks of the canal just seemed to be mud. What stops it seeping away into the fields? It's been artificially put there, after all.

Graeme leaned over the side of the canal, pulling apart the reeds and plants, and pointed to where there had at one time been a retaining wall. A small one, not full height, a drystone wall as opposed to brick and cement. 'Behind this little wall, they built a wall of clay, about a foot thick. That's what really keeps the water in. Well, mostly it does.'

Presumably the other problem is getting enough water in, especially in times of drought. How do they do that, Graeme? 'Oh, we have our own reservoirs all over the place. You must have noticed.'

Er, not really. He promised to point one out. In the meantime he stopped to show me a little brick building which I took to be derelict but which was actually an active pumping house, with its own generator. That's how they keep the canals filled. Along the canal bank are pipes underneath the towpath and outlet points where water can be pumped in and levels raised to keep boats afloat.

Surprising what one doesn't notice. When I'd walked the canal with my children, every stretch had looked much the same, but now Graeme was revealing features and facilities I'd never been aware of. At one lock gate, he took me behind where there were two large ponds, both fairly stagnant and overgrown. They are no longer in use, but they were vital at one time in controlling the level of the lock, using gravity and a series of gates which he carefully explained but I didn't really understand.

Another little building turned out to be a sanitary station. I did understand that, though I never knew such a place existed. It's where boat people dispose of the contents of their portable lavatories. 'Some people dump their sewage overboard, which, of course, is illegal.'

Mostly Graeme was going down his own memory lane, rather than explaining or instructing. As we walked, he was constantly remembering incidents that had happened, places where he had once rescued some water voles, or had a battle with some vicious mink, or sections where he had once worked, bits he had personally built, pointing with pride to examples of his handywork.

We came to part of the towpath which had been recently dug over and I asked if he had been working here.

'No, them's fibre optics.'

Excuse me? He wasn't quite sure what they were, but he'd been told by the bosses that it was the latest money-making scheme for British Waterways.

'Fibreway, it's called. They've laid about 400 miles of these fibre-optic cables along the canals so far. Easy to lay, when you think about it, compared with having to dig up roads and streets and pavements. They're sort of very thin bits of wire, you know, for communications. Least that's how it was explained to us.

'You have Tescos, right? They've got shops all over the country. When you buy a tin of beans in one shop, it gets recorded automatically on the till. With these wires, they can send messages from every shop to one central place. They then know what's what, and can send out more supplies. Well, I think that's it. Very clever, isn't it? I'm told it's about our best money-spinner. We could do with a few more. Otherwise we'll never catch up with all the work that needs to be done. It's a big worry. You can't make money from canals, can you, even with all the tourists. Costs millions just to look after them.'

Near the next lock we met another British Waterways workman, also dressed in green overalls, a friend of Graeme's called Mick. He comes from a family of bargemen who used to trundle up and down the Grand Union carrying coal. 'There were even schools for barge children in them days, before the war. Most people were born on their boats. Your dad would stop at certain places, when your mother was expecting, places where there was a midwife, and tell them what was happening. He'd then try to be there when it was due. He'd stop his boat for the midwife to come on board. That's how I was born in 1937.

'I started work with me dad on his boat when I was about 13, and then with me huncle. Then it all changed. The coal boats finished. The Waterways people took over. Now I'm a dredger.'

I'd never heard an 'h' in front of uncle before, but as soon as he used it, I noticed that Graeme also shoved the odd 'h' in front of various words. Could this be a bargeman tradition? I asked Graeme as we walked on, but he didn't know, or was even aware of his own usage, and was anyway too busy pointing out to me a crocodile. A what?

'A crocodile. Can't you see it, then? Look over there!'

I do happen to know what a crocodile looks like, having seen them when visiting our daughter in Botswana, so I leaned over the side of a lock. Not in the water, said Graeme, over on the other side.

In a little gap between some bricks on the other side, I could just see the head of a very little crocodile peeping out of a crack in a wall.

'See, I told you,' said Graeme.

I then put my specs on, for a close look – and I could see it was made of plastic. All the same, it probably gives some people on boats a bit of a fright as they rise up inside the lock, which must be a strange sensation anyway. Or a bit of a laugh.

'It's some kid's toy, I suppose. We found it floating on the water when we were working here, so we decided to build it in. A bit of a stunt, you might say. And over here, look, that's Mr Blobby. Can you see him? Look for the flash of pink. That's his head. We found him floating around on the water as well.'

Workmen have done this sort of thing for centuries, building in jokes or leaving their names, slogans or signs of their presence on bits they were particularly proud of. The Roman stonemasons did it on Hadrian's Wall, providing interesting research for our archaeologists. But in centuries to come, how on earth will anyone know who Mr Blobby was?

'I sometimes leave a time capsule as well. In fact, we buried one in some concrete foundation over there. Just in an old coffee jar, so it probably won't last long.'

But a good idea. I remember talking to Michael Grade when he was head of Channel Four, just after they had moved into their new and exciting building. He'd put a time capsule in the foundations which contained some commonplace objects of our times, including a condom.

So what did you put in it, Graeme?

'Well, I included a letter, saying who had worked on the job. I also wrote a bit about the bosses . . .'

Slagging them off? 'Yeah, a bit of that. Let's hope it's not dug up while I'm still alive or I could be sued . . .'

We came at last to the Beast, his work boat, on which he sails up and down the canal. It was moored beside a lock where he and his two mates were currently working on a stretch of brick paving. He showed me his handiwork, removing a plastic cover protecting the new work from any rain. I admired the colour and artistry of brick work. 'They're mostly Staffordshire blue bricks. They're dense and heavy, good for keeping out water. Sometimes we have to use old ones, not new ones, if the environmental people insist. They're spot on these days about conservation and protection. We're all now in the tourist trade, like, so things have to look nice and proper, historic and all that. Oh, I'm not against it. It's just that old bricks are hard to find. And harder to lay.'

The Beast itself seemed to be made entirely of metal, more like a lock-up bunker than a boat, and I could see no apparent means of entry, nor any windows. Graeme stepped on board, unlocked various padlocks, opened up the front section and went in.

I followed and found myself in another world. Outside it had appeared brutal, nasty and cold. Inside it was warm and cosy, secret and mysterious, as romantic as a gypsy's caravan. There was a coal-burning stove still on, with an old black kettle on the hob. In front of the stove was a large and battered armchair with more seating arranged along the wall.

On the wall itself were hanging a couple of calendars, with half-naked girls on the front, so naturally I averted my eyes, but pride of place on the wall was given to a much bigger illustration, a photograph of a face torn out of a newspaper. I immediately recognised Fergie. No, not the Duchess. The manager of Manchester United.

This was their mess, where Graeme and his two mates had their meals and breaks, and where they sheltered in the winter in bad weather. Behind it was another little room, their store room, containing their tackle and tools. Graeme slid the dividing doors apart and I could see it was dusty and dirty, much colder and less appealing than their mess room.

You could live here, I said. You could have your whole life here, your being, your work, everything. No need ever to go ashore, meet people, have a house and mortgage, pay bills, face the real world. It's the perfect escape, your very own castle, a working man's Shangri-La, a poor man's nirvana.

'You what?' said Graeme.

Come on, admit it now, Graeme. This was why you fell in love with canals all those years ago. It wasn't the bricklaying. It was having your very own Beast. Cut off from bosses, not messed around by offices, able to move up and down the canal, from job to job, unsupervised, unhassled. Brilliant, if you ask me.

'Er, not quite,' said Graeme. 'Not since we got one of these . . .'

Out of his pocket he yanked a mobile phone. I hadn't noticed he was carrying one, but then he is big and muscular.

'We got issued with them about 18 months ago. Now there's no escape. They always know where we are.'

Had he ever slept on the Beast, or taken his holidays on board?

'Not allowed. Though I have taken my kids on little rides, unofficially, like. They love it. But it has to be locked up totally at night. It's okay leaving it overnight round here, but when we're working in places like Milton Keynes, nothing is safe. Some kids forced an entry a few months ago. God knows how they got through the metal.'

Looking around, I couldn't see anything worth stealing. His chair, however cosy, looked as if it had come off a skip, and the black kettle wasn't exactly pristine. It would, of course, be a good place for someone on the run, or perhaps someone with a girlfriend.

'No, it's the tools they are after. Some are pretty valuable. Look at this stonecutter. How much do you think it cost? I'll tell you. It cost £1,000.'

He offered me a cup of tea, but I said no thanks. His kettle did look incredibly filthy. His mates had already gone off for their lunch, so I asked what he planned to do. Would he care to join me at a local pub – if, of course, he could spare any more of his valuable time? He had already given me a fascinating walk.

He didn't eat or drink at lunch time, he said. He always made do with a big breakfast. But the bosses had told him to look after me, show me round the canal, for as long as I wanted. So if I wanted to look at a canal pub, well, that would be fine.

So we walked up the canal to the next village, Stoke Bruerne, and went into a pub called The Navigation. Graeme took off his jacket, and his arms seemed even huger and his tattoos even mightier. Yes, bit of a mistake, he said. His mother was very upset when he had them done. His wife doesn't care much for them either. She's a nurse, working in a GP's practice. He used to have an earring as well, but that's gone — though I could see the mark left behind. 'I got it pulled off in a fight.'

Oh, he's calmed down a lot in recent years, so he says. At school he was a tearaway, always in trouble. 'I got bullied the first two years at secondary school. Yeah, might surprise you. I've always been fairly big. Then I decided to get my own back, to put it around. I wouldn't accept any authority. I hated anyone telling me what to do.

'I regret it now. Oh, yeah. Wish I'd stuck in more at school. I quite enjoy it now when I get sent on little courses. And I like teaching the multi-skill kids. If they want to learn, of course. When they don't want to know, which is how I was, then I can't be bothered with them.'

Over a few beers, it also came out that he'd been something of a football hooligan when younger, ejected from several football grounds while following Manchester United around the country. I'd noticed the Blessed Fergie, I said, but you come from Milton Keynes, don't you? Typical. Most people who follow Man United don't live anywhere near Old Trafford. Why hadn't he followed his local team, near where he was born and still lives?

'Luton, you mean? Must be joking. I got it from my dad. He followed Man United. And my gran. She loved Georgy Best. My oldest son Ben loves Man United. Lives for them. Got all the kit. He's got the home kit, the away strip, the lot.'

Man United were about to bring out another strip in a month's time, the 13th change in five years. Would Ben be getting that? 'Yeah, I suspect he'll have to have it. I'll give in. Of course it's a rip-off. It costs about £100 each time. But you've got to have it, haven't you?'

Alas, he rarely gets to see Manchester United play these days. Not because of lack of devotion. Just lack of mega bucks. The success of Man United in terms of marketing and commerce means that many ordinary, working-class people who traditionally supported them can now not afford it.

'I'm in the Members' Club, which costs £15 a year. So is Ben. You get bugger all for it, except Ben does get a Christmas card.'

The reason for joining is that your name goes into a hat for spare tickets, i.e those not already pre-sold as season tickets or for hospitality suites and commercial sponsors.

'The trouble is there are 120,000 members but only 40,000 tickets ever available. So you only ever have a one in three chance of getting one. In a season, I probably get to Old Trafford only three or four times. In the '70s and '80s I went to every match, home and away. Never missed. I would still, if I could get a ticket.

'You can see the thinking. They don't want the same people there all the time, do they? They wouldn't keep buying the merchandise, would they?'

And do you? 'Oh, aye. But I do it by mail order. I have a club credit card. I buy all the videos and stuff, all the books and that.

'I've been trying to tell the wife it would be a good investment to buy a season ticket. They cost a fortune, about £500 a year, but you can't get them anyway. There's a waiting list for years. But if I had one, I could sell my seat when I couldn't go. So I'd get some of my money back. She doesn't quite see it that way ...

'Yes, it's a disgrace, the way ordinary fans get treated. I blame that Martin Edwards. He must be worth millions by now. I don't blame Bobby Charlton. He's also a director, but he's my hero. I would never blame Bobby for anything.'

As it was man-to-man, pub talk, I then asked a really personal question. How much did he earn?

'My basic pay is £11,500 a year.'

Appalling, I said. A skilled bricklayer, 22 years' experience, married with three kids. How could he possibly survive?

'By doing overtime all winter. That's when the big jobs get done. I work seven days a week in the winter and that usually gets my annual pay to £20,000, with allowances and stuff.'

But he did sincerely love it and had no regrets? 'It's a different way of life. You have to have a passion for it.'

Would he like his son Ben to work on the canals? 'No. I hope he'll get something better. Nothing wrong with this, but I worry about the future. Will there be any jobs?'

There were current rumours that the government was going to sell off parts of British Waterways, the parts most attractive to developers, in towns where new buildings could go up – which would presumably mean the least attractive or least-used parts might be closed or left derelict.

'We've had so many changes over the years. Every time we do, it means more jobs go. I've always voted Labour, all my life. So has my family. I voted for them last time, and was pleased they got in. But they're just the same as the Tories. I blamed the Tories for all the cutbacks, all the changes and hassles we've had over the years. But New

Labour's just the same. In the long run, they're no more interested in us than the Tories were.'

And should they be? After all, it costs the government around £50 million, of our money, to keep the canals going.

'Of course they should. We're not only part of the tourist industry, helping to bring in millions of visitors. We're living history. That's what we are . . .'

He put on his jacket and went back to work. Back to the Beast. I went to have a proper look round the village.

* * *

Stoke Bruerne is a pretty little village sliced in half like a pretty little cake. The canal goes exactly through the middle and it was obviously a vital canal centre in the old commercial days, judging by the number of locks and bridges, canal cottages and buildings. Today, to my surprise, never having heard of the village before, it is one of the liveliest centres of modern canal life. It even has a canal museum. So I went in.

I never knew there was such a thing, I said to the museum's Interpretation Officer. He wore a badge with his title on. That's how I knew what he did. He looked slightly pityingly at my ignorance. 'Actually, there are now 18 canal museums.'

Goodness. I suppose this is the biggest, then? Wrong again. The biggest is at Gloucester, the National Waterways Museum. Stoke Bruerne is the next biggest.

It's on three floors, jam-packed with things to do with canals, telling their history over the last 200 years. There are lots of working models, bits of engines, boats, machinery, crockery, photographs, ornaments, lots of wall charts and diagrams. It was created by a retired boatman, Jack James, who collected bits for his own interest. In 1963 it became a proper museum, housed in what was once a corn mill. They now get 50,000 visitors a year.

I followed a party around and heard the Interpreter telling the history of canals, both national and local, which was jolly interesting. At the height of canal mania, there were 4,000 miles of navigable canals and rivers. Goods and materials from Birmingham and the Midlands to London took a rather circuitous route in the early years, down the Oxford canal, then along the Thames into London, which meant the boats were susceptible to tides and floods. So in 1805 the Grand Junction Canal was cut, going direct from Birmingham to London. All traffic changed to that route, making a handsome return for the canal owners. This route eventually became the Grand Union.

He explained how the nearby Blisworth Tunnel was built, the one which Graeme had first worked in, which is a mile long. 'The longest continuous bore in this country.'

I could think of several politicians who might beat that record, but didn't want to interrupt his flow.

'I use that word carefully,' he continued, after a pause. 'Some people might say that Dudley Tunnel is longer. And it is – but it's three tunnels, with air gaps in between. Blisworth is the longest continuous bore which is still navigable.'

We came to a display on the work of William Jessop. 'The greatest man you've never heard of. He built some of our most important canals, but now he's forgotten. He was eclipsed by Thomas Telford.'

'This village had two revolutions. The first was in 1800. Hundreds of people were employed in the canal round here. It was always very busy. Stoke Bruerne was where you hired the leggers. They were tough people. There were very often fights between the leggers.'

Leggers? My attention must have been straying, as I had been studying various displays as he had been talking. What did leggers do? Any connection with legging it, i.e. running away? Or with getting your leg over? Unlikely, as that's a modern term.

'The second revolution began after 1963, when this museum opened and we became a tourist centre. There was nothing really here in 1960. No work for the local people. They all commuted elsewhere. Now there's a lot of work right here in the village: restaurants, pubs, shops – all because of the canal being revitalised.'

We ended up back on the ground floor again, amongst the engines and models. The Interpreter was still sharing some of his accumulated canal wisdom, telling us the name of his own favourite canal-boat engine. I didn't catch its name. Most people looked equally uncomprehending.

'Horrible thing,' interrupted one of our party. He had said nothing so far, but was clearly a canal enthusiast. Canalist? Canalmaniac? I wonder what the term might be. 'My favourite is the Bolinder engine,' he enthused. 'Now that is beautiful.'

'A fine engine,' said our Interpreter, 'but it's got a hit-and-miss pump. You have four controls to play with, because there's no gears. I don't like it, nor its shape.'

'Well, I think it's beautiful. The noise is wonderful. I just love listening to it.'

'Well, I grant you, it makes an interesting noise, but I still don't like it.'

I left them arguing the finer points of canal-boat engines and went into the museum shop. It was jammed with canal ornaments and canal-boat souvenirs, all gaily painted in canal-boat colours and designs. There were also rows and rows of books on canals, by authors and publishers I had never heard of.

I went up to the woman at the till and asked about her best sellers, which stuff was currently flying out of the shop.

'Anything to do with boat memoirs. You know, by people who used to live and work on the canal boats. Oh, they sell very well. The people are all dying out now, of course, so they're hard to capture. And a lot won't talk to people. Oh, no. Even when you do track them down, they won't talk . . .'

Because they're bolshie or secretive?

'Oh no, just shy, I suppose. They dry up when they see a tape recorder.'

She pulled down a book called *Ramlin Rose*. It was all about the life of a boatwoman and was selling very well. I asked if Rose was a generic name covering all boatwomen. She laughed and said almost, it's always been popular.

'Now, this is good,' she said. 'You'll love this one. *Canal People* by Sonia Rolt. Lovely photographs, some of which I've never seen before. It's a gem, this book.'

Then she lowered her voice, as if worried that some fat canal controller might be listening. 'A lot of these canal books, well, they just use the same old photo, but don't say I said so.'

She walked with me round the shelves, all stacked with canal ornaments. She picked up one and shook her head. 'Look at this, a painted coffee pot.'

Looks pretty to me, I said. Nice colours, nice design.

'Yes, but they didn't paint their coffee pots, not the old boat people. They stood them on their stoves, didn't they? And these cooking pots and plates, they were never painted either. Or this rolling pin. Isn't it silly? The only objects boat people ever painted were their watering cans. The rest is just modern souvenir stuff. Made in China, probably. But I have to admit they all sell well.'

The most expensive item on sale was a large ornate teapot, highly decorated, priced £135. A modern repro, she said, not that she objected. Boat people did give each other such teapots as wedding presents, meant for display, not for use.

'They all used to go to Blackpool for their holidays, just like everyone else. They brought back souvenirs for their boats, but they went for lace plates. Like these, look. They have holes all round the edge, like lace patterns. They could then hang them up in their boat, usually with yellow ribbons. So these modern lace plates are okay. I don't object to them.'

Or the jars of canal clotted cream, canal jam or canal chutney? Not exactly produce one traditionally associated with the watery world of canal barges. 'Oh, every gift shop everywhere sells that sort of stuff these days.' True. Only the labels are different.

Outside, on the canal bank, I decided it was time for some light refreshment. The Great Interpreter had boasted about all the new places that had sprung up since the canal museum opened. Where were they? I could see a pub on the other side called The Boat Inn which had notices advertising its bistro and cocktail bar. What would the old bargemen have thought of that? It is even licensed for weddings. I walked over a little brick bridge – which was in excellent condition, no doubt thanks to my new friend Graeme – to have a look, but the pub was absolutely packed, with hardly any space to sit down. Couldn't see many cocktails being drunk, but a lot of beer.

I then spotted a French restaurant back on the museum side, so I crossed over once again, feeling I was in a M. Hulot film, that one at the railway station where they keep changing platforms. It looked rather posh, and quite pricey, but it was closed.

Then I noticed something called The Old Chapel. It looked suitably quaint and olde worlde English, so I had a look at the menus outside. Tonight, by public demand, they were having another Caribbean evening, only £14 for a three-course Caribbean dinner. On other evenings they were offering Thai, Greek, Italian or Tapas. You can hardly get more olde English than that, not these days.

Inside it was restrained and artistic, not at all plastic Euro-flash as I had feared. It had clearly been an old chapel, and had a lot of the windows and period features still in place. I sat down and ordered a cappuccino, having checked by peering behind the serving counter that they did have real coffee and a real cappuccino machine. One of my pet hates in life is Cona coffee, the sort they leave stewing in a glass goldfish bowl.

When I was paying, I asked a young woman at the till who the manager was. 'I am,' she said, looking at me warily, as if suspecting I was about to try and sell her something. I said I just wanted to compliment her. It seemed a nice place. Had it been open long?

'I started it six years ago,' she said.

She looked about 21, so I'd got that wrong for a start. Did you go to catering college?

'No, I'm a sculptor.'

It's quite common to find resting actresses running tearooms, but this was the first sculptor I'd come across. I asked how it all began, but she said she had to go into the kitchen first, to finish some cooking. Then she might be able to sit down and chat, but just for a few moments.

Sally Mays was her name, she was aged 29 and she had graduated in sculpture from Newcastle University in 1991.

'I couldn't get a job as a sculptor. The recession was on, and sculpting was about the last sort of work that was needed. I came back home, wondering what I could do. I grew up in a village five miles away. This is actually my boyfriend's village, but I knew it well. This chapel had been empty and derelict for some time. It seemed like a good place to do teas.

'I had no money and no training or experience in any sort of catering at all – but I had a nice bank manager and had an account at his bank since I was 16 and kept it on as a student, without running into debt. So I went to see him with the tearoom idea. He agreed to a small loan. After six months, when it was doing well, I then borrowed more. That's how it's carried on. I now have a staff of 12 altogether, including a chef, and we are still growing, but I've put everything back into the business.'

How about the fancy cooking in the evening?

'I just picked it up, from here and there. I was on holiday in Thailand last year with my boyfriend and spent two days of it on a cookery course.

'One of my problems now is getting decent help. Waitresses are easy to find, they're all students. But I've been contacting catering colleges for 60 miles around, asking them to send cooks, but with no luck. They are all technical cooks, who know all about microwave ovens and things like portion control, but they don't seem to know about proper cooking.'

With a staff of 12, things must be doing pretty well, so was she going to pack it in soon and return to sculpting?

'We're not doing that well. Not yet. It takes four years to get your money back. That's only just starting now.'

Well, let's say someone came along with a commission for some sculpting, offering the same money as the restaurant was making. Would she take it?

'I am going back to sculpture. It's what I love best. I am an artist. But I can't leave this now. I want it properly established first. In the next year or so, well, I'm hoping to cut down to four days a week, if I can find a good manager. I'll then spend the other three days sculpting. That's my fantasy.'

I asked if children came into her fantasy. 'Don't talk about them. All my friends seem to be having babies at the moment, and they ask me all the time. I'm not thinking about babies. Not at the moment. They are such a tie. Though, mind you, this is a tie. I'm thinking about it seven days a week . . .'

Her boyfriend is a surveyor, but he also spends a lot of time as the odd-job man around the chapel and gardens.

'That's what I've learned in the last six years. You have to be multi-skilled today. No use just having single jobs, or expecting to have a single career. At any moment, it might disappear.'

And what have you learned about yourself, now that you are approaching the great age of 30?

'I now know I like being with people. I've also realised I'm good at managing people. I wasn't aware of that. Though I suppose I've always been a bit bossy.

'The money side, I'm not so good at that. You have to keep very tight control of the cash flow. It's very easy to spend and find you don't have enough coming in. So far, I've kept on top of it. Now you'll have to excuse me. I've got to go into the kitchen and get going on the Caribbean dishes . . .'

When I came out of the tearoom, I felt cheered and encouraged. Such enterprise and self-awareness from someone so young. I had also enjoyed meeting Graeme, and slowly discovering his virtues. Oh, there's still hope for England today. Who says we're finished as a nation? Yours not at all disgusted, Stoke Bruerne, Northamptonshire.

I realised I was just a mile away from Blisworth Tunnel. I was a bit tired by now, but I decided to have a look at it and finish my canal walk where Graeme had begun his canal life.

It did look awfully dark and dismal, narrow and spooky. You can't walk through it, as there is no towpath. Horses couldn't get through it either. So how did the barges get themselves through, in the days before motors? Could it be something to do with leggers?

As I was staring into the tunnel, a boat suddenly emerged. I managed to draw my head back just in time. It was a Wyvern boat from Leighton Buzzard, one of a fleet of boats which you can rent. On board were a couple and three young children, all in yellow anoraks, hoods up to protect themselves from the drips and the wet of the interior of Blisworth Tunnel. They gave a little cheer as they emerged, having successfully negotiated almost a mile of darkness and also managed to miss this idiot bloke shoving his silly head in front of them.

They chugged on for another hundred yards, then drew in to the bank and moored their boat. I caught them up and said, hi, what was it like, back there in the middle of the tunnel?

'Wet,' said the man. 'But the children loved it. One of them has just asked if it is possible that we might be able to come again next year.'

His English was absolutely precise, but had just a hint of an accent, so I asked where he was from. Belgium, he said. He was a psychiatrist. His wife worked in computers.

'I read a book about your canals and always promised myself I would come here one day with my family. But I had to wait till they were old enough to be able to enjoy it.'

But Belgium has lots of canals. Robert Louis Stevenson's first book, *Inland Voyage*, was about a canal trip in Belgium. He went with a friend and loved it. Surely the canals are still there?

'Yes, we have lots, but they are still wholly commercial. There are no tourists' boats. You can't go for a sail on the canals. Same in France. In fact, I think you are the only country who has so far turned its canals into tourists' attractions. You should be proud of what you have done. Your canals are wonderful. It is the best family holiday we have ever had.'

Well, thank you kindly, sir. But how actually had he come to hire this particular boat on this particular canal?

'Well, first I read all the canal leaflets and information. We picked Leighton Buzzard to start from by looking at the map of England. It seemed an easy drive from London, yet was well into the countryside.'

It had cost them £650 for the week, including heat and water, which he thought was good for a family of five, compared with other sorts of holidays.

As he'd read so much, and done his homework, did he know about leggers?

Oh yes, certainly. Leggers, so he explained, could be hired when you went through a long tunnel, such as Blisworth. They sat on your boat, legs in the air, and propelled you through the tunnel by walking on the roof. Or you could have two leggers, one either side, who would walk along the walls of the tunnel.

'It was well-paid work, compared with being an agricultural labourer. So there was great competition, which very often led to fights and quarrels . . .'

Yes, he'd visited the canal museum on the way up the canal, and had listened carefully to the Interpreter. It does often take a foreigner to properly appreciate England's heritage.

Chapter Six

ALTHORP

I suppose I could have walked on to Althorp, another of Northampton-shire's tourist attractions, an ancient one which has also been given a new lease of life, but they might not have let me in. Scruffy bloke at the front gate, me Lord, on foot, says he's on a journey from London to Loweswater. Should I set the dogs on him or the paparazzi?

The real reason I drove there was the weather. My God, the weather. It was appalling. Floods all over the Midlands. Villages evacuated. Three people dead. Just as bad in the north. I rang our next-door neighbour in Loweswater to see if our house was okay, nothing blown away, the lake not arrived in the front garden, and she said it was horrible there as well, as cold as the Arctic. Oh, it's been quite good in London. People sitting having drinks in their back gardens. Oh shut up, she said.

London gets weather but never seems to suffer from weather. In the provinces they are fixated by it, fret and fuss about it, while the capital is above and beyond such trivial stuff, too grand and important to even notice it. Well, most of the time.

I remember in the winter of 1962, when we were living in a flat in the Vale of Health in Hampstead, our pipes were frozen for weeks and a standpipe was erected in the street. Then, of course, the hurricane of 1987, gosh, that was exciting. Trees uprooted all over London. We were in our house in NW5 by then. A pear tree in the back garden blew down, narrowly missing the house. Apart from that, not much. There have often been winters when I've not been aware of winter, not in the northern sense. Mild and wet in December, perhaps a spot of frost on the Heath in January, then mild and wet again till, very soon, it's summer and they are swimming again in the open-air ponds and at the Lido. Winter – did we have a winter? I must have missed it.

As a boy in Carlisle, the winter seemed to last about ten months, starting in August, when people went around saying, yis, aye, the nights are drawing in. No central heating, of course. Bedroom floors covered with lino, which froze your bare feet should you be daft enough to crawl out without having first got fully dressed under the blankets. Cycling to the Grammar School down Stanwix Bank was purgatory. My face would literally freeze, with icicles in my hair till break time.

Yes, that is one of the pluses about London life, or any urban life, compared with rural living. Life goes on, untrammelled, uncircumscribed, regardless of the climatic conditions. Streets and traffic, buildings and people, all have their own climate, which hardly seems to change. Nature is nullified. You are not aware of nature in London. Most Londoners never see it.

So I drove to Althorp, fearful of what nature was doing out there, scared by flood reports into thinking that I would never make it, that I might have to abandon my Jag, which would turn up floating on the *Six O'Clock News*.

My appointment at Althorp Park had taken me months to fix, as the house and gardens were still officially closed. Had been since 30 August 1997. A fairly minor stately home set in a fairly boring landscape in a fairly boring county, it had been of local interest only until one of the daughters of the house, Lady Diana Spencer, had married Prince Charles. Even then, it was merely of English interest, for those who knew from whence she had come. After her fateful death in that Paris car crash, Althorp turned into a shrine with an international fascination.

I stopped to buy a local paper in the nearby village of Upper Harleston. Only one shop, the post office, very pretty, twee and attractive, set back behind a front garden. A copy of your local paper, please. I didn't know its name, but knew there must be one. A woman was seated behind the counter with her arms folded. She had obviously seen me park outside, seen me walk up her garden path, seen me come into her shop, but she wasn't going to waste any time on niceties. With a curt nod, she indicated a pile of papers on the counter. They were copies of the *Northampton Chronicle and Echo*. I bought one, priced 28 pence.

As I paid, I asked her if she knew where the proposed car park was going to be, the new one for Althorp. She said nothing. I said, you know, the one which has been written about in all the papers.

'I'm not saying anything,' she said, folding her arms even more tightly, and her brows.

I told her that I'd got an appointment at the house at eleven o'clock, all arranged. I was just wondering about the parking problems which were bound to happen soon, when the house opened again.

'I'm saying nothing,' she said.

I left the shop smiling. Partly to annoy her, show her I was above her antagonism and suspicion. I might not be so amused when I got inside. If this was how one local felt, what sort of hostility might I find if and when I got inside the house?

I unfolded the newspaper and there was a shrieking headline right across the front page: WORLD EXCLUSIVE – EARL SPENCER'S FIRST INTERVIEW. I hadn't asked to see Earl Spencer, presuming he was living in his house in Cape Town, which was just as well. I'd been beaten to it by the local hacks.

I got past the security man on the main gates and drove slowly through the grounds. The main house looked a bit grey and grim, but then it was a dull, grey, rainy day. Celia Fiennes rather admired it when she passed this way in 1697. 'The front appeared like a Prince's Court of brick and stone, very fine.'

The stable block, where I was heading, was much warmer and more attractive, built of yellow Cotswold stone with an impressive archway at either end, a splendid edifice in its own right. It was built in 1732 on the lines of an Italian villa, complete with Tuscan porticoes and pillars, similar in style to Inigo Jones's St Paul's Church, Covent Garden. Pevsner, in his book on Northamptonshire, commented that 'It might well be argued that the stables . . . are the finest piece of architecture at Althorp'.

Alas, it appeared to have been turned into a building site. There was scaffolding everywhere, lorries and dumpers, piles of material, workmen scurrying around. There was even a mobile burger bar in an old van, tut tut. The sort you see on lay-bys or outside football grounds, not at stately homes.

I went into the internal courtyard, climbing over all the debris, trying to avoid the mud, and up some stairs in a corner, looking for the offices of David Horton-Fawkes, general manager of Althorp. His secretary said he had been delayed in some meeting with the builders on the site, but she made me some coffee and explained the correct pronunciation.

I'd been saying 'All-thorp' all these years, since I first heard about the place, and so had most of the world's media. The correct pronunciation is in fact 'Awltrup'. She pointed to an eighteenth-century engraving on the wall in which the house and estate is named as Althrop. She didn't know when the change in spelling to Althorp happened. Either way, the 'h' has never been pronounced.

Mr Horton-Fawkes, when he appeared, was much younger than I had expected. From his double barrel and position in life, I'd presumed he would be an elderly tweedy gent. He was actually in his early thirties but looked even younger with a modern close-cropped hairstyle. He could have been an off-duty footballer or a resting musician. He was wearing a jumper and was very casual and relaxed, in his clothes and his manner, with no hint of upper-class overtones, making it hard on first meeting to pin down his exact background. Which is, of course, what all Englishmen attempt to do on first meeting any other Englishman.

So how did you get the job, Dave? Didn't actually say that. Mr Horton-Fawkes for a while, then David from then on. Well, it all goes back to his schooldays, he said. And where was that, then? Eton actually. That's when his friendship with Earl Spencer began, when they were both aged 13, but after Eton their lives went in rather different directions.

'Oh, Charles was always the clever one, in all the top classes. He got three As at A level and got into Oxford. While I got, well, not very good results. Three Cs, I think it was . . .'

And so at 18, while Charles went off to Magdalen College, David went off to make beds, pour drinks and wait at tables for a salary of £46 a week as a management trainee at the Savoy Hotel.

'Yeah, a bit of a culture shock after Eton. We did everything, down to the filthiest jobs in the bowels of the hotel. There were 22 trainees started that year. Only two completed the five-year training. But I loved it. I'd always wanted to work in hotels.'

He says his father, a well-known sailor but with not much wealth, was all for it.

'But it was very hard. Sometimes I was doing 120 hours a week. I didn't really know much about London either, having been brought up in the West Country. That was a bit of a shock as well. For several weeks I was taking a taxi home whenever I finished later than 9.30 p.m. I thought all tubes stopped running after 9.30. This was because the first time I'd tried, I couldn't get into Charing Cross tube station. I hadn't realised that particular entrance was always closed early to stop vagrants sleeping there. Such ignorance. It meant I was spending most of the little money I had on taxis.'

After his five years' slog, he became deputy banqueting manager. One of his duties was helping to organise weddings. 'I did Mark Thatcher's, Rowan Atkinson's, someone from Duran Duran, and someone who turned out to be the biggest gangster in the East End. But your object is the same, whoever they are. You meet the bride and groom and say to them, "How are we going to make this a marvellous day for you?"'

He moved on to another London hotel as deputy general manager, where the standards were not quite as high as the Savoy's, then decided he wanted to move back to the country, becoming manager of a country house hotel near Bath, Huntstrete House. He'd by then got married to Christabel, an Austrian, whom he had met in the Savoy when she was working in accounts.

'Over the years, Charles had tried to keep in touch with me, as we had been such close friends at school. But in the hotel business you are always letting people down, your hours are so unsociable. I did lose track of most friends, but not Charles. So I'm grateful to him. I did see him quite often because he'd invite me here, to Althorp, as a house guest.

'When I became manager of my place, I invited him and his wife Victoria to come for the weekend. It was during that weekend he got talking about his problems at Althorp. It was costing half a million a year just to look after the house, repairing the roof, that sort of thing, but the income wasn't covering it.

'Althorp had been open to the public since the 1950s. The deal, as with all stately homes, was that if you let the public in for a minimum of 60 days a year, there were tax advantages to help you care for the house.

'Charles's grandfather had been obsessive about the house. He was known as the Curator Earl and had catalogued everything, down to the thimbles. He once had some chair experts visiting from the Victoria and Albert museum and he showed them the chairs he wanted them to look at – then he left the room. They heard him locking the door behind them, and then he shouted, "Don't touch anything else. I'll be back in half an hour."

'Charles's own father was not so obsessive and, of course, when he was married to his second wife, Raine, quite a few things were sold off and changes made, like, er, colour schemes that, er, didn't please everyone . . .

'They were getting about 28,000 visitors a year. That wasn't bad, plus there were a few things like car rallies in the grounds. But Charles wanted to try more corporate events, conferences and meetings. The more we talked, the more we realised he needed someone experienced in hotel and banqueting work – such as me. So in 1995 he offered me the job. I am not in charge of the estate; a land agent does that. Just the house and grounds.

'I made it clear from the beginning that if I was going to do the things he wanted, I had to be able to hire people who were experienced professionals, not old family retainers. Nothing wrong with them. I just needed people with the right priorities. For example, if I said that some corporate event was being held here, then those guests came first – not the family, or their guests, or the staff. I've visited stately homes where they say, ah, you can't go in that room today, the Duke is having his nap. You get places where the staff put themselves first, wanting to be able to park their cars near the house, making visitors park miles away. They tend to look upon visitors as people to be tolerated, not welcomed. I wanted them welcomed. Charles and I agreed on that – guests had to come first.'

One of the other things he wanted was PR support, an agency used to handling top-class clients. So he contacted a woman he had known when she was working at the Savoy press office. She had then gone on to run her own firm with some famous accounts like the Orient Express group. She was called Shelley-Anne Claircourt.

Oh, I know her, I said. Not met her, in the flesh, but spoken to her over the years when I've done travel stories. Yes, she is very high class. I had noticed her name, which is hard to forget, and seen her on television during the Earl's divorce case in South Africa, when she was described as his spokesperson. I'd wondered how she'd come to get that job. Now I knew.

At that moment, Shelley herself arrived, right on cue.

Just as well I'd been complimentary. By chance, she had a meeting at Althorp that day but had been delayed driving up from London. She'd got a flat tyre.

After she had settled down and had some coffee, I asked her about her background. I had always assumed from her pukka accent she must be posho English, but she turned out to be Rhodesian, didn't come here till she was a teenager. Her first job after school was at the Savoy Hotel, in a fairly humble position, before moving into their press office.

'I was reluctant when David first rang me,' she said. 'But he talked me into coming for the day, just to have a look at Althorp. I did – and fell in love with the place.

'Apart from promoting the event side, I also publicised the sale of some of his family titles, five Lordships of the Manor. He sold them to pay for some new plumbing work in the house. It got some good press attention, here and abroad, especially one which made you Lord of the Manor of Wimbledon. The sale raised £200,000.'

David also did well in increasing Althorp's income, attracting new events such as a British Telecom Forum. 'They were here for one month, demonstrating their new technology to customers from all over the world. For a whole month, I had to do lunch and dinner for 120 people. We've also done events for the Rolls-Royce Club, and concerts with people like José Carreras and Shirley Bassey.

'Charles was pretty good, I must say that. Even when they kept him and his children awake at night. He never started shouting, "Get these bloody people out!"'

So they were chugging along quite nicely. Then Diana died. Her brother decided she would be buried at Althorp, her family home, where she had grown up. That was when all the fuss and attention began.

'Until the day of her death,' says Shelley, 'I was getting about five or six press calls a week. No more than that. In fact, the month before she died I'd been trying to persuade *The Times* to do a piece about the business side of Althorp. The idea was in limbo, as they didn't seem very interested. The week afterwards, they rang up and said yes please. It was impossible. We were by that time getting 500 press calls a day – and had decided that no one was being let into the house or grounds.

'It was difficult. As a press officer, you want to help, give information, but mostly all I could say was "no comment". They wanted to know all the family details and plans, as if they had a right to know everything, ignoring the fact that she was someone's sister.'

'We were overwhelmed by people's kindness,' said David. 'There were just so many decisions to be made, with the whole world watching.'

And a lot of people criticising many of the decisions and comments and statements, though when the Earl spoke at the Princess's Westminster Abbey funeral service, his speech was universally admired for its passion and sincerity.

'But he did get a letter from a famous Tory politician the very next day – who gave him a warning. He said the speech was great – but he had offended the Establishment and the press. "And both will try to bring you down."

'I couldn't quite see how he had offended the Establishment. But it was true he had attacked some sections of the press. It was his sincere belief that the press had played a significant part in his sister's death.'

Understandable, in a way, after all he and his sister had gone through, but his antagonism towards the press did seem a bit over the top at times. Had he always been like that, as a boy?

'Not at all. He had no views either way about the press, not until Diana got married. Then she was hounded, and he was hounded. They made out he was some sort of Champagne Charlie, a rich, self-indulgent aristocrat. But he was never like that. He might have thrown a few buns around in his youth, done some silly things, as we all do, but their image of him is all wrong. He's a highly intelligent, very sensitive person. He can be tough and he has some faults, like everyone, but their caricature of him is grotesque. I suppose the fact that he has won several legal cases against the press has not endeared him to them.

'What people always forget is that he didn't cause or want any of this. He wasn't a pop star, someone who courts the press when starting his career. He was dragged into all this by chance, when his sister got married. None of this was his doing.'

Then came the Earl's divorce case in South Africa at the end of 1997, which might not have been reported had he been anyone else. Shelley went out there to help, as his spokesperson, and David, as his friend.

'I sat through every day of the trial,' says Shelley, 'and I just couldn't believe some of the things which were written.'

But surely the press can only report what has been said?

'Yes, but they took things out of context, blew them up, made rumours appear as facts. I was so depressed by what happened in South Africa. It made me cynical about the press, and about Britain. I really didn't want to come back here.'

David also felt he'd had enough. On his return, he didn't know how long he could carry on working at Althorp, with all the pressures and the media attention.

Althorp had been closed totally after the funeral, to the corporate entertainment circle as well as the public. 'We felt we couldn't let the firms in if the public were not allowed.'

Now, a year later, they were getting ready to open again. The Earl had decided they would open for their normal 60 days in the summer. With the anniversary of Diana's death coming up, it was pretty obvious hundreds of thousands would want to come. It was also decided to have a sort of Diana exhibition.

'The logistics of handling the possible numbers was horrific,' said David. 'On a scale none of us had ever dealt with before. We knew that the cars, for example, would cause chaos and bring the county to a standstill. Where were they all going to park?'

After discussions with the local authorities and parish council, they decided to turn a nearby field, owned by the estate, into a car park. That led to protests from some locals, one of the many stories picked up and fanned by the national press.

'I suppose we did make a mistake there,' said David. 'With hindsight, we should have personally contacted every local resident. We thought we were doing the right thing, doing it through the parish council, but, of course, people don't pay much attention to what their parish council is discussing till it's too late.

'So at the moment we are not tarmacking or concreting the field.

After the two months, it will go back to being a field. Let's hope it's not wet in those two months, like today. Eventually, it's obvious we will have to have proper parking. If not in that field, then somewhere else.'

To find out how to cater for a massive intake of visitors, David made a tour of similar places which had experienced similar problems. He went to Blenheim, to see how they coped after Churchill's death. To Castle Howard, to see how they managed after *Brideshead Revisited* brought in the coachloads. To Buckingham Palace, after they opened their gallery, and, most of all, to Chatsworth.

'Chatsworth is the leader in this field. They are masters in handling the masses and laying on proper facilities. They were very helpful, and gave lots of good advice on things likes shops and loos.'

So at Althorp they had put in 17 new lavatories – 11 for women, 6 for gents – and a cafeteria with seating for up to 300. There's also a shop, but it won't sell Diana postcards, Diana souvenirs or anything with her name or image on. 'We never sold postcards of her even when she was alive.' The total cost of all the new works, buildings and improvements, will come to around £3 million.

The exhibition is contained in six rooms in the stable block, where most of the building work was being done that day. One room is devoted to past Spencer women. 'That will include, of course, Sarah, Duchess of Marlborough. She was very important, the Spencer who married the Duke of Marlborough. People don't realise that's where the Spencer came from in Winston Spencer Churchill.

'There is, of course, a room dedicated to Diana's childhood. Charles has collected items including cine films and her school lunchbox. We didn't want to make it a morbid exhibition. More of a celebration, about the life of a woman who came from a well-established family, became an icon, made a difference, but was still someone's sister. Perhaps people looking at the exhibition will think they might be able to make a difference too . . .'

When booking began and a telephone number was given explaining how you could buy a ticket, priced £9.50, it was made clear the exhibition would be open for only two months and for a maximum of 152,000 people. At once, the calls came pouring in. 'Some 220 separate lines were set up,' said Shelley, 'and we still couldn't cope. BT estimated there were eight million calls. Many, of course, couldn't get through, because some people would go on for ages, asking about buses and train times and how to come from the far north of Scotland with a pram and a dog.' They were also working on a concert, tickets £39.50, to be held in the grounds with international stars from the world of opera and popular music, such as Julian Lloyd Webber and Cliff Richard.

'I know some tabloid newspapers have said we are exploiting Diana's name, but all profits are going to the Memorial Fund. And we will publish the full accounts, so everything will be seen to be above board.

'We had to do something. The demand was enormous. This is where she is buried. People want to come. We had to open again in the summer anyway, whatever had happened.

'We had a thriving business before her death. We didn't have to do all these extra things. But we realised people would come considerable distances and wanted more than just to pay their respects.'

For your £9.50 entrance fee, you get a tour of the house and gardens, entry to the exhibition and a walk round the edge of the lake where she is buried. It was still raining but they said, yes, I could have a tour, so Shelley got on her wellies and David put on his Barbour.

The house itself was much warmer and more attractive than it had appeared from outside, in spanking condition, yet a lived-in sort of house, with books and presents, flowers and ornaments scattered around. Over the fireplace in the main living-room I noticed a Gainsborough and a Reynolds, so not quite your ordinary lived-in sort of house.

Visitors are restricted to the ground floor. The ornate ceilings might not stand the strain if people were allowed upstairs. But they took me up to see the enormous picture gallery which goes the full length of the house, where ladies of the household took their exercise on rainy days. It is hung with portraits in massive gold frames, most of which seemed to be of yet another royal mistress.

We then walked through the grounds, towards the lake, passing the arboretum where members of the Spencer family since 1833, including Diana, and visiting members of the royal family have planted rare trees.

I half expected the lake to be little more than a large pond, but it is a good size, some 50 metres across to the island in the middle. Its official name is The Round Oval, and it was designed by Capability Brown's chief assistant, Samuel Lapidge, in the eighteenth century. The rain was still lashing down, the clouds dark and dismal, and it all seemed suitably funereal. Around the island, from the far side of the lake, came gliding four black swans, almost on cue, as if a hidden film director had released them for his moodiest shot.

'We were given the swans,' said Shelley. 'There were thousands of calls after Diana's death. One of them was from a man, hundreds of miles away, who said he had some black swans. Would we like them for the lake? I didn't think we would, and nearly said no thanks. But I took his name and number, just in case.

'A few days later Charles was walking round the lake, discussing various arrangements, when he said, "You know what – it would be marvellous if we had some black swans." We were able to say at once, "No problem. We've already got them." It's not often in life you can say that.'

We walked the circumference of the lake and came to a large, ornate summerhouse, looking a bit like a temple, facing towards the island. Another extra attraction for visitors? Not quite. It was put there in the 1880s by the 5th Earl, who was First Lord of the Admiralty. It had previously been in the gardens of Admiralty House in London. He thought it would look nice beside his lake and bought it second hand for three pounds.

We sat inside it, sheltering from the rain. I noticed two bunches of flowers, still in their wrapping. The public had not yet been allowed in. So how had they got there?

'Oh, Charles was here last week,' said David. 'He had a few house guests. Someone must have left them. We still get a dozen letters a day from strangers, and bunches of flowers. We don't mind, of course, as long as it's just bunches of flowers. The problem is disposing of the cellophane.'

Inside the old Admiralty temple, the present Earl has added three plaques in memory of Diana. I could read the writing, and some verse, done in ink fading somewhat with the rain, waiting for the stonemasons to arrive and create a permanent record.

In the distance, I could hear a rumbling sound. It grew louder, as if getting nearer. Thunder? No, too constant. Traffic on the dreaded M1? Too far away. It was a goods train, trundling away on a railway line not far away. It's a regular sound, down by the lakeside, depending on wind direction. Rather moody and atmospheric. A film director would approve, though he would cheat and add it on later.

There are remains of a little stone pier at the lake's edge. At one time, Spencer children used to row across to the island. In the middle of the island is a clump of about a dozen trees. Diana buried her pet cat Marmalade and a couple of her pet dogs on the island when she was a child. This is where Diana's body is now buried. An 18-foot-high memorial urn has been placed there by her family.

David invited me to his own house for lunch, which was nice, but a bit hard on his wife Christabel, bringing home an unexpected guest. She took it in her stride. 'I was going to the supermarket today,' she said as she opened the door. 'But the weather has been so bad I just couldn't get there. So it will have to be scraps, I'm afraid.'

Which, of course, it wasn't. It was cold meats and salad and some jolly interesting bread. While we all ate, their five-year-old son Peter played around us with his Lego, bringing exciting bits to the table for us to admire.

It must feel a bit isolated, living in the middle of a vast estate, with a young child, yet cut off from other families. They didn't think so. Peter goes to the local primary school and loves it, so they said.

Their house was a small detached lodge a mile or so from the main house, built in the same colour of stone as the stables. It goes with the job, so they kept on their old house near Bath, just in case.

They didn't see themselves living at Althorp for ever but, for the present, David was enjoying all the challenges. That afternoon he had a meeting with an access group for the disabled. They had already laid a new gravel path to the lake, but on muddy days, it was now realised, it wouldn't be much good for wheelchairs. 'After them, I've got a meeting on self-binding gravel. Apparently, that's the stuff which will provide a better surface in bad weather. Yes, I'm learning a lot in this job.

'Transport has been a headache, because we are not on the normal tourist route. Tourists didn't pop in here on their way to Stratford-upon-Avon or York. We have now agreed with Virgin Trains that they will provide a bus shuttle service from Milton Keynes railway station, and from Northampton.

'Next year we might do some things differently. We might, for example, change the ticket system. Buying the software for an automatic computerised phone system can cost £60,000. Or we could hire more human beings, which is what they do at Buckingham Palace. Or we might sell our tickets on the Internet.

'I am sure everyone who comes will be overwhelmed by Althorp, but this is not our final way of doing things. This first year has been very much a learning curve for all of us . . .'

★ ★ ★

Before I left Northamptonshire, I decided to talk to the editor of the local paper. Well, he had got a world scoop. And talked to the Earl himself, which I hadn't done. It also must have been a learning curve for him these last few years, finding himself at the centre of such exciting goings-on.

Mark Edwards is 34, born and brought up locally in Kettering. He did an English degree at Middlesex Polytechnic, then returned to Kettering as a trainee on the *Kettering Post*. He became editor of the

Northampton Chronicle and Echo in 1995. It's an evening paper, with an editorial staff of 38, not to be confused with the *Northampton Evening Telegraph*, which is in the same group, all part of Johnson Press. His paper covers Northampton and the southern part of the county. The *Telegraph*, based in Kettering, covers the area around Kettering and Corby. I hope I've got that right.

'We have dealt with Althorp on a regular basis since Diana's death and found them helpful. Just the nitty-gritty stories with a local angle. We let the tabloids do the rumour stories. We only investigated if it was local. There was a rumour at one time that she wasn't buried on the island. We contacted the Bishop and he released the burial certificate. So that story was poppycock.

'Yes, we did interview local people complaining about the parking problems, but that is our job. I think Althorp understood that. We've never fallen out with them.

'I put in a request for an interview with the Earl some time ago. I felt we would get it some time, being the local paper. It was when they finally got all the planning permissions, that's when they agreed. He couldn't have been kinder. I had about two hours.

'Because it was a world exclusive, we decided to run it in the group's two local papers, which confused most of the national media who lifted the story from us. They couldn't work it out. *The Times* described us as the "Northampton Chronicle and News", which doesn't exist. Funnily enough, only the *Sun* got both names right.'

So what did he think of the coverage? And the national press ripping off his world scoop?

'Shelley warned me what would happen. She said they would all come back to me for more stuff. What did surprise me was how they lifted things out of context, blew them up and exaggerated them. One of the tabloids had a headline saying the Earl had "blasted the Diana Memorial Fund". He hadn't blasted them at all. All he'd said was that the fund should have a finite lifetime. They made up the "blasting".

'It has been a strange experience for us, watching the national media at work. I don't want to criticise them, of course, but I can now understand why the Earl thinks he's had such a hard life with them. They do take things out of context, lift quotes from elsewhere, then put their own spin on them.'

Presumably it has been a profitable time for him and the paper?

'Not really. We decided we would give the whole interview to the PA, for free, plus photographs. We didn't want to make money from the story. We didn't want to get into all that.'

But surely you do sell stuff, in the way provincial newspapers normally do? You must have some sort of pool, whereby the journalists on the staff share any proceeds?

'What I do here is allow individuals to keep their individual money. They can sell any story they like to the nationals – as long as it's post production.'

And do you personally do that?

'I did, but now, as editor, I don't do any writing. Except for this story. When I came back to the office with it, several people pointed out that if I resigned immediately from the paper and flogged it myself, I would be very rich today.'

And did you contemplate that, just for a second?

'Certainly not.'

Although he had given the story to the PA for free, and it had subsequently been used by every British newspaper, there were now requests coming in from all over the world from people wanting serial rights for the story and photos. It was something they had never experienced before.

'We've decided we're going to give it to an agency to handle, someone who specialises in syndication. But we'll give away all the profits. Not sure who to yet. Probably some local charity in Northampton.'

'There has been a reluctance generally to cash in. There weren't postcards of Diana on sale in Northampton, even before her death. But I should imagine the local tourist-board people are quite pleased. They used to describe Northampton as "The Secret of the Shires". This was because most people never came here, going right past on the motorway. They'll probably have to change that slogan now.'

Even though he and his paper had not made any money directly from the scoop, their sales must have jumped up tremendously. I noticed that he had spread the story over three days. To milk it even further and sell more copies?

'No, that wasn't the reason. It was really because there wasn't enough space. So much else was happening locally. A lot of big news.'

Oh, come on.

'Our normal circulation is 27,800, but we have been well over 30,000 for the last week. All because of the floods.'

The floods?

'The Diana story has helped, but I know we've done well mainly because of our flood coverage. We've done special reports all week. Didn't you notice them?'

I looked at the paper again and, yes, there were four whole pages on the floods including the centre spread, where an editor normally places his best or biggest story. The photographs were pretty good, showing villages totally surrounded by water, people saving their furniture, pubs abandoned, firemen rescuing people from buildings.

I suppose if you live in Northampton, knowing each village, each street, each pub, you will want to keep these photographs as a record, to show to the grandchildren.

Reassuring, in a way. Local people did retain local priorities, even when the rest of the world was losing its head once again over Diana.

Chapter Seven

THE SUSTRANS WALK

Also, I could have walked. All the way. On footpaths. Not just canal towpaths. It is possible these days to walk all over Britain, up and down, in and out, coast to coast, town to country, on pretty paths, easy tracks, quiet byways, without ever having to use a nasty main road or a nasty motor car. And all with legal access. It hasn't been possible, on the present scale, during these last hundred years, though the beginning of the access movement goes back a bit further than that, to the end of the nineteenth century, when activists like Canon Rawnsley of Keswick, one of the founders of the National Trust, began demonstrating against landlords who wouldn't let the great unwashed put one foot on their fields.

The king of the modern access movement, to whom we owe so much, is hardly known to the general public. I was about to walk on a stretch which he had created, so I arranged to meet him before I set off. He had long been one of my heroes, a genius of our times, though I had never met him.

A genius? Come on. That's going it a bit. Well, I do use the term rather lightly. In my lifetime, let's see, I have used it about Lennon and McCartney, Wainwright, Glenn Hoddle in his Spurs days, and now John Grimshaw.

The HQ of his organisation is in Bristol, which wasn't on my route to Lakeland, but he had to be in London for some meeting with railway people about taking over some disused railway tracks. So I arranged to meet him for coffee at the Groucho Club in Soho. I am a founder member and have shares in it. It is one of the modern London creations which I am sure Priestley would have approved of heartily. A club for hacks and people in the media, open to men and women, dress casual. I often wish there was a branch in Loweswater.

Mr Grimshaw's organisation is called Sustrans, a dopey, not to say confusing, name, one of the reasons why their achievements have been scarcely recognised. I've known of the existence of Sustrans for some years because I once did a book about walking old railway lines. I've rung them up, spoken to their officials and even done an unveiling ceremony for them when they reopened an old railway bridge in Cockermouth – but I've never actually understood who or what they are.

All I knew was that they were goodies, jolly interested in converting old railway lines into cycleways and footpaths, but how did they begin? Did they have paid staff and a proper structure, or were they just an assorted collection of hairy-legged amateurs?

I realised they must be bigger than I had imagined when I read a news story about them in 1995. Sustrans had been awarded £42.5 million of Lottery money. Strewth. The biggest award for any privately run environment scheme so far. Not exactly amateurs.

John Grimshaw arrived on his bike, natch, and tied it up outside the Groucho Club on the railings which are more normally accustomed to supporting drunks and the over-excited. The bike was beat up and dirty, his trouser bottoms all dusty. He was very tall, a bit like an overgrown public schoolboy in a tweed jacket with leather patches on the elbows. By comparison, his bike looked small and fragile, hardly able to take him anywhere, but he is never without it.

I said it must be hell riding it in London, but he said no, no worse than in Bristol. 'I've only ever been knocked over once, so far. But I have been done for reading while riding. I lived in Kensington at the time, and was working out at Heathrow. The bike ride was so long and boring that I used to read while cycling, till I got stopped by the police . . .'

He was born in 1945 in Guildford but brought up in East Africa, where his father had a job with the Church Missionary Society. Aged nine, he acquired his first bike while living in Nairobi. 'I won it in a raffle. It was a Raleigh, very big and black and upright, too big for me, really, so I swapped it for a smaller one. I've been riding bikes ever since. Not for touring, just as a means of transport.'

He cycled at school, Monkton Combe, near Bath, and then at Cambridge, where he read engineering. For the next 15 years he was a full-time professional engineer working for some big firms, like Taylor Woodrow, on some big projects, such as the Heathrow Cargo Tunnel. He got married, started a family and moved to Bristol.

'I always rode my bike to work, but I did have a car for a while. A Volvo estate, of course, like every engineer. But I gave up my car about ten years ago. One of the first rules of family life is not to have a car when they become teenagers. Otherwise you'll spend the rest of your life ferrying them around. It made my children independent, because they had to be. We sent Joshua by train to London on his own when he was eight. He burst into tears when I gave him the two tickets, because he thought someone must be coming with him. I had to explain the other ticket was his return. The following year he was on another train ride on his own and fell asleep and missed his stop. That was worrying, till the stationmaster at Cheltenham rang to say he was sitting on the platform.'

A bit dangerous, letting young children travel on their own? 'Look, here are the facts,' he said, getting out two fountain pens from the inside of his tweed jacket. One had red ink and one had blue ink. He then proceeded to baffle me by drawing lots of colour-coded graphs and tables. The one I did take in was that for every child murdered by a stranger there are 50 killed by motor cars.

During the 1970s in Bristol, he was active in several anti-motorway movements, but he never personally demonstrated. 'All I did was produce papers and plans for alternative schemes, hoping they would influence the authorities to change their minds.'

His proper piece of action came in 1978 when the local council announced it had sold off some cranes on the Bristol docks. Not particularly old or pretty cranes, but they had been looked upon as a traditional part of the dock landscape. Lots of locals were jolly upset. Instead of signing the usual petitions, writing to the local papers, generally huffing and puffing, John and some friends found 50 people to put up £100 each.

'We tracked down the person who had bought the cranes, who was a scrap merchant. We plonked down our £5,000 in cash in front of him, knowing he had only paid £4,500 and still had to pick them up. So he was making £500 for doing nothing. Naturally, he agreed. We then wrote to the council and said, you know those cranes you sold, well, we own them now. We plan to leave them where they are, but we'll pay you £1 a year rent for the site. Eventually, we gave them back to the council. They're still there. In fact, they're now the symbol of the Bristol Industrial Museum.'

They did a similar bit of creative action when there was a ferry closure they didn't agree with, believing there was still a local demand. They bought their own ferryboat, hired a ferryman, and reopened the service. Eventually they sold the boat to the ferryman, who now runs five ferries.

'What we learned was that if bureaucrats won't do it, and you think it really needs to be done, there is always a way of doing it yourself.'

He then became part of an action group, Cyclebag, which wanted proper cycleways established in the middle of Bristol, but for two years they didn't get very far. 'That sort of thing is much harder to do on your own. You can't actually buy up roads in the middle of towns.'

So they turned their attention to a stretch of old railway which was lying empty. 'We leased five miles of the Bristol–Bath line in 1979 for £1 a mile. All that summer, we had volunteers clearing it. We got some money from Clarks, the shoe people, persuading them that supporting public pathways was good for them because people would wear out more shoes. When finished, it was a simple dust path, but it was phenomenally popular. So we took over another 15 miles in 1980. The Bristol–Bath route is still the most successful cycle and walkway in Britain. It carries over one million trips a year.'

So that was how it all began. Converting one local disused railway led to others in his local region. In 1980, John was approached by the Department of Transport to do a study of all disused railway lines in England and Wales. This was when he gave up his proper job, as a staff engineer, to become a freelance consultant.

Out there, doing nothing very much, going nowhere in particular, were 8,000 miles of disused railway. This was the figure I estimated in 1982 when I wrote a book called *A Walk Along the Tracks*. I did it for my own amusement, being a walker and a railway enthusiast, when I realised that thanks to Dr Beeching there were all these old railways you could walk, if you didn't mind trespassing and didn't mind some very rough, overgrown terrain. As I travelled round, I found there were little pockets where local action groups such as John's had done their own conversions, though I never met John himself, who was by then working on his master plan.

'In 1983 I was contacted by the Countryside Commission and asked if our Bristol group would be interested in buying the York–Selby line. We had only leased until then. And we had only done it in our own region. That was when we decided we should set ourselves up properly as a charity.'

And so Sustrans was born. He admits it probably isn't the snappiest of names. It stands for 'sustainable transport', meaning transport which sustains itself. By 'sustain', he means something or somebody which does no harm or damage to anyone or anything. You now hear the word 'sustainable' tripping off the tongue of environmentalists all over the globe, a non-religious mantra of our times.

'We did think of calling it Greenways, but that sounded a bit recreational. I don't think the name in the end really matters. Our job is simple: to persuade people to walk or cycle.'

Out came his pens again, with facts and figures for cycling, walking and car driving in Denmark, with lots of diagrams, proving that what happens in Denmark can be done everywhere.

Throughout the '80s, Sustrans created several thousand miles of public cycle and pathways all over Britain. 'We were helped in a way by the unemployment problems. We were able to take advantage of all the government schemes and Manpower agencies set up to provide work for the unemployed. At one time we had 800 unemployed on our books, working on routes all over the country.'

They also proved highly successful at doing deals with local councils and countryside bodies and in getting government and other grants. This culminated in their £42.5 million Lottery money, awarded by the Millennium Commission, the condition being that they had to create 2,500 miles of public routes by the year 2000. Sounds a lot.

'The Lottery money is only a quarter of the money needed. We have to raise a further £150 million ourselves. But we'll easily do it. It sounds a lot of miles, but we are in partnership with around 400 councils. Almost all are now on our side. We still have a few problems with some private landowners, but having the Lottery money behind us means very few people or bodies can finally stand in our way.'

Out came another sheet of paper as he took me through a current drama on a line near St Austell. They own 20 miles of pathway – but have failed for 18 months to take over a vital stretch just 100 yards long. 'In the end, we've had to buy four properties, actual houses with gardens, because certain people wouldn't give us access round the edges.'

Having bought the houses, their public path will be laid out, then they'll resell the houses, this time with smaller gardens. They might even get all their money back, or make a profit. What the money did was give them the muscle to make possible what they wanted.

'The Lottery money is both a boon and a curse. People think we have more money than we have. Our success has also made some people fear that all our paths are going to have millions of people walking and cycling along them.

'But we are well ahead of schedule. I now hope that by the year 2000 we will in fact have opened more like 4,000 miles, not the 2,500 we promised. I also like to think we are the only truly national millennium project. The Dome, after all, is local, in the sense that it is fixed in one place. Our Millennium Routes are throughout the whole country, available to all.'

* * *

Off he went on his bike and off I went to rural Leicestershire, to the next county on my journey north, to walk one of his Sustrans routes.

I'd made an appointment with their regional manager, Patrick Davis, to meet up with him and have a pub lunch at the Malt Shovel in the village of Worthington. I was there well on time, unusual for me, and found the pub locked up. Not again. What is happening to the countryside? I then found a notice which said they no longer opened at lunch times.

Patrick eventually roared up on his motorbike which didn't seem exactly sustainable transport, but I didn't say anything as he was immediately full of apologies for having chosen this pub. It was open for lunch last time he was there. But not to worry. There was another pub at the next village, so we could start walking now, give ourselves an appetite.

As we walked, I asked him about his accent. It wasn't pronounced, or easily identifiable, just sort of soft southern rural. 'It's Bernard Miles rural. You can hear it across a whole stretch of southern England, from the Isle of Wight, up through Hampshire, into Herts and Bucks. It's now being drowned by Estuary English, flooding out of London.'

He is aged 51, comes from Bucks, went to Oxford Poly, did a degree in planning and then postgraduate work at Edinburgh, where he met his wife, who is Irish. He worked for Leicestershire County Council for 21 years as a landscape expert, till in 1996 his department was downsized and he was made redundant. He then joined Sustrans, with whom he had worked on various joint projects.

'I had by then become tired of feeling fenced in, never visiting villages or places if they were just a few yards outside our council boundaries. With Sustrans, there are no boundaries.'

He said all this with a smile, semi-mocking, but at the same time there was a glowing, spiritual feeling to him, as there had been with John Grimshaw, although in Grimshaw's case I could sense there was a tougher nut underneath.

We got to Osgathorpe, a name I found hard to pronounce so tried not to. Very pretty village, affluent air, nice gardens, neat houses – but all dead. No signs of people, no signs of life. We got to the pub Patrick had in mind. It was closed as well.

A woman with a baby in a pram was coming backwards out of a house, negotiating the steps. She jumped when I spoke to her, as if living in this village meant never seeing another human being. I asked if she knew of a pub which might be open and she directed us to the other end of the village.

'We don't do meals,' said the woman behind the bar. 'This is a wet pub.'

I had an image of umbrellas at the bar, or swimming suits and underwater cocktails, floating glasses and synchronised drinkers raising their glasses in unison from a sea of lager. What she meant was she did drinks only. But she did have some cobs, and could do us a cheese roll.

I told her about the other two pubs being totally closed, offering nothing at all. 'I would be, if I employed staff. You can't afford to open at lunch time round here, not if you have wages to pay. But this is my pub. I do it for the community. Not the money.'

There didn't seem much of a community, as the pub was empty, but a real fire was burning and a television blaring away, so some sort of company was expected. She said yes, the same five or six people came in every day. They didn't want food. They just drank their two or three pints each, chatted to each other and watched the television, if there was any racing on.

Sure enough, five blokes wandered in, one after the other, all roughly in their sixties, in old pullovers and trousers, looking suitably rural and local. One even had mutton chop whiskers, direct from Central Casting. They took what was obviously their regular place at the bar, made their regular hellos to mine hostess, ordered their regular drinks.

On entry, each gave a cursory glance in our direction, betraying by the faintest flickering of an eyelid that, heh up, strangers present, then resumed the sort of conversation at the bar they probably had yesterday and would probably have tomorrow. The owner stood behind the bar, elbows splayed, nodding away, making her contribution to the community. I was hoping to overhear some village gossip, some scandal or minor drama, but all I could hear was a discussion on the finer points of Teletext, how it worked, what you could get on it.

After our snack, we walked back through a totally empty Osgathorpe and Patrick explained what an important village it was, how vital it was in the greater scheme of things to the Sustrans firmament.

'It's like a motorway junction. Two of our major routes join each other here.'

Amazing. Who would have thought it? Yet there was no sign of another human being, a bike or even a lone dog.

'One of them is Route 6. That starts in Sheffield and goes down to Milton Keynes. Then there's Route 52, which starts in Stratford-upon-Avon, goes through Warwick Castle, Leamington Spa, Coventry and Nuneaton, which, as you know, is the exact centre of England.'

No, I didn't know that, Patrick. How can you be so exact when the shape of England is so irregular?

'Ah, well it's just been worked out by the Ordnance Survey people, using computers. The exact spot is 273 yards south of a bridge over the A5. It's actually on one of our routes and we hope to make a big feature of it, putting up a special piece of sculpture.'

As we walked, we were eventually overtaken by a few cyclists following the Sustrans route. 'That couple will have come from Sheffield this morning,' said Patrick confidently. 'That man will have started in Stratford-upon-Avon.'

Or they might just have been taking a bike ride round the block, but I let Patrick have his way. After all, he was the area negotiator. Whatever that means.

Well, part of his job is looking after their existing routes, supervising maintenance and such like, and part of it is looking out for new routes. All of which he does from his own home, making his own hours, making his own work. That very morning he had finished off the final application forms for planning permission for a route of some 22 kilometres they had acquired in Warwickshire, part of the old Rugby–Leamington railway.

It had taken months getting all the right applications in place as there were 30 bridges to be dealt with, landscape work to be done, bogs to be drained, scrub to be cleared, before any path could be laid down. 'All the forms have been lying on my desk like a paper elephant, but today I got the last one done.' The cost of the conversion will come to around £1.2 million, but a lot of that will come from local councils and grants from national and European bodies.

'My job is really imagineering. I see where a route can be created, or people tell me where a route might be created, then I go and investigate. I work out how it should be done, how we might be able to add other stretches, link up with existing bridleways, canal towpaths, use bits of minor roads or whatever.

'I have to imagine how we can do deals to get what we want. Then I have to guesstimate how much it will cost. Finally, I have to imagine how we are going to pay for it. What you do is invent cash.'

What?

'We do live in the real world. We know that everything has to be paid for. But it's the opposite of working for a local council. With them, you know what your budget is before you begin, so you don't start anything if you haven't got the money. With our work, we start off without any budget at all. Just an imagination.

'My first job is to sell the idea to the local community and local authorities. If you get the council involved, you hope they will contribute. I suppose a major part of my life is spent fundraising. To do that, you have to know how councils work, how grants are made, which bodies have funds, how you qualify for them. You don't initially need money; what you need is the knowledge of how to get money.

'When I first put up a scheme, I am often told "no chance". By the inflection in the voice of someone who's turning you down, you can tell if it's worth changing the emphasis, altering the approach, altering the route, till eventually you hope they will say, "Ah, if you are doing it that way, then we might just well agree."'

His years as a council official have clearly come in handy, knowing the ropes, knowing the language, knowing how to get permissions, but fundraising must have been new to him. '"Milking the trusts" it used to be called. Now it's a full-time profession, with Resource Consultants who do nothing else but raise funds. We have used them on occasions.

'We have Golden Goose training days in which we are told how to do it ourselves. I went to one last week. A specialist fundraiser explained on a blackboard how by starting on a project with £100 you firstly get local individuals or bodies to put up one pound for every pound you have raised. Then you move on to national bodies, into Europe, then on to world bodies, till eventually you have managed to turn £100 into £1 million.

'It can be done. It's all a matter of mixing and matching, coaxing, pleading, battling for grants. Europe is very good at the moment. There are, for example, special grants at present for areas with rundown quarries or coal mines. We in Leicestershire do well with them.'

I was imagining what training days for Sustrans managers might be like. Not exactly happy clappy, but perhaps a mixture of TM spiritual uplift and American-style business exhortation which my niece has experienced doing telesales.

'It is a time to share our visions. You don't get whingers working for Sustrans. There is no real hierarchy or wage structure. Some people who work for Sustrans have been successful in other professions, have often made a bit of money, so they join Sustrans to work for not much more than the warm glow.'

As we walked and talked, he happened to mention that one of his favourite writers was Bruce Chatwin – a writer I happened to have sacked. Patrick stopped in his tracks, horrified at such a sacrilegious deed. I was editor of the *Sunday Times Magazine* back in the late 1970s, and all I did was not renew his contract. I decided the magazine had had enough of enormously long purple-prosy landscape features. So Chatwin went off to Patagonia instead. I probably helped him. Patrick still seemed shocked at what I'd done, but fortunately we had come to the beginning of a reclaimed country lane which he wanted to tell me all about as it had been a long and complicated drama.

It revolved around a local quarry with whom they had had poor relations at one time. Sustrans had stepped in and bought a length of old railway track which divided the quarry's estate. They had not been best pleased. A few years later, the quarry wanted to extend one of its sites but was having planning problems with the local council. Eventually a deal was done whereby the quarry was able to expand while at the same time allowing Sustrans to reopen the old lane and extend their route. So everyone was well pleased. I think I've got that straight.

It reminded me of the inner-city deals that were done during the property boom of the '60s, when developers gave local councils land to widen roads, in return for planning permissions for high-rise blocks. Such quid pro quo deals, some of them more devious than others, have always been struck between public bodies and capitalist developers ever since the railways arrived. What is new is that modern-day deals are often brokered by one of the participants doing it for worthy, charitable, environmentally friendly reasons rather than for financial or political gain.

Having got his extra mile, Patrick then had the problem of converting it. It was totally overgrown and very swampy in parts, so they organised a summer camp for volunteers to do the hard graft of clearing the site. 'They came from all parts of the country. Some stayed in local B and Bs, others camped on the site. All gave their labour for free, then disappeared again.' The quarry itself, now best friends with Sustrans, pleased to have such an environmentally attractive feature passing through their property, provided their digging machines and some of the materials.

We stood in the empty lane, quite pretty, quite short, but unremarkable, which I would have walked down and never remembered but for Patrick giving me a blow-by-blow account of all the problems and dramas which had had to be overcome.

'Six months ago, it was impossible to use this path at all,' said Patrick, gazing around with pride. 'Now look at it.'

Yes, very nice. The actual job of laying the final surface was done by two of Sustrans' own workmen, whom we came upon a few hundred yards further on. They were two brothers, Kevin and Ian Mannion, beefy blokes in their late forties, each with an earring and close-cropped hair. Ian had worked for Sustrans since 1989. His brother had joined him three years later, coming off the dole. They are the only two full-time labouring staff employed by Sustrans in the East Midlands. Half of their time is spent on maintenance, cutting hedges and verges, repairing bridges and fences, keeping clear existing routes, and the other half is spent on new projects. That's the bit they like best.

'It can be a bit boring cutting hedgerows,' said Kevin. 'You can work solidly all day, then stand back and look and you hardly seem to have moved. Laying paths, we have to do 80 metres in a day, if the path has been cut out first and laid with stone.'

They were laying a stretch with tarmac, which seemed a bit, well, urban, but it was a particularly swampy bit which needed a good surface. The tarmac arrived, hot and steaming, on a lorry. Then they had to lay it using their dumper and roller, shovels and muscles.

They'd had a problem the previous week when they'd arrived for work to find that a cyclist had chained his bike to their dumper.

'He must have seen we were working here, but he just thought it was a safe place to lock up his bike for the day and go off for a walk. But we managed to track him down and bring him back.'

Their problem that day was a series of people on horseback who had been riding on the stone path further on and had left deep ruts in the dust. Riders are meant to use the grassy path to the side of the stone path especially laid out for them, leaving the stone path for walkers and cyclists.

'They make these ruts, then they get bigger and bigger. When it freezes, they break up the whole path. Makes it hellish bumpy for cyclists. They're right arrogant buggers, some of these horse people. Won't be told. I'd ban them, if it was up to me . . .

'What I like best is seeing families come out on their bikes at weekends. You see little kids wobbling away, taking their first rides, knowing they can do it here in safety, with no traffic.'

They both enjoyed working for Sustrans. The wages were about the same as working for the council, but they had problems explaining who they worked for. 'We never say Sustrans. No one knows what it means. So we just say we work on cyclepaths.'

Further along the route we came across various bits of sculpture, one of John Grimshaw's personal passions. He likes to have his routes artistically decorated. I took the first lot to be a couple of rough lumps of limestone dumped by the quarry till Patrick took me closer and pointed out where the insides had been sculpted. They had been shaped internally like the two parts of a nut – the shell and the seed – or it might have been male and female organs, about to fit exactly and intimately together. Patrick said he liked it.

He wasn't so sure about an ornamental milepost, one of Sustrans' main signposts on their National Cycle Network. It indicated that Derby was 12 miles ahead, Loughborough 10 miles behind. I liked the idea of these new walking and cycling routes across the nation having their own milestones, as the railways did and, long before that, the Romans marking the way across Hadrian's Wall.

This milestone was about six foot tall, shaped like a totem pole. At the bottom was written 'Millennium Project, supported by funds from the National Lottery.' No mention of Sustrans.

The totem pole bit was covered in ornamental designs and shapes, none of which I would have worked out without Patrick's help. It started with the carboniferous age, symbolised by some fossils, and went up to the modern age, symbolised by a car's steering wheel. Finally there was a petrol can, with the last three drops being poured out. Meant presumably to indicate that the age of fossil fuel and the internal-combustion engine is over. It's now back to walking or pedal power. Bloody clever but, er, a bit . . .

'Naff?' asked Patrick. 'Some people have said so. Personally, I prefer the style of mileposts we have in Scotland, which are more sculptural.'

Patrick himself gave up owning a car in 1982. I pointed out he still had a motorbike, using nasty fossil fuel, but he said he needed that for outlying parts of his region which he otherwise couldn't get to. Mainly he did use public transport, or travel on foot.

'Local and national governments are on our side today, thinking in sustainable terms, but the strange thing is, the general public hasn't yet caught up. You just have to look at all the motoring magazines. The shelves are full of them. People still love their cars. But that will change. Young people are much more concerned. Schools are very aware of the dangers.

'One of the other projects we are working on in Sustrans is creating safe routes to schools. This began in Denmark, but we are trying to make people aware of it in Britain. We all know how the roads are filled with cars every morning and afternoon with kids being driven to school, often just a few hundred yards, often a huge station wagon taking one child. The rationale is that parents are scared of their kids being knocked over or being molested. So we are working on purpose-made routes to schools. On roads there will be quiet places where they can be crossed with toucans, which are another form of pelican crossings. The object is to get cars off the street and get people walking.'

When I left Patrick, he gave me some membership leaflets for Sustrans. I hadn't actually realised you could become a member, but it turned out they already had 35,000. I wondered what the advantages might be. Unlike the National Trust, they don't have stately homes which charge entry fees for non-members. Or British Waterways, where you have to pay to sail on their canals. Sustrans owns or manages open space. Their paths and routes are free to all. Which, of course is brilliant, wonderful, marvellous, and definitely creative. But what extra does membership bring, Patrick, apart from presumably a membership badge and a newsletter?

'You'll get a warm feeling,' he said. I smiled.

'Oh, you must never underestimate the unstoppable force of the Holy Glow . . .'

Chapter Eight

DERBY

I know two things about Derby. They have a football team, Derby County, who surprised the football world by twice winning the First Division in the 1970s. And Bonnie Prince Charlie visited Derby in 1745, before giving up and turning back.

I know the former because I am a follower of football and the latter because my wife once did a biography of Charles Edward Stewart. I had an enjoyable year accompanying her on research trips to Rome and Italy and romantic parts of Scotland such as Skye and Eriskay. We never got around to visiting Derby. Not quite as romantic. As a football fan, I'd never got around to it either. I've often wondered why. After half an hour in the town, I decided I'd never been there for possibly the same reason that Charlie gave up. It's a dump.

Well, probably not really a dump, but that was my first impression. So much traffic, such complicated ring roads, nowhere to park, and it all looked hideous. I went round and round endless featureless roads trying to find a parking place, following signs indicating City Centre which all pointed towards buildings which looked horrible and nasty, so why was I bothering to fight my way in anyway?

I stopped at a garage in Traffic Street. Neat name. Spot on for aptness. I got some petrol and paid for a car-wash token, as I'd arranged an appointment with a person who works in an area where they tend to judge you by the nature and freshness of your car. I couldn't get the car wash to start, despite pressing all the buttons and lights I could see, by which time another car was hooting impatiently behind me.

I was fuming by then, so I got out to remonstrate with the driver of the other car. It was a beat-up BMW, white wheels, rows of flash headlamps, bits hanging off, disco music blaring away. Its driver got out as well. He was young, bulky and much bigger than me. I returned quickly to my car.

It was obviously all my fault, being stupid with the instructions, failing to understand the plastic token I had been given, unable to work out its arrows, or the arrows and instructions, drawn in a childlike hand, which were on the car-wash machine itself. I kicked the machine, in a childlike, stupid way. Still nothing happened. I went to get an attendant who looked about ten but was at least in long trousers. He explained it was his first day, he was on work experience, or possibly life experience. He took my token and put it in the wrong way, which even I had worked out was the wrong way. He turned it over several times, examined it for hidden codes, wiped it, then said he'd go and get another attendant.

Meanwhile the queue behind was stretching well down Traffic Street. Probably into Heart Attack Street and Coronary Thrombosis Street. I had allowed myself two hours to spare before my appointment, which I'd planned to spend in downtown Derby. 'A vibrant city, steeped in history, yet lively and up to date, rich in culture, waiting to be discovered.' So the brochures said. At this rate, I'd be spending all my Derby time in a dead car wash. If not dead.

The Brute in the BMW had got out and was standing beside me, menacingly, while I tried to smile and apologise, saying it's not my fault, actually, this stupid machine is bust, actually. He stared at me, half threatening and half confused. In my mind I still have a strong northern accent, hard to identify, but not posh or even BBC, certainly not, though I have presented several BBC radio programmes over the years. But the strange thing is, when I am in the north, or even the Midlands, nay, anywhere beyond Watford, I can hear myself sounding, or being perceived as sounding, not the rough, natural, genuine northern chap I think I am, but, well, middle class and London. Was he going to hit me, just for the way I spoke? 'Fuck off,' he said, getting back into his car. He reversed away at high speed, tyres screeching, rubber scorching, exhaust belching.

The senior attendant got the car wash working in seconds and even advised me where to park and how to walk into the city centre through an underpass. No need to drive there. Have a nice day.

I found myself in something called the Eagle Shopping Centre, which didn't seem at all nice, not compared with Milton Keynes. Nasty cheap shops, nasty cheap shoppers. I take that back about the shoppers. How can I tell things about people just by looking at them? We all do it, of course, though perhaps not as rudely as J.B. Priestley on his arrival in Birmingham, when he chanced upon a whist drive.

'First, I was struck by the extraordinary ugliness of most of the people. Nobody has ever called me handsome, and I do not ask for a very high standard of good looks in other people. They were for the most part downright ugly, rather unpleasant to look at closely. The women were either much too fat or far too thin. The men looked like lopsided oafs, gnomes, hobgoblins.' Priestley was honoured in his time, but I don't think he got the Freedom of the City of Birmingham.

I then came into an ancient market hall which was much more attractive, with a splendid roof and lots of old-fashioned stalls. We have a fine Victorian covered market in Carlisle, but, alas, they decided to modernise it, replacing the old wooden bench stalls with plastic fascia and strip lighting. The old stall-holders couldn't afford the new modernised rents, and the public prefer really modern shops, so Carlisle's tarted-up ancient market became half empty. Derby's old market still looked old – and was doing excellent business. Well done, Derby. When I said dump, I didn't really mean it. Yes, an Hon. D.Lit. from the University of Derby will do nicely. If they have one.

A signpost directed me to the tourist office, which was beside the Assembly Rooms, an ugly red-brick building where that evening Ken Dodd was due to appear. I once saw him at the Palladium and he was brilliant, making people ill with laughter. I then interviewed him, and was a brilliant failure. In 30 years of interviewing so-called famous people, I don't think I've ever got less out of anyone. Certainly not about his personal life. So I wrote it as a non-interview, how not to do it. It wasn't used.

'Scuse me, I said to the tourist assistant, I have an hour to spare, what should I see in Derby? She recommended the cathedral. I didn't know they had one. At least, I didn't know they didn't have one. It had just never struck me. After all, the football team is called Derby County, not Derby City, and I can't remember ever hearing about a Bishop of Derby. She also suggested Derby Museum and the Pickford Museum. A museum for furniture removers? No, it was a famous local family, she thought, probably. She was actually new to the job.

The cathedral only got cathedral status in 1927, which is why it's not so well known. It felt cool and modern, light and white, very airy, with some pleasant pillars, and instantly it reminded me of somewhere else. But where?

As I walked around, a well-dressed woman of about 40 wearing a smart red jacket came up to me. 'Excuse me,' she said, 'do you work here?' I said sorry, though I was quite pleased to be mistaken. Did she think I was a verger, perhaps even a canon? Not the Bishop. I do know that bishops don't hang about cathedrals. It's the Dean who's top man. The woman looked very disappointed. I wanted to ask what she was after, but that seemed a bit direct, a bit rude.

'Have you, er, got an appointment?' I asked, cunningly, if a bit daftly. Even if she had, I couldn't possibly help her, being a total stranger.

'No, no appointment,' she said nicely, giving me a big smile. She proceeded to follow me around the cathedral, stopping to look at things as I stopped to look at things, till I began to think there was something strange about her.

'I'm just walking the streets,' she said.

That made two of us, and I probably seemed pretty strange as well. I did a quick turnabout down the main aisle and left sharpish. When I got out, I remembered what the interior of the cathedral had reminded me of. A Pizza Express. Some of them are highly attractive, architecturally and artistically. There's one near us in London, in Kentish Town, which has been converted from an old college. If Derby Cathedral falls on hard times, it could easily become a Pizza Express. Wouldn't cost much to convert.

I then went to Derby Museum. Inside, this reminded me of Hampton Court Maze, stairs and corridors going up and down, back and forwards, leading to dead ends, with no signs, no apparent exits, all confusing and higgledy-piggledy. I began to think I would never get out. I had no ticket, as entry was free, which meant there was no proof I was inside, lost in the maze. I could collapse and die and no one would ever know.

I stumbled into a room marked Bonnie Prince Charlie's Room. Not his actual room, but panelled with the original wood from Exeter House, now demolished, where Charlie had stayed in Derby in 1745. A table was laid out with old maps and parchments and at it sat a wax figure of Prince Charlie, dressed in a long red coat. Weren't the English the redcoats? Or did they all wear red coats? A question for my dear wife. Not that she'll know the answer. When you do a biography, you live and breathe it for two or three years, think of nothing else, but once it's over, it's like sitting an exam – it goes out of your head.

There were candles burning and it was all suitably dark and atmospheric. I leaned over, reading the ancient documents, and got a huge surprise when I suddenly heard bagpipe music. Then a disembodied voice started talking in an Italian Scottish accent. A rather hard accent to do, unless you've been brought up in the ice-cream trade. I looked around for an ice-cream van, then realised I must have activated some audio-visual wizardry, just by my presence.

The population of Derby in 1745, so a wall chart told me, was only 6,000, so it was fairly dramatic when Charlie's army of some 10,000 soldiers and assorted hangers-on arrived in the town on their way to London, hoping to kick out the King and install Charlie's father as the rightful monarch. They had marched triumphantly down from Scotland, conquering all before them, taking towns and villages, including Carlisle. Most places had given in easily, with women swooning and local lordlings either scarpering or deciding to join in with the Jacobites.

The Mayor of Derby was one of those who did an immediate bunk, leaving Charlie and his officers to commandeer decent accommodation. They then set about raising a tax of some £3,000 from the townsfolk of Derby to help with their march south. Just 126 miles to go and they would be in complete control. It was worth paying the tax, if just to keep in with them.

That night, news reached Derby that the Duke of Cumberland had assembled his army and was heading their way, just a few miles away at Lichfield, ready to stop the Jacobite march to London. It was in fact duff information. He was much further away, but several of Charlie's advisers got scared, fearing they wouldn't be able to beat Cumberland's army. It was decided to give up. The next day, 6 December, Charlie's army turned around and left Derby, heading the way they'd come, retreating in ignominy and eventually utter defeat at Culloden.

My retreat took almost as long, back down the corridors, up and down stairs to the front door of the museum, before I was out into the streets of Derby again.

I celebrated my escape in a pub in Irongate called The Standing Order, the biggest, handsomest pub I've ever been in – but then I don't normally go into pubs. It was formerly a bank, which explains its size and grandeur. All around the sides were little book-lined cubicles filled mostly with women of a certain age, sitting drinking little glasses of wine and gossiping. No one was reading any of the books.

I took a seat and studied the tourist brochures I had picked up from the tourist office. I wondered if I might still have time before my appointment to see the arboretum, 'The first public park in England'. Could that be true? Derby, so it also said, was the first town in Britain to have piped water and the UK's first Virtual City, whatever that means. Almost any place I have ever visited has managed to boast that it has the biggest, smallest, newest, oldest, first, last something or other.

That's how tourist offices work. That's how tourist officers get promoted.

I had just half an hour to spare, and therefore had no time for arboreta or virtual cities. Instead I walked around the streets, looking for mobile phones. It had struck me that I had seen only one so far, being used by a young girl in the Eagle Centre. Had I at last crossed England's mobile phone barrier? I'd noticed loads in Milton Keynes, apart from those buskers. In the old days, Londoners talked about north of Watford as being off the map, 'there be wild beasts', the limit of civilisation as we know it. Perhaps the new boundary is Derby, judging by the sudden disappearance of mobile phones. I was no longer in the London orbit, influenced by London attitudes and affluence. I had at least reached the Midlands.

★ ★ ★

My appointment was at Derby County. Priestley, when he was roughly in this region, went to see a Derby match – but in the other sense of the word: Nottingham Forest versus Notts County. His comments about football, written back in 1933, could almost be repeated today, word for word.

'Nearly everything possible has been done to spoil this game: the heavy financial interest; the absurd transfer and player-selling system; the lack of any birth or residential qualifications; the absurd publicity given to every feature of it by the Press; the monstrous partisanships of the crowds.'

He didn't know the half of it, or the hundredth of it. In 1972, when I wrote a book about a year in the life of Tottenham Hotspur, football was very much as it had been back in 1933, give or take a few price increases. Spectators mostly stood. Many of the stadiums were around a hundred years old. There were no advertisements in the ground at Spurs, nor at Arsenal, nor in their programmes.

That was considered rather vulgar. Top clubs were above such things. Shirts were virgin territory, unsponsored, unsullied by nasty commercial names or logos. There was no marketing and little money came in from merchandising or television. A First Division player made £5,000 a year, with a handful of top players getting £10,000 a year, about the same as in many other crafts and professions.

In the last ten years, almost everything in football has changed dramatically. The money, for a start. The average wage for an established senior player in the Premier Division at the end of the millennium is now £350,000. An England international will get around half a million, and a superstar £1 million a year, doubling that if he is suitably glamorous and willing to put himself about, posing and preening for advertisers and sponsors. Even at Derby County, not one of the more glamorous or wealthy clubs, most players, if they have decent careers, should be millionaires by the time they retire, with no need to work again for a living.

Then there is the racial mix. In 1972 there wasn't one black player in the Tottenham team – and only one in the whole of the then First Division (Clyde Best of West Ham, born and brought up in Bermuda). Now around a third of professional footballers are black, far more proportionally than in the population as a whole.

Even more surprising has been the arrival of foreign players. When Priestley moaned about players not being qualified by birth or residence to play for their clubs, he was thinking of the apparent anomaly of Scotsmen playing for Arsenal or Geordies turning out for Manchester United. Never for a second was he thinking of real foreign johnnies playing for our famous clubs. There are now 150 non-British players in the Premier League alone, attracted by the huge wages. Football is now enormously popular amongst all classes and in most regions – as long, of course, as you are at or near the top, which in England means the Premier League.

Derby County is amongst the most English of English clubs, formed in 1884 by some members of the Derbyshire County Cricket Club looking for a way to boost their income. They were one of the 12 original members of the Football League when it was formed in 1888. Yet today they are amongst the most foreign of English clubs. In 1998, they had at one stage 11 overseas players in their squad, drawn from a wide range of countries. They also have a brand new and most impressive stadium, Pride Park, opened in 1997 after 102 years at their old ground, the Baseball Ground.

But I wasn't going to see them play. You can get all that on the telly these days, five nights a week and twice on Sundays. I was going to watch them train at their handsome little training ground at Raynesway, on the outer ring road of the city. In the car park I could see several Mercedes and BMWs, a sure sign of today's young professional footballers.

Out on the pitches, despite the foreign influx, I could hear all instructions and expletives being shouted in English, which, of course, is the basic language of football. England gave football to the world, the rules as well as most of the words. And footballers, like spectators, are brought up in the same global village of football, using the same gestures and expressions.

Afterwards, in the training ground's dining-room, there was much talk and banter about who had got that day's yellow bib. Bib as in training top, worn for practice matches. A yellow is awarded each day at Derby on a free vote to the person deemed worst at training – which means next day he'll have to wear it and suffer the appropriate mockery and ridicule. Footballers are very strong on ridicule, taking the piss, winding up their fellow players – all in good humour, of course. So they think. Not so much fun for anyone who happens to be habitually picked on.

On a central table were lined up a row of Derby County shirts waiting to be autographed by the players, along with several footballs and giant-sized 'get well' cards for children, all destined for worthy local causes and hospitals. Players, when they finished training, stood and dutifully signed their names on the items laid out, usually while still talking, still shouting. That scene hasn't changed in the last 25 years. It was the same at Spurs.

Igor Stimach was finishing his pasta and salad. Now that has changed since 1972. Most players were on chips and mushy peas then, and they were all Brits. Stimach stood out as a mature figure amongst the younger players he happened to be sitting beside, many of whom appeared mere gawky youths. He is six foot two, a tough, resolute defender, but he also has the aura of a senior prefect amongst schoolboys. Understandable, in a way. He is the team captain, and footballers, like schoolboys, live and work in hierarchies, with captains and senior players commanding respect. They also respect his intelligence, as he is able to converse in several languages, an achievement well beyond the scope of most British players – and British people generally, come to that. They also know that Igor has seen things, witnessed events, which in their life, football or otherwise, they are unlikely ever to experience.

'Pass the fucking juice, then,' he said to one of the younger players across the table. I'd somehow not expected him to swear, as if his life might have put him above swearing, which was silly. A football club is an industrial setting, populated by working-class men, so they use the appropriate language, mostly without thinking. That's how a newcomer fits in. I remember going to see Kevin Keegan in Hamburg when he had just joined them, and he was already swearing in German – but found he'd stopped swearing in English. He only spoke English at home, to his wife. And, naturally, he didn't swear at her.

The juice was blackcurrant, poured from large, industrial-sized cartons into jugs on each table. At Spurs in the '70s all they drank with meals, or during breaks from training, was tea, full of sugar. Igor asked if I'd like a tea, calling to a waitress behind a hatch to make me one, please.

When he'd finished his meal, we went into a little office, looking for a quiet place to talk, but the phone kept ringing.

Actually, I said, I'd rather talk at your home, if you don't mind. That would be more relaxing for you. More interesting for me. Any chance of it?

With a well-known London or Manchester player, there would be little hope today of getting into his home. Even getting ten minutes after training is hard enough, as they are surrounded by agents and advisers, liable to demand money for interviews or say their clients are too busy and have to rush off for something much more important – i.e. lucrative – such as opening a supermarket, doing some advertising, shaking some corporate hands.

'No problem,' said Igor, getting up. 'I'll just go and get changed.' He was wearing flip flops with bare feet, T-shirt and jeans, having come straight from his post-training shower to the lunch table.

I stood waiting in the dining-room and noticed Jim Smith, the manager, come out of his office. Football fans know him as the Bald Eagle, a jovial Yorkshireman in his late fifties who has seen many English clubs as a player and manager. He was never a star as a player, nor has he played or worked abroad. Strange, then, he should have signed so many foreign players. But then that is where the bargains are today, if you are running a middle-ranking club.

He gave me a beam and a welcoming wave as he was talking to one of his coaches – something Bill Nicholson of Spurs would never have done if he'd spotted a stranger on his premises.

I'd rung the club a couple of days earlier, asking to see their captain, so presumably the request had gone through his office. He came over and shook my hand, said he'd read my Spurs book. Many years ago, of course.

I asked him about all the foreign players in his team. Did they cause any problems? 'Oh, not at all, they're all grand lads. The coaches find it more interesting, having players from different countries.' The different languages were not a problem either, thanks to Igor. 'He's the only one at the club who can speak Italian to our two Italians. And he can also speak Spanish to the South Americans.'

Settling them into a different culture, though, that must be a problem. I know that at the big London clubs it is normal for new players to spend months on their own, stuck in some anonymous hotel, feeling very lost and fed up.

'No problem here. One of our directors has a building firm, so they all move into one of his houses. The more foreign players I sign, the better his firm does. I should have been an estate agent, not a football manager . . .'

Igor got into his Shogun four-wheel drive – his Mercedes sports car was being serviced that day – and I followed behind in my Jag. Quite pleased it was a Jag, if four years old, and glad I'd got it cleaned. These things matter in football, if not in life.

We drove for about 15 minutes to the outskirts of Derby. He lives on a new estate in Littleover, at the end of an enclave of what looked like show houses, so new and sparkling they appeared unreal, like Toytown houses. In this enclave live most of Derby's foreign players, which had recently included two Italians, two Costa Ricans, two Croatians, plus a Dane, a Dutchman, an Estonian and an Irishman.

The wives and children are in and out of each other's houses all the time, providing vital support for each other in a foreign land. Being a footballer's wife, foreign or otherwise, is not as glamorous as it might appear. It means living an unusual life, having plenty of money but limited contact with the local community, liable to be uprooted at any time. Their husbands are with their team in a hotel usually one night a week, suffer extreme highs and lows, are unbearable when injured, and even when fit don't have much energy or interest in the world at large.

Inside, his house looked as sparkling as it had from outside, as if all the sofas and furnishings had just been unpacked that day. Igor's wife Suzana was at home when we arrived. She looks after everything domestic, does all the bills, organises their two young children. She made us coffee and laid out a large plate of biscuits and nuts, then went off in her car to pick up their children from school.

Igor was born in 1967 in Metkovic, Croatia, a small town of 20,000 on the border of what is now Bosnia, though at the time both Croatia and Bosnia were part of communist Yugoslavia. His father was a director of the local electricity board, a responsible job with a good salary, but inflation was high and there wasn't much to spend money on. He has two brothers, one older, one younger. At school during the late '70s Igor carried a schoolbag emblazoned with the names of Keegan, Dalglish, McDermott – the whole Liverpool team, in fact, which then dominated England, and Europe. It was his older brother's bag which Igor had inherited, but he was proud to carry it, as he loved football. He was always at school an hour before the bell rang in order to play football with his friends. He also collected Beatles records and had every LP.

He played for all the local youth teams and at 15 was offered a place at a football school in Split, some 100 miles away, run by one of the country's two big teams, Hadjuk Split. (The other big Yugoslavian team was Red Star Belgrade.) Several thousand boys passed through this school each year, many just on two- or three-week courses, but Igor was one of the 300 permanent pupils who received all their normal education, plus football training.

'It was the greatest football school in Europe. I remember when Ajax of Amsterdam were setting up their training school, they came to Split to see ours. Character training was as important as football training.'

Education and accommodation was free, but his parents had to send him pocket money. At the age of 17, two or three boys each year progressed to signing professional forms. Igor was one of them. 'There was no signing-on fee, which there is now. I was just so happy to be signed.'

He was paid according to a strict scale beloved of communist countries, with three categories. Within each category everyone was paid the same rate. The top category was for seniors, which meant mostly international players. Then there were middle professionals and new professionals.

At 18 he hadn't made the first-team squad, so he left for Dynamo Vinkovci, still in the first division, but a smaller club where he had a better chance of first-team football. While there, he was picked for Yugoslavia's Under-21 team which went on to win the World Under-21 Cup in Chile in 1987.

'That was a marvellous team. We had players who are now world stars, like Suker, Boban, Jarni, Prosinecki, Mijatovic. I could have signed for a foreign club after our success in Chile, but I'd always supported Hadjuk Split, so I went back to them. I'd left them as a small door, as we say in Croatia. I returned as a big door.'

Over the next six years he became a regular in the Split side which did well in Europe and he was made captain. 'In the last game of the 1990–91 season, just when the war started, we were in the Yugoslav Cup final against Red Star Belgrade. We beat them 1–0. Boksic scored. Seven days later, Red Star beat Marseilles to win the European Champions' Cup.'

Despite the war and all the bombings, shootings and ethnic killings, football somehow carried on. New leagues were established and Hadjuk Split went into the newly formed Croatian league.

'It was our job, so we just got on with it. The crowds were a lot smaller, but people still wanted to watch football. When we travelled by coach to away matches, there would be road blocks, gunfire and fighting in the hills. On the way to play at Zador, the Serbs put bombs on the road to stop us, but they didn't go off. In one match, there was a bomb explosion on the terraces. The game was abandoned, but no one died. You couldn't escape the war, so you just lived with it. When the sirens went, you sheltered like everyone else.'

They also suffered like everyone else. Igor had an apartment, but for months on end there was no water or electricity and for a long time they were not paid. 'As captain, I had to go and complain on behalf of the players, which didn't make me popular with the club.'

Hadjuk Split had always traditionally been a Croat club, but, like most teams, they had a sprinkling of players from all regions.

'When the war began, we had a few Bosnians and Serbs. They were our friends, our colleagues. They wanted to stay playing with us, to earn their money, but they began to get warning letters, threatening them. In the end they went. Some of our younger players, the Croats, gave up football completely to go off and fight for Croatia.' So why didn't you?

'It was felt that the top players, the internationals, had a duty to carry on, play their best and be ambassadors for the country. When we played for Croatia, we were letting the rest of the world know that Croatia existed. It was very emotional, playing for Croatia in those early matches.'

After the first Croatian season finished in 1993, Igor felt it was time to leave. 'But it was the wrong time. No one wanted to come to Croatia and look at players. So I took the first offer that came along, which was Cadiz, in the Spanish first division.'

Igor had got married in 1990 to Suzana, whom he had met in a night-club in Split when she was 17. She had been Miss Yugoslavia and become a model. Even in wartorn countries, footballers manage to live like footballers anywhere.

'Cadiz was a mistake. I hadn't realised how much they were struggling when I signed for them. They had sold their better players and we got relegated. Next season, we got relegated again. I was doing well playing for the Croatia national team – and we beat Spain 2–0 in a friendly in 1992 – but not well with my club team, so after 18 months I decided to come back to Hadjuk Split.'

He stayed there two years before Derby signed him in October 1995 for £1.5 million. 'I had signed for Vicenza in Italy, but at the last moment my club was not happy with the terms, and it fell through.

That's when Jim Smith came along. He didn't come and see me play, but watched me on tapes.'

Igor had never been to England, though his wife had, competing in a Miss World contest in 1988. 'It was just as I expected. No surprises.' Oh, come on. 'Well, I knew all about English football, having followed it and watched it on television. Perhaps the people were a surprise. I had been told English people would be cold and unfriendly, but everyone has been warm and very kind. Perhaps because I'm a footballer. I don't know. I wasn't known here at all when I arrived. In Split, everyone knew me. I couldn't go anywhere without being recognised. Here, people didn't know me or anything about Croatia, even where it was.'

He had heard of Derby County, so he says, even though when he arrived they were languishing at 17th in the First Division. 'We played Tranmere on my debut game. I scored but we got beaten 5–1. I wasn't depressed, because I saw the quality and realised we could only get better. We were unbeaten for the next 20 games – and won promotion.' Now they are a respectable Premier Division side, lying that day in seventh position.

Igor was then joined by a fellow Croatian, Aljosa Asanovic. 'I told Jim Smith about him, said he was my friend and he wanted to come to England. I said he was very experienced, and would do well for Croatia in Euro 96. He should look at him now, because afterwards his price will be much higher. He got him for only £960,000 just before Euro 96. He played well, so his value rose to £3–£4 million.'

Igor finds the football here much more physical, with refs letting players get away with things they wouldn't allow in Europe. 'Here you hardly see the ref in a game. In Europe, they are blowing their whistle all the time and stopping the game. In Croatia we pass the ball more, keeping the ball. English players used not to be so good technically as Europeans, but now I think they are.

'Footballers themselves are the same the world over. You get the jokers, the ones who moan, the ones who never spend any of their money, the ones who disappear the moment training is over.'

But he has found English social habits a bit different. During his first Christmas, there was a team party which started at two o'clock, after training. By four o'clock, he'd had more than enough to drink. All the British players were still pouring down the beer, pint after pint, hours and hours later.

'I still don't know how they do it, how they have such a capacity. After a couple of glasses of wine, a normal footballer in Europe on a night out will think now, where can I get a nice shag, or where should I go for a nice meal? In Britain, they just think, where should we go to keep on drinking? It's amazing.'

The training system is also different in England, though with more European managers arriving this is beginning to change. 'We still don't train in the afternoons at Derby, which we did at Split and in most of Europe. A game is normally on a Saturday afternoon, so if you are used to training in the afternoon, the body's metabolism is ready for it.'

In Split, they did three whole days of training, plus two afternoons. So is football here easier, with less training?

'Not at all. We play more matches in England, so that leaves less time for training. But England is getting more like Europe all the time. Since I've been here, the gaffer has hired a club psychologist, which Derby didn't have before, and two more physiotherapists who look after things like diet and fitness. And we've got our brilliant new stadium, which I never expected when I came. I couldn't have chosen a better time to come. The set-up at Derby is now as good as most places in Europe.

'One of the nicest things that happened was during Euro 96. The club shop bought 500 Croatian shirts, all because of my connection. They were for the fans to buy — and they were all sold out in a matter of days.

'People still don't know much about Croatia, but they know we exist. Your politicians were not helpful. They supported the Serbs when they were killing our people. When I explained the true story to ordinary people, then they understood. Most people in England are very insular, the country being an island. You think anything of importance in the world only happens here. I suppose other people think that as well. We have a thousand islands in Croatia, and when you visit any of them, the people there have no idea what's happening in the rest of the world.'

There was the shouting of children in the front hall. Suzana had arrived home, bringing Mia, aged two and a half, and Luka, their seven-year-old son who went straight up to his bedroom to change out of his school clothes. Mia had brought home a little Danish girl with incredibly blonde hair, daughter of another Derby player. She asked Igor, ever so politely and in perfect English, if she could have a biscuit. Igor said yes, of course. Mia got out a children's video and asked her father to put it on, speaking to him in Croatian. He replied in English, saying she could do it herself, just work it out.

Igor couldn't speak English when he arrived. Now he is fluent.

During our conversation, there had not been the slightest hesitation with any words or ideas. The only confusion had been when I asked if he had an agent and he said no, he used Encounter. I said that firm was new to me. Later on, his mobile phone rang and when he put it down he said, 'That was my encounter.' I then realised he'd meant accountant.

'When I arrived, I thought I would be able to say a few words of English, as I'd done some English at school, but I couldn't understand one word.'

Presumably Derby laid on some intensive tuition, along with the lovely house on the lovely estate?

'No. I've had no lessons or tutors. I picked a lot of my English up from television. I found that movies were the best. They speak more slowly and it's clear in most situations what they must be saying. But it's mostly due to speaking English all the time at work. As captain, I come off the pitch exhausted as much by talking as by playing.'

His mobile phone rang again. It was a woman this time, the mother of the little Danish girl. 'Let me see, my dear,' he said in very posh English. 'I think she's still here. I'll go and see.'

Their own two children speak English without a trace of an accent, but at home with their parents they speak Croatian. Every evening, Suzana gives them Croatian lessons, so they learn it properly, including the grammar.

'Luka will often use certain English words when he is speaking Croatian to us – technical terms, to do with the video or computer, which he doesn't know in Croatian. He also uses English words like "Monday", to save him thinking of the word in Croatian. But no, he's not confused. He knows when he's speaking which language.'

They are pleased with the children's progress at school, where they seem very happy. I said it will be a great help, wherever they go in the future, having learned fluent English. 'What matters is that they grow up to be good people,' said Igor solemnly, 'who respect others and respect themselves.'

Suzana's own English was better than Igor's when they arrived, so she says. She couldn't actually speak it, but she remembered more of the grammar. She has picked up a lot from watching Oprah Winfrey on television, but her English is a bit more hesitant than Igor's. She doesn't have the constant practice, stuck at home on her own for most of the day.

Igor acquired his Spanish while in Cadiz. As for his Italian, he has never lived or worked there, but his part of Croatia is near Italy and he often went there shopping or on holiday. 'I just picked it up.'

They both love their English house. 'Anything in England would have seemed wonderful to us, coming from a war zone like Split,' said Igor. The four-bedroom house, with a large garage, cost them only £125,000, bought at a discount through the club's director. Even so, the price seemed very low compared with similar houses favoured by London footballers. Denis Bergkamp, for example, lives in a house on a new estate north of London which cost him £650,000. (I know the price because a journalist friend, Richard Littlejohn, lives in the same street.)

Suzana says she likes almost everything about her life here, even more than in Split. 'I see more of Igor in England. He is home every day at two o'clock, after his training. In Split, I hardly saw him. It wasn't just the longer training, but every five minutes he was off somewhere, meeting friends, football people, doing things, doing business.'

Igor has no business interests in England, though he would be willing to consider any offers or suggestions. Derby County is not a very fashionable team, nor are they in a large conurbation, so the chances of promotional work are limited. But back in Croatia, he is a veritable entrepreneur.

'I bought my first discotheque in Split 18 months ago. It's called Mississippi. Yes, in English. My two brothers look after it, and we try to go for most of the summer. Recently I started another club and restaurant, which I built myself. It's on an island called Brac in the town of Bol. This is where the young and rich go, the jet set of Croatia. Oh yes, we have them. The club is called Faces and can hold 4,000 people. It's been a big success. Next I'm going to buy a hotel in Split.'

He got out holiday brochures for the island of Brac and it looked wonderful, with white beaches and a perfect sea, more Caribbean than Adriatic. One day he will go home to live in Croatia, but in the immediate future he sees himself at Derby.

'I have a two-year contract. I have given Derby my heart, so why should I change? I am happy here. The fans like me. The atmosphere at all English matches is brilliant, far better than Europe. I am proud to be the captain. I am a strong character and I like to be leader. I like to be positive and support players, do the best for the lads.

'I've been lucky. This is a great time for football in England. Everything is booming. And it will get even better. I think in five years, players will earn ten times what they get now.'

Ten times? But they're getting so much already. 'Well, even more than they are now. But this is definitely the best time to be in English football.'

What happens then, after Derby? 'I might have a final year playing for Hadjuk Split. Then at 33 I'll retire. I don't want to keep playing when I'm past it. I don't want the crowd shouting, "Go Home!"

'I might then go into coaching. I want to stay in football, so if a coaching job came up, in Croatia, England or anywhere, I would be interested. I want to help young players to do what I've done.'

During his two years in England so far, he's seen a lot of English football, watching every possible match on television, reading the football pages in the *Express, Mail* and *Telegraph*, but he hasn't seen much of Britain. Their only family trip has been to Alton Towers, which is not far away. They haven't yet been to Stratford, the Lake District or Scotland. Igor shrugged and said he hasn't got much energy left after training. He'd also had a back injury for the last ten weeks. When not training, he was supposed to be resting.

But he and his wife did have a day in London, not long after they arrived. 'We went on the tube, visited the Tower, saw Big Ben, Trafalgar Square, Piccadilly. London's not a British town, really. It's a cosmopolitan, world city. It would take a month to get round it. I'm glad I'm not at a London club. I like Derby. It's easy getting to the training ground and the club.'

Suzana said she liked Derby as well and was very fond of the Eagle Shopping Centre. I made a face. Coming from Split, any modern shopping centre must seem pretty wonderful. When going out in Derby, to a restaurant or a cinema, they don't get pestered much by fans. 'Well, people might shout "Hi Igor", but they are all nice people. At a place like Man United, the players must be under a lot more pressure all the time.'

The only thing they don't like is the traffic. Derby and Split are similar in population, each around 200,000, but there is no comparison in traffic. 'There is so much here, so many hold-ups.'

Nor do they like the weather. 'In Split, we have 300 days of sun a year. Here it's more like three days. In the winter, you are stuck indoors all the time. In Croatia, we live our life outside.'

Suzana cooks at home in the Croatian style, which she says is much healthier. 'I buy the same food from the same places as everyone else, but we eat a lot of vegetables and fish, rather than meat. I cook them in the Croatian way.' I couldn't quite follow what the difference was, except she always uses olive oil in salads.

'Life in England is very easy,' she said. 'Everything is easy. But then things are always easy if you have money . . .'

Very true. There seems little doubt that Igor will end up with a lot of money when he does retire, though in the summer of 1998 he didn't manage to spend much time with his investments back in Croatia. He was otherwise engaged in France, the backbone of Croatia's team which stuffed Germany 3–0, beat Holland 2–1 and ended up third in the World Cup, with his friend and colleague Davor Suker winning the Golden Boot for scoring the most goals. We won't talk about England, or Scotland, who got eliminated much earlier.

Igor has done pretty well, for a foreigner in our land. But he also gave back a bit of interest for all football fans in Derby, watching the progress of one of their lads.

Chapter Nine

CHATSWORTH

From new blood to old blood, new money to old money. One of the places Igor and his family could easily visit during his sojourn with us at Derby County is Derbyshire county's greatest single attraction. Chatsworth is roughly due north, turn left at Chesterfield and follow the signs. Can't miss it. That's if he doesn't feel too tired, too stressed, with too many aches and pains, and wants to observe something of olde England getting to grips with the modern world.

Visitors have been coming to Chatsworth for the last 450 years, ever since it was first built. They got in for free until relatively recent times, and naturally they felt grateful to the Cavendish family, praised their taste and munificence as they admired the buildings and gardens, marvelled at the fountains and artificial lakes, gazed in awe at their enormous estate, stretching across some 50 miles of the Derbyshire countryside, containing villages and small towns, all part of the Cavendish domain. Chatsworth is not just one of Derbyshire's wonders, the Palace of the Peak District, but England's answer to the Palace of Versailles. Althorp, by comparison, is a mere bungalow.

From a distance, it looked like the opening shots of an expensive television classic serial. The main house is so well positioned, so impressively lit, so cleverly set. Jane Austen was staying nearby when writing *Pride and Prejudice* and it's thought Chatsworth was the inspiration for her fictional great house Pemberley, home of Mr Darcy.

Long before the television people came creeping with their long lenses and lady novelists with their pens and inks, famous English travellers made a point of taking in Chatsworth if they possibly could. Celia Fiennes in 1696 raved about the Duke's garden, his statues and ornaments, especially his piped water, spouting all over the place. Daniel Defoe came twice and on his second visit, in the 1720s, was amazed to see a new stretch of water, some 314 yards long. 'The Duke has removed a great mountain that stood in the way . . . I was perfectly confounded, for I had lost the hill and found a new country in view.'

Horace Walpole was not so complimentary on his first visit in 1761, saying he found the gardens 'tiresome and disappointing' and he personally would get rid of the 'absurdity of a cascade tumbling down marble steps'. On a later visit, he changed his mind, noting that many 'foolish water ways being taken away, it is much improved'.

J.B. Priestley gave it the cold shoulder. On his 1933 journey, he did wander around Chesterfield, take a look at the crooked spire and think there 'was an air of cheerful madness about the whole place', but then he moved swiftly on, heading for Yorkshire to attend a reunion of the soldiers he had fought with in the First World War (one of the best bits in his whole book). Perhaps he failed to get an invite from the Duke or Duchess.

It is noticeable in the millions of words recorded by visitors to the house over the last 450 years that they all go on about the gardens and the watery bits, but very rarely do they have any personal stuff about the Cavendish family themselves.

The dynasty – along with the house – was created by a woman, Elizabeth Hardwick, later known as Bess of Hardwick, the daughter of an impoverished and obscure Derbyshire squire. Her first marriage was relatively short-lived but she went on to become one of the richest, most powerful women in Elizabethan England. Bess's blood is still flowing today in the veins of many of our ducal families and the royal family.

Her second husband was Sir William Cavendish, who came from Suffolk and had done well working for Henry VIII, helping him to dissolve the monasteries, managing in the process to acquire a lot of ex-monastic land. Bess persuaded him to sell most of it off and move to Derbyshire. In 1552, she set about building Chatsworth, choosing a site beside the River Derwent, surrounded by hills and moorland. While she was at it, and had the money, she went on to build another stately home not far away, Hardwick Hall, which was almost but not quite as grand.

Sir William died in 1557, causing only a slight pause in her inexorable rise, and she went on to marry twice more, ending up as the Countess of Shrewsbury. Her husband, the Earl of Shrewsbury, was made custodian of Mary, Queen of Scots by Queen Elizabeth, which is how it came about that Mary was a prisoner at Chatsworth, looked after by the redoubtable Bess.

Despite four husbands, Bess's only children were by Sir William, so their son William Cavendish inherited Chatsworth, becoming the Earl of Devonshire in 1618. It was the 4th Earl in 1694 who became the 1st Duke, a reward for having helped bring William of Orange to the British throne. Once established, the family improved its finances by further advantageous marriages to equally wealthy and aristocratic families such as the Boyles and the Comptons, inheriting further estates and further handsome houses.

Over the last 300 years, they have managed to avoid one of the pitfalls which can weaken even the best and richest of families – they have had neither a totally mad Duke nor a totally wild, extravagant Duke who wasted all the money. On the other hand, they haven't had many who became national figures. The 4th Duke did become Prime Minister, but only for six months in 1756. The 8th Duke, a leading figure in Gladstone's cabinet in the 1880s, was thrice asked by Queen Victoria to be PM, but always refused. Lady Dorothy, daughter of the 9th Duke, became the wife of a Prime Minister, Harold Macmillan, whom she deceived by having a long-standing affair with one of his Tory colleagues, Bob Boothby.

Over the years the family has turned up two notable scientists. Not something one normally expects from landed lordlings. Henry Cavendish (1731–1810), grandson of the 2nd Duke, is credited with recognising hydrogen as an element and was the first man to weigh the world. William Cavendish was a scientist and a scholar, Chancellor of Cambridge University and founder of the Cavendish Laboratory.

The Dukes themselves have spent most of their time caring for their estates and their houses, collecting art treasures or just messing around at Chatsworth, usually with the watery wonders, an obsession which goes back to Bess. If she hadn't chosen a rather dodgy boggy site beside the river, they would probably never have bothered themselves with watery matters.

It was the 6th Duke, the only bachelor, who hired the 23-year-old Joseph Paxton to be his head gardener at Chatsworth. Paxton, uneducated and self-taught, built a massive conservatory at Chatsworth (now gone), teaching himself to be an architect in the process, going on to build Mentmore and then the massive glass building for the Great Exhibition of 1851 which became the Crystal Palace.

While Paxton was still head gardener at Chatsworth in 1843, the Duke told him that Nicholas, Emperor of Russia, was coming on a visit. The Duke had been to Russia for the Tsar's coronation and stayed at his palace, where he'd been most impressed by his great fountain. For the Tsar's return visit, he decided he would have an even greater fountain. So Paxton set to work.

In six months, with men and horses working at night-time using flares, they built a conduit of pipes two and a half miles long across the moors which dropped into an eight-acre reservoir, some 350 feet above the height of the house. The fountain was, of course, gravity fed, there being no other power. The bigger the mass of water, the bigger the spurt. And boy, did it spurt. The water shot up to a record height of 296 feet. So they called it the Emperor Fountain, in honour of the Emperor. Alas, he never came. His visit was cancelled. But the Emperor Fountain is still there and is a splendid sight to this day.

I could see it as I approached the house, but spurting it was not. It was December, the spurting season over as far as visitors were concerned. I went through a massive arch, past the porter's lodge, along an avenue of tulip trees to the front door, or what I assumed was the front door. There are so many grand entrances and exits, it could be a Noel Coward play.

The Duchess's secretary Helen had obviously seen me through a window and opened the door to greet me. Then the Duchess herself appeared with a girl from Texas, another visitor to the house, to whom I was introduced. We had an inane conversation about Texas. That didn't last long, then the Texas girl went and the Duchess led me into her private room.

Small, homely, overcrowded, lived-in, a bit like a large cupboard. Quite easy to describe, really, the Duchess's room. Just because you live in a house with 175 rooms, some of them the size and grandeur of the Albert Hall, and you have 27 bathrooms, 56 lavatories, 17 staircases, 359 doors, 3,426 feet of corridor, 1.3 acres of roof, 2,084 light bulbs and 7,873 panes of glass to clean, it doesn't mean to say you don't personally prefer a small room in which to live.

I remember going to Blenheim once to see the old Duke of Marlborough and being shown into a large and formal room. I wandered around it, opening doors, and stumbled across the Duke at the end of another room, behind a draught screen, sitting at a bare table with a jar of Nescafé and a white cup, looking like a dosser at Arlington House. He didn't see me, so I retreated quickly and waited for his formal, ducal appearance.

Another time I was doing a radio interview with Prince Philip at Buckingham Palace and was kept waiting in a posh library, watched by a flunkey. I was walking around it, looking at the books to see if there were any of mine. Prince Philip suddenly appeared through a secret door in a bookcase I hadn't realised was there. As he came into the library, I caught a brief glimpse of from whence he'd come – a much smaller room, overcrowded, where he obviously lived, which was heated by a pathetic, tatty, one-bar electric fire.

John Lennon had this amazing mock-Tudor place at Weybridge in Surrey. He'd spent a fortune decorating and furnishing all his large sitting-rooms, yet every time I went to see him, he was crouching in a small back room, perched on a sofa squashed against the wall, about five feet away from his television set.

The moral, friends, is that people, however rich, however aristocratic, however famous, are human beings, built on a human scale. Regardless of their surroundings, their outer public shell, they live their real life like a human being.

'You are a sport,' said the Duchess, shaking my hand. 'Coming all this way.'

I felt as if I'd come across the North Pole, or from Mars, and was doing her some enormous favour just by turning up, but then that's another thing about the upper classes. Well, some of them. They do have this over-the-top charm, this exaggerated politeness, telling absolute strangers they are brilliant and marvellous and wonderful. Better than rudeness and abruptness, treating you as if you weren't there. Which can also happen.

The Duchess of Devonshire is the public face of Chatsworth. She has a sociable, extrovert nature, while the Duke is shyer, his health not so good, and, anyway, he prefers to stay in the background. She is quite tall and attractive-looking, long skirt, black shoes, lots of arm gestures and enthusiasm, then sudden stops in the flow, in the gush of words. A bit disconcerting at first, till I got the hang of it.

'Oh, what a pest, what a bore,' she said, picking up her phone to dial Helen for a name or number she's suddenly forgotten. 'You'll think I'm going gaga.'

Not for a moment would anyone think that, not with those bright eyes and that quick, agile brain.

The Hon. Deborah Mitford was born in 1920, the daughter of Lord Redesdale, and the youngest of the famous Mitford girls. The importance of being extrovert and lively, not to say occasionally eccentric, was in them from the beginning. Unity was the one who was a friend of Hitler and later committed suicide. Diana married Sir Oswald Mosley. Nancy wrote the books and moved to France. Jessica, the left-wing one, wrote books and moved to the USA.

I met Jessica several times socially when she came to London and I interviewed Nancy in Paris when her book *The Sun King* came out. I remember thinking how strange her life seemed, shutting herself away, all on her own in Paris with no apparent partner. It wasn't till after she died I learned there had been a Frenchman, married with his own family, who lived nearby and who had been her secret lover almost all her life.

'Well, you wouldn't have expected her to have told you that,' said the Duchess. 'Come, now . . .'

None of the Mitford girls really went to school, she said. They were mainly educated at home by governesses. 'Unity was sacked from three schools – from St Margaret's, Bushey, Queen's College, Harley Street, and there was a third . . . oh, what a pest, the name's gone. My memory really is appalling. Nancy went to a school, but only for a short time. As for me, I lasted two days at school.'

Two days? Sounds like a Mitford exaggeration. 'No, that was all. I was the youngest, so there came a time when I was the only one at home. It seemed a waste to keep on the governess just for me, as we were quite hard up. To save money, it was decided I would go away to school. I was sent to Wychwood in Oxford. I hated it so much, was really miserable at being away from home, so after two days I asked my mother if I could return home. She said yes and they rehired the governess. So, you see, I had all my education at home. Such as it was. That's why I know so little today and am totally unintellectual . . .'

I ignored that one. But were the Mitfords ever really hard up? Okay, they were never as wealthy as the Cavendishes, but then who is? They weren't poor, were they?

She looked me straight in the eye, pausing for a few seconds, considering the hidden implications of the question.

'Of course we were never poor. It's all comparative. Compared with the agricultural labourers around us who had to manage on 35 shillings a week, we were wealthy. But we had to practise economies.'

Such as?

'Well, my limit when I bought a pony was £45.'

Sounds a lot, for the 1930s.

'What are you saying? You got a terrible pony for £45! I always had terrible ponies. They were the bane of my life. And I had to ride them to all meetings, as we couldn't afford a horse box.'

In 1938, aged 18, Deborah came out, presented at court, did the season. 'I can't remember meeting the King and Queen, though I must have done. Poor things, imagine having to put up with all that, having girls presented, but I loved every minute of the season. Oh, it was wonderful. My older sisters found it utterly boring, but I think they were unlucky. I was fortunate to come out with some very good friends. I was out dancing every night of the week for the whole season, which lasted, let me see, from the beginning of May to the end of July. Oh, it was wonderful.'

Every night? 'I mean five nights a week. It was just like going to work.'

You must have got through a lot of frocks. 'Not at all. I had only two dresses for the whole season. I told you, we were not a very wealthy family.'

It was during that season she met Lord Andrew Cavendish, ex-Eton, then at Cambridge, younger son of the 10th Duke of Devonshire, at a party held in Browns Hotel, Mayfair, given by her aunt, Lady Blanche Cobbold.

Love at first sight, or were there other boyfriends at the time?

'Well, I didn't pick out anyone I liked better.'

They married in 1941, the year they were both 21. Andrew and his older brother William, Marquess of Hartington, heir to the dukedom, both served in the Army during the war. Andrew joined the Coldstream Guards and was awarded the MC.

His brother William married Kathleen Kennedy in 1944, sister of John F. Kennedy, later President of the USA. Four months after the marriage, William was killed in Belgium while on active duty with his regiment. His widow Kathleen later died in an aeroplane crash in 1948. They had no children. Thus Andrew unexpectedly became his father's heir. Even then, it was presumed he would not inherit the dukedom for many years, but in 1950, when his father was aged only 55 and apparently fit and healthy, he collapsed and died. He was engaged at the time in one of his favourite occupations – chopping wood.

Deborah and Andrew were living locally, in a house on the estate, but spending a lot of their time in London. They had two children: Emma, born in 1943, and Peregrine, born in 1944, who became Marquess of Hartington and heir. They then had a second daughter, Sophia, born 14 years after the first in 1957.

'It was all so sudden. We didn't quite know what to do. Andrew had never expected to be Duke. He would probably have gone on to have a normal job. I don't know, perhaps in publishing. But suddenly he had to put his mind to the estate.'

In 1950 Chatsworth was lying empty and had been for some time, none of the family living there. Even before the war, the 9th Duke had hardly used it, spending most of his time in London or abroad, serving as Governor General of Canada. The 10th Duke had taken over in 1938 but only lived there for a few months. During the war, it was taken over by a girls' school from Wales.

'This was very clever of the Duke. It was likely to have been taken over by the Army, as many big houses were, so he arranged for a school to have it, managing to get a girls school, knowing that soldiers would not be allowed entry to the park.

'After the war, he was just too distraught by the death of his older son and couldn't face moving in. So it was just left empty, until he died.

'But that wasn't the worst of the problems. Death duties were 80 per cent at the time. If the Duke had lived only three months longer, there would have been nothing or very little to pay. As it was, the death duties were enormous. We had to find £6 million. They took away ten of our best things – a Rembrandt, a Greek head, a Holbein drawing of Henry VIII, oh, I can't remember them all, but they just came and took them away.'

Who took them? 'People. Officials. In lieu of death duties, don't you see? He also gave away Hardwick Hall, which Bess had built. That went to the National Trust, along with 3,000 acres. A lot of other buildings and land were sold as well. It took us 17 years to pay all the money.'

Next came the problem of what to do with Chatsworth, which had now been lying empty for almost 20 years. 'We considered all sorts of solutions, such as making it an offshoot of the Victoria and Albert, or a part of Manchester University.

'It was our then agent who suggested we should move in. The only way to look after it properly, he said, was to occupy it, have someone living there who would open the windows.'

It took two years of basic repair work to make it habitable. A new central heating system was installed along with a new kitchen, and six flats were created for members of staff. 'I went through the Yellow Pages, looking for seamstresses to make curtains. There was a limit of £150 at the time on house improvements, whether you lived in Chatsworth or a small house.'

They eventually moved in 1959 and began the job of making the house and the estate pay its way, as well as paying the death duties. 'It took me two years to set up a farm shop. None of us knew how to be shopkeepers, so it started very quietly. There was the problem of planning permission. At first we were only allowed to sell meat for the freezer, which meant half a lamb, or one eighth of a beast, that sort of thing. We couldn't sell cutlets. I was told we would be unpopular with local butchers. Oh, I had a frightful time, getting it going. But now it's a huge success.'

There was a knock at the door and in walked the present agent for Chatsworth, Roger Wardle. 'You wanted me?' he asked. 'Oh yes,' said the Duchess, raking through piles of letters and papers spread out on a stool in front of her. Her two dogs – Bracken, a springer spaniel, and Nobby, a lurcher – sprang up from lying in front of the gas fire, thinking the Duchess's sudden movement meant they were going for a walk.

'Yes, two people have written wanting a job. They look quite interesting.' She handed the letters to Roger.

'I bet you wish you had a First Class Diploma in the Countryside,' he said, smiling, reading one of the letters.

'Yes, isn't that a scream,' she replied. 'But the laddie looks quite good. Perhaps you might take him, hmm? He says he's already got accommodation, so that's a help.'

'Oh, we're not too bad at the moment,' said Roger. 'There is some room in the Den of Iniquity. That's what we call our bothy,' he explained, for my benefit. 'Where we put up single people.'

They discussed various estate matters while I idly looked through some newspapers and magazines scattered on a small table. Amongst them I noticed a Beatles magazine, produced for the opening of a *Hard Day's Night* in 1964. Strange reading matter for a 77-year-old Duchess.

Roger left, agreeing to give me a tour later, depending on his appointments. When he'd gone, and before I could ask the Duchess about her interest in the Beatles, she immediately led me to a corner of the room to show me a massive hand-tooled book, beautifully decorated, done in copperplate handwriting.

'We got this as a surprise present last night. From Roger and others. Isn't it marvellous? We had a party for the heads of departments and doctors and lawyers, locals who have worked for us for, oh, 40, 50 years.

'I knew they had organised a surprise for us and through my mind went the image of my new great grandson, suddenly arriving. It turned out to be this marvellous book. Look, it's been signed by everyone who works on the family estate. Isn't that wonderful?'

At the beginning of the book, after some fancy scroll work and heraldic devices for Andrew and Deborah, it congratulates them on having been Duke and Duchess longer than any others in the past.

The signatures were by department, starting with the agent, Roger Wardle, going through the ranks to the 21 gardeners, then on to drainers, fencers and wallers.

'I know that name,' she said, flicking through and stopping at one page. 'He's a brilliant waller. Wears an earring. They're all brilliant, in fact. Not a bad apple in the barrel.'

The book also included permanent staff at their three other estates: Bolton Abbey in Yorkshire, where Lord Hartington lives, Lismore Castle in Ireland, Compton Place in Eastbourne, and their London home, 4 Chesterfield Street. There are also two hotels, one local and one at Bolton Abbey.

Apart from the 160 permanent staff at Chatsworth, there are 260 who work seasonally, when the grounds and house are open to the public. Added to them are 500 tenants, who live on farms owned by the Chatsworth estates. Finally there are 100 pensioners, retired estate workers, who live in estate houses. So altogether, counting up on both hands, both feet, the total number of people dependent on the Chatsworth estate as we enter the twenty-first century comes to the enormous total of 2,000.

Not quite a feudal family. More a modern industry, turning over some £12 million a year. The farm shop, for example, brings in £2 million a year. The gift shop makes £1 million. Visitors to the house and garden average 350,000 a year. Another 110,000 visit the farmyard. No wonder my friend from Althorp popped up to see how the big boys do it.

There are also 'behind the scenes' days, where visitors get to see how visitors are catered for. Special parties are guided around the kitchens, workshops, library, archives, watching conservation work being carried out, painted ceilings preserved.

Has anything not been thought of? Well, the next excitement was going to be a new adventure playground. 'We looked at playgrounds all around the world and, I'm sorry to say, the German equipment was best. So that's what we're having.'

How much will it cost? 'Quarter of a million pounds. Of course. Everything costs quarter of a million pounds, don't you know? You simply can't make a move these days without spending quarter of a million pounds.'

The estate would now appear to be a big success, perhaps running at a profit? The Duchess pooh-poohed the idea of profit. 'We do have many departments which are purely spending departments. They just spend, spend, spend, with no income at all. But let's say things are much healthier than they have been.'

And she herself would appear to be the main inspiration behind many of the projects. 'Oh, no, I just fiddle around. My husband makes all the final decisions. And our son is now chairman of the Trust. Thank God we all get on, unlike some families.'

In a way, she and the Duke were lucky, taking over when the estate was at rock bottom, house empty, massive death duties. What's left for the next Duke to achieve?

'Oh, I'm sure he'll think of something new and amazing. Our hotel here, the Cavendish Arms at Baslow, is owned by us, but we don't actually run it. But he does run the hotel at Bolton. So that's a new enterprise and very exciting.'

The Duchess has written two books about Chatsworth, one on the house and one on the estate, and is working on a third. 'I try to do a bit first thing in the morning when I wake.' What time's that?

'Oh, about five o'clock each morning. I make my own breakfast in my room, just coffee and toast, then I sit and scribble away till the phone starts ringing. I did do a column for the *Telegraph* for six months, just on country matters, but that's finished.' You got the sack? 'Certainly not. I gave notice. Doing it every week did become a struggle.'

There was another knock at the door and in came a young man carrying some photographs whom she introduced as William Burlington, her grandson. She looked at the photographs, which were of the house and gardens, and exclaimed, saying they were marvellous, just marvellous. 'He is a photographer, you see. And, of course, I think he's a very good one.'

The young man blushed. As Earl of Burlington, born in 1969, son of the Marquess of Hartington, he is next but one in line to the dukedom. The lineage would thus appear to be in healthy condition.

But, of course, one never knows what might happen. If, for example, her own husband had died in middle age, as his father had done, she would not have been Duchess these last 40 years. Her status, as the widow, with a new Duchess on the scene, would have been completely altered.

'Oh, I've always realised that. I would be immediately out of a job. I could not have stayed here, doing the same job. When the man dies, the woman takes a back seat. That's how it is.

'I got on very well with my own mother-in-law, but thank goodness we've never had to live or work together. She took a back seat when I became Duchess. I think that's all to the good.

'So I would move out of Chatsworth if my husband died. I'd live elsewhere. Outsiders might think this is all unfair, that my house and position both depend on my husband. But I think it's a good thing. It means you always get new people coming in.'

I take it you are not a feminist? 'Absolutely not. I mean, it's jolly good if women have a vocation, to be a doctor or whatever, and they can fulfil it, but I think women are personally happier not being out and about.

'I see the friends of my daughters who have gone on to have careers, some of them very good careers, then they come home from work and find the nanny's upped and gone. How do they cope? How do they manage that sort of thing, a family with a career? I feel feeble at the very thought.'

So what would she have done in life, if by chance she hadn't become a Duchess? 'A stable girl. And I would have been perfectly happy, I think.'

As a child, according to Mitford family legend, she had little intention of ending up as a stable girl. In fact, she was hoping for something at the posher end of the social spectrum. When the six Mitford girls were fantasising about who Mr Right might be, she was the one who fantasised about 'Duke Right'.

'Yes, I'm supposed to have said that. I probably did, as a joke, because we had all kinds of jokes as girls, but I can't actually remember it.'

Now, after all these years, she can hardly remember not being a Duchess. I had noticed that most staff addressed her as 'Your Grace'. Even members of her own family treated her with unfashionable deference and politeness. Did she like all that?

'I suppose I've grown used to it, but I do believe all humans beings are made of the same stuff. A Prime Minister is no better a person than a gamekeeper. Those with a vocation, who always wanted to be, oh, I don't know, a dentist, they are the luckiest of all. I have been very lucky myself, being able to live in this wonderful house and estate, but I know I am just the caretaker, looking after it for the next generation. All you ever hope is that you leave it in a better state than you found it in.'

On the surface, she would appear to have everything, surrounded by masterpieces and minions, with access to millions, able to go anywhere, do anything, indulge the smallest whim, if she felt so inclined.

Money and wealth do bring happiness, oh yes, creating better health and greater confidence. I have personally observed this happening when writing a book about 24 Lottery winners. At the end of a year, following all the changes in their lives, only one out of the 24 could in any way be said to be enjoying a less happy life. Accepted wisdom is that having sudden money ends in tears, but this is purely a compensatory myth which we like to believe to make up for us not winning.

However, nonetheless, notwithstanding this, the apparently rich and privileged can be just as constricted as anyone else, liable to jealousies and depressions, bugged by people and things which might appear ridiculous to outsiders, prone to feeling pissed off, bored and irritated, happy to enjoy the simple pleasures in life which don't cost anything. Just like everyone else.

So, your Duchessness, tell me, from where you are sitting, what do you personally consider one of your little luxuries in life?

'Nothing in the book,' she said, quick as a flash. So quick I wasn't quite sure what she meant. Which book? 'My appointments book. I would love to wake up one day and find no people waiting to see me, no meetings to attend, no decisions to make, able to just get up and do absolutely nothing, go out and take the dogs for a walk, just do what I like, when I feel like it . . .'

But surely you can do that already, any day you want, as long as you plan it ahead?

'I suppose so, but I don't. At 77, I am beginning to get tired at times. There are so many things I do which I know are voluntary, but I still keep taking them on, keep agreeing to them. So, to answer your question, to wake up with nothing in the book, that would be a wonderful luxury.'

But a negative one, all based on not doing something. I was thinking really of a more positive pleasure.

'You mean like new potatoes or a fine day in May?'

Yes, that sort of thing.

'Right then, new potatoes. That would be my luxury.'

I could see she was tiring a bit, that my time was up, then I remembered her Beatles booklet. Could I look at it, as I am a Beatles collector? It was in excellent condition, clean and shiny, but as I turned the pages I found one stained with chocolate, as if a Smartie had been squashed into it.

'Oh, I just found that in the nursery. I suppose Sophia must have bought it when she was young. She was born in 1957. So she probably got it sometime in the mid-'60s.'

It is real, I said, not a reproduction, though there are lots of them around now.

'How much do you think it's worth?'

I estimated £25, that's what a dealer would charge. But she would be lucky to get half that.

'Oh, is that all? Well, you can have it if you want.'

I said how kind, but no thanks, I already have several copies. She should keep it herself.

As I got up to go, I noticed on her mantelpiece, which was crammed with photographs of her various dogs, a cut-out image of Elvis Presley, stuck into a mirror. Something else found in the nursery?

'Oh no, that's mine.'

You mean you are an Elvis fan?

'Am I an Elvis fan!' she exclaimed, clapping her hands, rushing around her room to find other bits and pieces of Elvis memorabilia to show me. Then she stopped.

'Just remembered. Nothing Elvisy is here at the moment. My collection is on show at Buxton.'

She recently bought some drawings by telephone, making her secretary Helen do the actual phoning in of her bids, which was all jolly exciting.

'It all started just three years ago. I was watching some TV programme about Elvis, some anniversary I think. Watching it made me remember just how brilliant he had been. I suppose I knew all about him at the time because of my children's interest, but I hadn't taken a great deal of notice. Now it struck me how amazing he was — so I decided to study him more.

'I've been to Graceland this year. Oh, yes. I just joined a party of Elvis fans and went to America to look at his house. Oh, it was brilliant. I brought back lots of souvenirs. I have a large phone in the shape of Elvis, holding a guitar. When you pick up the phone, he starts playing the guitar and singing. It's marvellous.'

I do like collectors, having so many collections of my own, and I do like enthusiasts, for anything, however dopey. So I left promising that in future, when I'm looking through catalogues for Beatles stuff, I'll let her know if I spot any Elvis stuff. We collectors must stick together. Oh yes.

* * *

Roger Wardle, agent for the Chatsworth estate, did manage to spare some time for a guided tour. We went first to the village of Edensor — pronounced 'Ensor' — which is totally owned by the estate, including its post office and tearoom. Then to the village of Pilsley, bigger and busier, which has its own primary school where estate workers send their children. Work for Chatsworth, you see, and they will look after you from cradle to grave, from school to old-age pension. Positively feudal.

Ah, but in feudal times they didn't have such a thing as The Club. It was originally a form of working-men's club, where estate workers could have a pint in the evening and play dominoes, but now it's more like an upmarket Country Club, with masses of facilities and attractions. Apart from bars, a snooker room, tennis courts and a hall big enough for dances, parties and shows, it also has its own golf course. There's even a heated indoor swimming pool. I agreed nothing can ever be too good for the workers, but I didn't quite believe the heated pool. Must be very titchy, I said suspiciously. But no, it is big enough to be used by local schools when not being used by estate members.

It is actually a club, with 600 members, membership fees and a waiting list. Ordinary Membership is just £10 a year, but you have to be part of the Cavendish estate, as an employee, a tenant or a pensioner. Then there is Associate Membership, a bit more expensive, which is for local doctors, clergymen, contractors, people whose job means they serve or supply the estate. Finally, there is Affiliate Membership, for those who have no work-related connection but happen to live locally and would love to be able to use the club. For this there is a waiting list of several years.

We then toured some of the farms, all of them looking like model farms, as clean and unreal as their two model villages and the model social club, all of it on a model estate, free from any of that nasty, dirty urban stuff we call modern life.

I laughed out loud when we eventually came to the famous farm shop. It was straight from the television commercial. Lots of jolly, smiling women in jolly straw boaters emblazoned with 'Chatsworth Farm Shop' lined up behind sparkling counters ready to serve you with Old English-style delicacies. The smells were delightful, the goodies enticing, more like Fortnum and Masons or Harrods' Food Hall than some rough-hewn farm shop. In fact, shop is not even the right word, as they have a staff of 40. It's a superior delicatessen, run on the scale of a supermarket, packed with hundreds of varieties of cheeses, meats, breads, wines, beers and assorted sweetmeats.

The park itself had been empty of visitors, as it was winter and the house was closed, but the farm shop was absolutely packed. 'Oh, December is always our busiest time,' said Roger. 'People come from Sheffield, just to buy their Christmas goodies.'

One whole area was selling Duchess of Devonshire goods – bottles, packets and jars of jams, marmalades, chocolates, all bearing her name. How neat, to have her very own line, but what a mouthful, in every sense of the word. 'Duchess of Devonshire Dark Chocolate Dipped Grapefruit' must prove quite a test for anyone working on the lettering, let alone someone working their way through the goodies. I examined some 'Duchess of Devonshire Cumberland Sauce with Port', wondering about the geographical clashes and confusions which must ensue when you start such concoctions. The Duchess of Devonshire has, of course, no connection with Devonshire; nor with Cumberland, nor Portugal.

Much of the produce, said Roger, is in fact made on the premises, such as the pâtés, breads and cakes. The rest is local or from elsewhere in Britain. That's one of their selling points. Your actual olde English delicacies.

What about the Duke, then? I know he's shy and retiring compared with the Duchess, but, looking round, I couldn't see his name slapped across any fancy bottles or beribboned boxes.

Roger led me to the butchery department. There on a plate were the 'Duke's Favourite Sausages'. Just a simple label. None of the four-colour fancy flummery of the Duchess's lines. This is the only product he allows to bear his name. 'But his sausages have just won a silver medal.'

We then went for a pub lunch at the Wheatsheaf in Baslow — not part of the Cavendish estate, though we could have lunched at the nearby Cavendish Arms and kept everything in the family.

It must be strange, I said, for people like him, and the 2,000 or so others who live and work in the shadow of the Cavendish clan. What if you fall out with them? Does it mean you have to leave the district? 'Oh, that doesn't happen. People are very happy to work for them.'

Yes, but now and again someone must get the sack, and end up hating the Cavendishes? Roger could only think of one person who had been sacked since he arrived.

'I know it does sound feudal, but it works. If you think about it, it's no different from working for a big company like ICI, the sort which looks after you, has clubs, gives you a pension. That's all we do here, only the line of control is much simpler and easier. The Duke makes the final decision — and makes it quickly. The Duchess is Front of House. She's the one people meet. She dazzles with her ideas. The Duke is the steady hand on the tiller. He is naturally more shy, and now his eyesight is not as good and he's had two hip operations. But I would say, from my experience, he is the wisest person I have ever met. When I go to him with a problem, he gets the situation in seconds, and always comes to the right solution.'

Oh, come on, Rog. I know he is your boss, but that is a bit brown-nosing. He smiled but said no, he truly believed it.

Roger seemed affable and classless rather than county and posh, but suitably country-looking in the inevitable tweed jacket, faded cords, patterned shirt and club tie. Cavendish club tie, of course. He is aged 51, comes from Chester, trained as a land agent and began his working life in a local estate agency but quickly got fed up selling houses. He moved back to the land, getting a job as an assistant agent on a large estate of 150,000 acres in the north of Scotland. By which time he had a wife and two children. As they got older, he decided to move somewhere less remote and got a job with the National Trust in Nottinghamshire. He came to Chatsworth in 1981 as deputy agent. In 1994, he became agent.

He is in a sense the firm's managing director, with the Duke and Duchess as chairman and vice-chairman of the board, responsible for the day-to-day running of the house and estate, some 400 employees and around 35,000 acres. Mineral rights, limestone quarries and coal mines also come under his control. (Bolton Abbey and Lismore in Ireland have their own resident agents.)

As the Chatsworth agent, he divides his empire into 12 different departments: farms, woods, house, collections, shops, catering, garden, game, domain, accounts, survey, building yard. Each has got its own head of department whom he meets with every month. And almost every week he sees the Duke or Duchess, especially when there's something they need to decide.

'I am all for benevolent dictatorship. I think it's the best way to run things. That's how Bess ran it, and it worked. Within the system, people are encouraged to show their initiative. Would Paxton have been given his head at 23 in a normal firm? I don't think so. Once you have committees, everything is watered down and takes forever. Here we get instant decisions.

'At the same time, I admit it is partly feudal, not to say medieval. We insist that people in tied houses have to partly paint them in blue and cream, our corporate colours. Satellite dishes must not be visible and preferably not on the roof but on the ground. You cannot park a caravan on your front drive, as it looks untidy. You must look after your front garden.

'Yet at the same time we are up to date. We have modern non-contributory pension schemes with index linking. We use digital cameras and GIS maps.

'Traditionally our workforce was predominantly male, because the work was predominantly manual. Now it's fifty-fifty. We are determined to keep things fair so that a female worker can have the same rights as men. Widowers should also be treated the same as widows. The old rule was that for a widow to inherit a tied house, she must have been married for ten years before her husband's death.

'I can see why some people would object to one family owning and controlling so much, but it works. If you have the right people in charge, it works for everyone, and for the nation.'

Oh, come on, Rog. How does the nation gain?

'Well, if you believe in conservation, which most people do today, this is the best way to conserve Chatsworth and the Park. It's open to all to enjoy. It doesn't cost the nation anything. Its future is assured. An alternative would be to nationalise it, have it state run. That could be done, but the government wouldn't want to do it, not today. They'd think it too expensive. So then the National Trust might take it over. Yes, that would work, and would ensure its future. But I've worked for the National Trust. I don't want to criticise them but, well, the National Trust is an institution. Once you institutionalise anything, it loses its personality.

'Of course, if the next Duke turned out to be a pig, I might well change my mind. But the next Duke, and the one after, are both very human, very intelligent. I know they will be resident Dukes, caring for the estate. They won't be dissolute and waste it all.'

Good defensive argument, Roger, well put, but what about all this 'Your Grace' nonsense, as if they really were superior beings?

'Yes, that was about the first thing I asked when I arrived – how did you address them? Now I find "Your Grace" very handy, easy to use. Doesn't worry me at all. In my eyes, they haven't just been given a title, they have both earned it, with the effort and work they've put in over the years.'

Roger himself was addressed as Roger, so I had noticed when going around the estate with him, not Mr Wardle or Sir.

'Years ago the agent was always called Sir, but then one did become a knight, Sir Roland Burk. In his day, he was looking after 85,000 acres. He was indeed a big cheese. Since the problem of those death duties, the estate has shrunk to 35,000 acres.

'When I arrived 15 years ago as deputy agent, I was writing letters to tenants, addressing each of them "Dear Mr Smith, Dear Mr Brown," or whatever. I was told that was not done. They all had to be addressed as "Dear Sir", as that was considered to be more polite, not by their names. The then agent said, let's ask everyone in the office, see what they think. So we had a vote. It was decided to address them by their real names from then on.

'I personally don't want to be called Sir. I am happy being known as Roger. But some of the older people don't like it. That's fine by me.'

One of the most popular social events of the year for the staff was soon to take place – the annual Christmas party given by the Duke and Duchess in the Big House for the 100 or so children on the estate.

'It's very traditional – white tablecloths, jelly and ice cream. After the meal, they all go into the inner courtyard and look up and see Father Christmas on the roof. A spotlight picks him out and you see him clearly, with his reindeer. Then they rush inside into the Painted Hall, gather round the big fireplace and all shout for Father Christmas. They shout louder and louder – and finally he does appear, stepping out of the fireplace. Oh, it's a wonderful sight.

'No, no child ever says it's a trick. It is, of course, limited to under-11-year-olds, which helps. Yes, we do have two Father Christmases. One has been hiding all the time in the fireplace, which, of course, is enormous. And the reindeer on the roof is actually a deer's head, carefully positioned behind a parapet so that's all you see.

'When they leave, every child gets an individual present with their name on, given by the Duke and Duchess. You should see the children's faces. It's magical.'

Catching the children young, one might say, indoctrinating them into the ways of the estate, to acceptance and dependency.

'But that's what companies do, whether it's ICI or Toyota. Good ones look after their staff. You do feel you belong to a family. People fit in.'

You mean they know their place?

'It's not that. People realise there is an order to everything. Nothing is written down, but everything is clear and people are comfortable with it. People automatically fit in, whatever they do. They are not thought less of because they clean the loos. We all know that's more important than sitting in a warm and cosy office. Visitors soon complain if the loos are dirty, or there's litter around. They won't come again.'

Right then, Roger, you have got to admit that, despite all the lovely life, the lovely people, the lovely systems, you have in the end been conned in one respect – you won't end up with any capital. A normal working person, over 40 years, will have paid off his or her mortgage and end up with a substantial property. In London, I bought my house in 1963 for £5,000 and in 1999 it was worth £600,000. In this pretty part of rural Derbyshire, it wouldn't have gone up as much, but I bet it would still be about £300,000. You, with your tied life, however cosseted, however comfortable, will end up owning nothing.

Roger looked thoughtful. Yes, he was in that precise position. He does not own a house of his own, though he will, of course, have a pensioner's house when he retires, if not the one he is now living in, which is rather grand.

'I couldn't possibly have afforded to have bought or even rented the house I am living in. It's grade 2 listed. Same with the ordinary agricultural workers on the estate. They couldn't possibly compete for houses with the Sheffield commuters. Like me, they have a handsomer house than they ever could have expected. And by not paying rent every week, they can afford to buy their round in the pub.

'In my case, I have been able to educate my two children better, send them to private schools, have better holidays. I have a life insurance policy, so when I go, my children get something.

'I don't let it niggle me, not being a homeowner. If it does, you should get out. But I consider myself lucky to live in a lovely house in a beautiful village. I've had a damn good life. So no, I don't regret not ending up a houseowner. Though, in actual fact, I probably will, from my own parents . . .'

* * *

The Duchess had arranged a lift for me to Chesterfield railway station. Which was nice. She has her own car, a Mercedes, with her own chauffeur. So has the Duke, with his own chauffeur.

It was the Duke's car, a Bentley, just a few months old, which took me gliding through the snow which was lashing down across the moors, driven by the Duke's chauffeur, Joe Oliver. He was wearing a black suit, black tie and braided cap and was as immaculate as the car.

Joe has worked for the Duke for 40 years. His brother is comptroller of the house. Their father and grandfather also worked for the family. As does Joe's son today. Naturally, Joe had not the slightest word to say against the Cavendishes, and why should he? So we chatted about football. Over the Christmas holidays, he hoped to manage a visit to Chesterfield. They used to have some good goalkeepers, so we talked about good goalkeepers we have known.

The next day, Joe was driving the Duke and Duchess to Eton, for some old-boys' ceremony. He was hoping the snow would be clear by then. He talked about possible routes he might take, depending on the weather. He doesn't get to London much these days, now the Duke is not so active. But there is still the chauffeur's two-room apartment in their Mayfair house for his use. Oh, he spent half his life there, in the old days, the happy days.

I said how amusing Deborah had been, how lively and entertaining.

'Her Grace,' said Joe.

And Roger, I said, seemed a nice bloke, friendly and helpful.

'Mr Wardle,' said Joe, as if merely clearing his throat.

Thanks, Joe, I said, when he dropped me at the station. It was only afterwards I wondered if I should have called him by his surname.

Chapter Ten

MANCHESTER AND SALFORD

My first job in life was in Manchester. On 1 September 1958, when I was 22 and had hardly been further south than Penrith, I got a letter from the news editor of the *Manchester Evening Chronicle*, Bob Walker. I have it displayed in a collection called My Life, Volume I, along with my baptismal certificate, infant's weight card, school reports, letter from Carlisle Education Department giving me a university award and my graduation certificate. The letter confirmed my appointment at a salary of £14 a week. Oh, what joy. My father had never earned as much as that in his lifetime.

I was supposedly a graduate trainee, but there was no training in those days, no courses, no diplomas. Kemsley Newspapers, soon to become Thomson Newspapers, took on a handful of graduates every year and spread them around their provincial newspapers, most of which were in big cities. I also got an offer from Westminster Press, but their newspapers were smaller, located in smaller towns.

The *Evening Chron* had a readership each day of one million, so it boasted, which seemed phenomenal. I couldn't imagine such a figure. And Manchester itself was awesome compared with Carlisle, where I had grown up. Most awesome of all turned out to be 'Kemsley House, Manchester 4', the address on Mr Walker's letter where I was going to work, generally known as Withy Grove and said to be the biggest newspaper printing plant in Europe. There were rumours about a bigger one in Brazil, or we would have been the biggest on the planet.

So many newspapers were being produced and printed there that I could never keep track. Not just the *Evening Chron* and the northern editions of all the other newspapers in the Kemsley group, such as the *Sunday Times, Empire News, Sunday Graphic* and *Sunday Chronicle* but also the *Daily Mirror, Sunday Mirror, News of the World, Daily Telegraph* and

Sporting Chronicle. They changed, depending on contracts and ownerships, on newspaper wars and deals, as papers were born, amalgamated or simply died, but it meant that for decades the vast building had never been silent, never still, producing up to 20 million newspapers a week, with noise and excitement and bustle all day and all night long.

The ink-stained printers were kings, of course, top men of the working-class craftsmen. All the journalists considered themselves kings of their craft as well, looking upon Manchester as the Fleet Street of the north, with a similar pay structure and national status.

We on the *Chron* were in daily and deadly rivalry with the *Manchester Evening News*, sister paper of the *Guardian*, each of us producing up to six editions a day, most of them with four pages or so of local news covering outlying parts of Cheshire and Derbyshire as well as Lancashire and Greater Manchester. If you went on a murder story or some tragedy first thing in the morning, you had to go round the dead and injured and say, 'Anyone here from Buxton?' You'd get the appropriate quotes, and they would go in the early edition which covered Buxton. An hour later you'd have to find a Macclesfield angle, then Knutsford and Altrincham, followed by Wigan and Eccles, till finally, as the day wore on and you kept the story up to date as well as finding the local angles, came the last edition, for Salford and central Manchester.

A senior reporter, Barry Cockcroft, looked after me for the first few weeks. That was about the only training you got, after which you were on your own. I thought he was the most amazing, most brilliant, most gifted person I'd ever met. We'd rush to the scene of the story, get quotes from the police chief, the fire chief and witnesses – and then Barry would dash to a phone box and straight out of his head dictate to copy-takers a story that made total sense, colourful yet logical. Incredible, so I thought. How did he do it?

A month or so later, when it came to my turn, I crouched behind the telephone box for an hour, scribbling and rescribbling my story, before eventually phoning it over. I got the most awful bollocking from the dreaded deputy news editor, Harold Mellor, for missing two whole editions. I lived in fear of Mellor. He didn't approve of graduates, especially those who couldn't spell and who tried to be clever with intros instead of just sticking to the facts and getting them over fucking quick.

In the end, I realised it was all a trick, not too difficult to acquire. Barry had about five different intros and frameworks for any news story. Almost every incident or tragedy could fit into one of them. Barry later went on to become a distinguished television director, well known for his work with Hannah Hauxwell.

One minor thing I never got the hang of was Manchester's habit of referring to itself as the north-west. When I first saw it in an *Evening Chron* headline, I thought heh, imagine us having a story about Carlisle, or at least Cumbria. If you look at a map of England, the north-west is clearly Cumbria. No question. That's us. That's where we are. By comparison, Manchester is the deep south, practically the Mediterranean. It confused me all the time, seeing the NW in headlines. I suppose it was Manchester striving to be a provincial capital, head of its own country.

I got moved from Manchester after nine months and came to London. I have hardly been back since. Quick visits only, in and out, because, well, it's just so horrible. At the time, I loved working there, but not living there. Even then, when I had little aesthetic appreciation or interest in my surroundings, I could tell it was nasty, dirty and ugly.

Daniel Defoe, in his 1720s tour, admired the trade and manufacturing of Manchester, which he said was well known to everyone, but he rather put any civic pride in its place by describing it as 'one of the greatest, if not really the greatest, mere village in England'. He put the boot in by noting that it didn't even send any MPs to Parliament.

On his 1933 trip, Priestley didn't spend much time in Manchester, and rather cheated in that he really went for the opening of one of his plays, then moved on sharpish. He still managed to get in a few swipes, but then he was a Yorkshireman. 'Between Manchester and Bolton the ugliness is so complete that it is almost exhilarating. It challenges you to live there. That is probably the secret of the Lancashire working folk: they have accepted the challenge – they are on active service.'

On my arrival in 1958, I took the first room I could find which was near the office, knowing nothing about the local geography or social pecking order of each district. I found myself in Cheetham Hill in a rundown street which was filled with Eastern Europeans doing sweated work in little raincoat factories. A drunken Polish bloke came through the window one evening, as I was asleep. My girlfriend, now my wife, woke up and screamed. The bloke apologised, said he'd got the wrong window and climbed out again. I went straight back to sleep. My wife never forgave me.

She was still at Oxford at the time and had come to visit me. I was supposed to be living in the room alone, not just because the rent would have been higher for two but because you could not have a woman in your digs who was not your wife. One day the landlord made a sudden visit, wanting his rent, while we were in bed. Margaret immediately hid under the bedclothes. I jumped out and stood in front of the bed, hoping to hide her. It wasn't really a bed, just a battered let-you-down couch. At that moment, it decided to put itself up, jack-knifing with Margaret still inside. She couldn't be rescued till the landlord left.

My first friend in Manchester was Harry Evans. I had been given his name because he'd been at the same college as me at Durham, some eight years earlier, and was now assistant editor of the *Evening News*. He invited me for a meal at his house, which was in posho Altrincham, so I later invited him and his wife back to my place. When Margaret was staying with me. I wasn't going to work out how to cook a meal. And still haven't.

Margaret made my room look as attractive as possible, covering the awful bed-settee, buying candles to create a bit of atmosphere. The meal was fresh herring, yum yum, but Harry immediately started fretting about the bones, jumped up and switched on all the lights, revealing the full horror of the room.

Some eight years later, when I had been on the *Sunday Times* for six years and was writing the Atticus column, Harry arrived. I was about the only person on the paper he knew, so he looked me up, rented a house nearby and came for a meal. I said he was mad to come to London. He was a provincial journalist, really. He'd won prizes and done excellent work as editor of the *Northern Echo* in Darlington. Why come to the *Sunday Times*? They would just eat him up. What was the point? The next morning, when I was getting into my Mini to go to work, I noticed that someone had written in the dust on the roof the word SEX.

Harry went on to edit the *Sunday Times*, then *The Times*, becoming a legend in his lifetime, at least amongst journalists. Last heard of in New York. I wonder if he has been back to Manchester in recent years?

I got the 6.55 train from London, determined to be in Manchester as early as possible. The train was absolutely packed, with hundreds of mobile phones beeping and burbling, before we'd even left Euston.

At Manchester Piccadilly, I rushed out to get a taxi and found a hundred people in the queue – and not a taxi in sight. When I lived here, I could never afford a taxi. Now that I can, there isn't one. How bloody annoying. I walked towards Piccadilly itself, which has been the limit of my Manchester experience in recent years, staying at the Plaza Hotel after doing some TV or radio thing. On the way, I passed a trolley-bus named Sir Matt Busby. Trolley-buses, running on tram-lines, are recent arrivals, snaking silently and efficiently across the heart of the city, giving Manchester a European, cosmopolitan feeling, however fleeting. Piccadilly was as horrible and dreary as I remembered it, but there was at least a taxi vacant.

The driver said yes, it was stupid, the lack of taxis at the station. 'They now charge you £350 a year to use the station. Well, I'm not paying that, it's a bloody liberty.'

I said I wanted to go to Withy Grove, but he didn't appear to know what I was saying. I had always called it that, 40 years ago, never realising that the name referred to a minor side street. I said it used to be Kemsley House. Never heard of that either, but he'd only been in Manchester 30 years. Ah, Thomson House, that rang a bell. His accent seemed southern, so I asked him where he was from. 'Holland. I followed a girl here, didn't I? But I'm not going back. I love it here.'

The whole of central Manchester appeared to be a building site, gaping holes in the ground everywhere, old buildings coming down, new buildings going up, most of them as horrible-looking as the ones they were replacing. The IRA bombing of the Arndale centre had caused a lot of the damage, but the city was apparently determined to rebuild and rearrange everything in sight.

I couldn't work anything out. I'd either forgotten the geography or streets I'd once known had moved. I walked up and down Corporation Street, looking for Withy Grove, either the little street itself or that monster building where I had once worked. I still couldn't recognise anything. Mainly because there was nothing to see. The whole building had gone, except for a bit of frontage covered in scaffolding and plastic sheeting. A large notice said, 'Printworks – a major entertainment development by Richardsons.' I wondered what sort of entertainment was being planned. Amusement arcades, leisure centre, health spa or what? There was a number printed on the notice for further enquiries, so I rang it. Very exciting plans, I was told, which would include Manchester's first 3-D cinema. I'm sure when I was a lad I saw a 3-D film in Carlisle. Or was 3d the price? You had to put on silly specs. The film was rubbish.

Nice, at least, that the site's history will be remembered in the new building's name, Printworks. Printing, of the cold metal variety, is now, of course, prehistoric. It's all computers today, with images of pages sent instantly around the country to various streamlined print plants. And yet, and yet, the strange thing is, with all these amazing new developments and state-of-the-art technology, newspapers, in Manchester or London, produce fewer editions than they did in the old steam days. Harold Mellor would have no need to scream at his reporters to catch all the different editions. He would be out of a job anyway. The *Chron* has long gone, absorbed by the *Evening News*. Manchester is no longer a centre of national journalism, not since the *Guardian* moved to London, and most northern editions of the dailies have disappeared. London papers now get by with just one reporter covering the whole of the north.

I walked to St Anne's Square, the only half-decent, half-attractive part of central Manchester. Then and now. It was at Kendal Milne's in Deansgate that I bought My Jacket. What a day that was. Still the finest, most expensive item of clothing I've ever bought. I consider clothes utilitarian objects, to be acquired as cheaply as possible and worn as long as possible, but I was talked into this jacket by my dear girlfriend Margaret. The poshest shop I'd ever been into until then was Burtons in Carlisle, where I'd bought my first and only suit on going up to Durham. Charcoal grey, off the peg but pretty smart. This jacket cost a fortune. I can remember it costing a fortune, all the moans and groans, but I now can't remember how much. Definitely more than a week's salary, which would make it £14. It cost so much because it was designer made – though I don't think the term was used then – and imported from Denmark. It was a tweed jacket, but in an unusual grey colour, with a thin stripe. Awfully distinguished. I never saw anyone wear anything like it. I wore it for the next 20 years, till it fell to pieces.

Kendal Milne's was, of course, frightfully exclusive, where the quality shopped, ladies from Cheshire, wives of Lancashire magnates. From the outside, it still looked pretty smart, but no smarter than Binns in Carlisle or any department store in Oxford Street. The first counter I came to was cosmetics. No sign of any customers, just a woman behind the counter, lost in space, lost in make-up. I asked if she could help me. She said she'd try.

I'd noticed, coming into the shop, that it was now called Kendal's. Last time I'd been in, admittedly some time ago, it was Kendal Milne's. When did the change occur?

'I've been here since 1978,' she said. 'And it was called Kendal's when I joined.'

Eeeeh, you must have seen some changes.

'I certainly have,' she said, making a face. 'We don't get the type of people we used to get. Everything's changed, alas, hasn't it? Everything's changed.'

How true, I said.

'But not everything,' she said.

That's also true, I said.

She gave a sigh, picked up a colour chart for Guerlain and pointed to a list of perfumes.

'That one was introduced in 1853 – and we're still selling it today. This one goes back to 1895.'

Goodness, I never knew perfumes had ages, like wines have years.

'Well they don't, not any more. Not the new ones. All these modern perfumes, they're just produced by make-up artists who don't know anything, nothing at all . . .'

She looked in her late fifties, though hard to tell with all her make-up. Why do assistants on such counters layer it on so thickly? Even the youngest, freshest-faced ones cover themselves with whole beauty cabinets so that when they first turn around it's a shock, as if you've wandered on to the set of a horror movie. Do they see it as a perk of the job or an industrial hazard, like having to wear helmets on building sites or boiler suits in petrol stations.

'Tomorrow is the last day,' she said. I wondered if she was being philosophical. Tomorrow never comes, so in a very real sense it is the last day for everyone. I nodded.

'I'm leaving tomorrow.'

Oh, I see. Would there be a gold watch, a touching speech?

She made another face. 'They're doing nothing, but I'm having a bit of a do. With lots of wine. I know there'll be lots – because I bought it today.'

Would she be pleased to retire, after all these years?

'Certainly not. I like the job, didn't want to retire. It's my husband's doing. He's retiring next month, and he wants me to retire as well.'

He worked in a warehouse, which he hated, but he had formerly worked as a docker on Salford docks. Which he had loved.

I said surely that had been a nasty, dangerous job.

'Oh, no. Best job he ever had. He still says that every day.'

I wished her good luck for her retirement, left Kendal's, jumped into a taxi and said, quick, take me to Salford docks. Or where they used to be.

* * *

That had been my main object in coming to Manchester. A wander around Withy Grove, down memory lane, had been self-indulgence, akin to Priestley coming to watch his own show. I was here to observe something new and exciting. On the journey so far I had done enough ancient buildings and traditional activities. Now for a modern wonder, a thrusting, pulsating state-of-the-art creation, getting ready to propel us into the new millennium.

Salford docks, at the end of the Manchester Ship Canal, were one of the wonders of their day when they were opened by Queen Victoria in 1894. The world gasped at the cost, some £16 million, and at the leap of the imagination involved in turning Manchester into an inland port where transatlantic ships arrived, bringing raw materials from all over the world and taking out Manchester's manufactured goods. They finally closed in 1982, by which time the world had changed, container ships had taken over, Manchester was no longer a port, the Ship Canal had become a sewer, the surrounding buildings either derelict or slums.

That was yesterday. But today, ah ha, it is all so very different. By the end of the year 2000, some 39 hectares of docklands, where nine crumbling piers once stood, will have been finally transformed into a spanking new development which will have cost over £350 million, providing jobs for over 13,000.

Half of the jobs, and the new buildings, were in place already, but on the day I arrived, the heart of the new industrial empire, the crowning glory, was still being completed – the Lowry Centre. Its name might make it sound as if it will be little more than an art gallery, but in reality it will be a palace of our times.

L.S. Lowry, 1887–1976, was not just Manchester's best-known artist but one of Britain's most distinctive artists of the twentieth century whose matchstick men can be recognised by almost everyone with or without any artistic knowledge.

I did meet him once, when he was quite old, and didn't get much out of him except a lot of laughter, as he was very amused by the status he had acquired. But I did know one of his girl friends quite well, Sheila Fell, the Cumbrian artist. 'Girl friend' in the platonic sense, for he would appear to have died a virgin. But from his fifties onwards, he took up with a series of very young girls, often as young as 13, whom he would befriend, buy meals, even take on holidays to exciting places like Sunderland, where they would stay in some crummy hotel – in separate bedrooms, of course. This would create sensational headlines in the tabloids today, but nothing unbecoming ever happened. Even looking back in middle age, most of these girls remember his friendship as innocent and pure. What was going on in his mind, of course, we will never know.

When the girls got to their twenties, met a man and got married, Lowry would give them a wedding present, then that was usually it. The connection stopped. He was on to the next girl.

When he died, it was found he had left everything to a woman he had hardly seen for 20 years, one of those he'd met when she was 13.

She later got married, but her husband and two young children had died in a plane crash while the husband was piloting the plane. She was in the sea for nine hours, clinging to the wreckage of the plane, before she was rescued by an RAF helicopter. She later wrote to the RAF man who had rescued her, started a correspondence – then married him.

I wanted to write a book about the lives of these women who had been friendly with Lowry as well as about the life of Lowry himself, but it never happened. I couldn't get a certain agreement, though most people concerned were very helpful.

I went first to call at the offices of the Lowry Centre Trust. They were in a two-storey building beside the canal, where a chief executive and a team of 12 were working away until they moved into the completed building.

The chairman of the Trust also happened to be there when I arrived, an energetic, glamorous-looking woman called Felicity Goodey. I recognised the face but couldn't quite place her, until I remembered she used to be a BBC reporter. Unusual to find media persons doing good works.

'Oh, it's a long story. I was sent by the BBC to Manchester to be the northern industrial correspondent. My editor told me Salford was a no-go area. Their council was fed up with the media because all we ever seemed to report was bad news. I went to see them and said I wasn't going to ignore bad news but I would go out of my way to find and report good news. So I made a sort of pact with them.

'What they had was an enormous black hole in the middle of their city, a vast, dirty, stinking, derelict wasteland. No one wanted it and they didn't know what to do with it. They had attempted to give it away to a developer who was going to raze it to the ground, fill it in, then create a vast car park. He was going to get the land for nothing, but at the final meeting he said he wanted half a million just to take it off them. That was it. They hadn't the money. It was the depth of the recession. But they carried on, hawking around various plans and schemes to various bodies, and were mostly laughed at.

'Then they found an architect who was interested. He had done work at Lancaster University. He came up with a plan and I did an item about it, standing on the stinking docks while he looked up at the sky and at the water and said, some day, this will all be wonderful. My editors thought I was barmy for taking it seriously.

'But the plan went forward. Salford Council managed to secure grants for the first stage, about a tenth of what it would cost. They started without knowing where the money would come from. They saw it as a bedrock development, to revitalise a whole area, raise everyone's hopes and aspirations.

'What was also remarkable was that from the beginning they were willing to make deals with private and commercial concerns. They were an old-fashioned Labour council in many ways, yet they were so ahead of their times.

'They had started long before the National Lottery was even thought of, but once that came into being, they created a steering group to bid for funds. This was in 1994. I was invited to be its chairman. It was a huge undertaking, but we did get some money.'

How much?

'£64 million.'

How did you feel?

'Ecstatic. And I still do.'

I could see out of the window all the new developments, houses and offices, glass and concrete blocks. Nothing as high-rise as the London docks, no one building anywhere near as massive as Canary Wharf, but I would guess by the look of the ultra-modern new offices that the jobs would be equally ultra-modern, of the sort my niece was doing at Milton Keynes. Not exactly the sort for which ex-dockers would be qualified, or most people living on the sprawling local estates at Ordsall or Langwarthy.

'That's true. Of the 7,000 people working here already, many come from elsewhere. And they live in south Manchester or Cheshire. That's because the first jobs are high-tech. With the next stage, we will be on to the service industry – hotel staff, taxi drivers. By then we'll have Metrolink trams coming right to our front door.'

The chief executive of the Lowry Centre is Stephen Hetherington, slender and dapper in a black Armani-style suit and a tieless shirt buttoned to the neck. He started out in his professional life as a trumpeter, after graduating from the Royal Academy of Music in London. He played in various famous orchestras, then at 27 decided his future lay not as a trumpeter but as an agent for conductors. He moved on to become an all-round music and arts consultant setting up and running artistic projects, including a new theatre at Wycombe in Berkshire.

In 1995, he was approached by the Lowry Centre Trust to help them with their Lottery application, producing a plan on the lines required by the Millennium Commission. He went off to fetch it from his drawer. I thought it might be a couple of sheets but it went on for hundreds of pages, outlining the legal situation, the ultimate aims and principles, how many would be employed in the centre. It even listed, day by day, what exactly would be going on for a whole year. As he flicked through it, I could see the names of real shows, real stars. Did he just make them up?

'No. These were the productions available in 1995 which I could have booked. I knew how much they cost, so I was able to do exact budgets and business plans. On that year, I projected an income of £4 million from tickets.'

When the Lottery money was awarded, the Trust was set up and the position of chief executive advertised. Stephen applied – and got it.

The Lowry Centre will have two theatres, the Lyric, with 1,730 seats, and a smaller, adaptable theatre with 450 seats. There will also be other spaces for smaller shows and exhibitions. And, of course, there is the art gallery where 330 of Lowry's paintings will be permanently on show. This is the biggest collection of his works, owned by Salford Council but now loaned to the Trust.

The whole project will be run without direct grants or subsidies, neither from Salford nor any government body. Not even from the Arts Council?

'I have strong views on the Arts Council – not all of them printable. Our object is to receive shows, not create them. We'll be like a retail outlet, a department store, as opposed to a factory, so we won't have the risks. We'll be buying in productions, then selling tickets for them. And we aim to run at a profit.'

So will that mean going for mass-market, popular shows?

'There is this misconception that "popular" equals lower standards. That's just not so. We'll be doing a full range. We might book, say, an esoteric dance company for two shows only in our smaller theatre, but that will be 800 tickets sold, enough to cover their costs. If you put on, say, the Chippendales, then they might run for more nights. If it's legal, and we think there's a local market, we'll put them on. I'm not in the business of dictating public tastes. What you find is that public taste is not actually limited to any one thing. What you need is constant variety. We aim to have the Lowry Centre running like a TV set – always lots of different things on, all the time, offering a choice, all the time.

'It is very rare for a centre such as ours to have such a creative breadth, but that is one of the advantages of not being Arts Council or publicly funded. Once you are controlled by the politicians or the bureaucrats, they impose upon you their idea of what the arts are. They pre-define it. Which is total bollocks. The arts can't be pre-defined. They are a human activity, so you can't pre-define them, only celebrate them.'

His main problems so far have not been the building works, which have been making excellent progress, but the bureaucracy of the funding process. 'That has been my greatest frustration. We succeeded in getting the awards, which seemed a massive struggle at the time, but that was relatively easy compared with what happened afterwards.'

The complications arise from the fact that their money comes from different sources. The £64 million Lottery grant itself is made up of monies from three bodies: £41 million from the Arts Council, £15.65 million from the Millennium Commission and £7.65 million from the Heritage Lottery Fund. Then there's £70 million from commercial developers, £16.3 million from European Regional Development, £6.15 million from the private sector, £5.1 million from English Partnerships, £3.5 million from North-West Water, £3.2 million from Salford City Council, £1 million from Salford University and £300,000 from the former Trafford Park Development Corporation.

Even just writing down the names exhausted me. Think of what it must be like dealing with them, keeping in with them, for all of them require a monitoring process. If there's no such thing as a free lunch, then there's never a free million. It comes doled out in bits and pieces, dependent on certain conditions and constraints. Not just saying please and thank you but following stringent procedures and rules.

'They don't all cause the same problems, but they all have a bureaucratic process which slows us down – and is very expensive. Our legal bills alone are enormous.

'We can't tolerate delays, not when we are in the middle of building something. We can't just stop work because certain money has not come through at the time we need it. So we have to borrow money till the next lot of funding comes through. And the cost of borrowing money is appalling. We've mainly done it through Salford Council, who have been very helpful, but we still have to pay them interest.

'I have had sleepless nights. I never stop worrying about it. But so far, touch wood, we've not lost a day's work. We have now achieved 78 per cent fixed-price deals with all the contractors on the site, so we do feel in control of what is happening – but at a price.

'All these problems will, of course, disappear once we open and have no further need of funding. But it's made me see once again that the only way to work in the arts is to do it privately. Governments and Arts Councils can't run things. I have a Board of Trustees, but I can get a decision out of them very quickly.

'I've felt sorry for the people trying to run the Millennium Dome. The government, in its wisdom, decided that it was in control. The Dome has therefore been put under a lot of pressure and has been abused unfairly, so I think, criticised because exact plans and details were not made public. But it's not normal with such a project, whether it's the Lowry Centre or the Dome, to have to give public answers to all questions as you go along.

'If, say, Andrew Lloyd-Webber is commissioned to do a musical for the opening, he doesn't have to tell you the details in advance. Nothing wrong with you asking him – but there's also nothing wrong with him saying "I'm not telling you".

'With any new arts venture, you have a marketing plan, everything timed and worked out, so you want the maximum publicity at the right time, when tickets can be sold. But because of the government involvement, they are doing what politicians always do – reacting to media pressure, giving out bits and pieces as they go along, instead of saving it all up.'

Apart from all the worries over the funding, there was another moment of worry when someone walked into their offices one day and asked what they'd done about the bomb.

'We said, "What bomb?" He said, "The wartime bomb. It landed on the docks, but never exploded. Didn't you know about it?"' There was some panic as the police and security experts were called in and historical records analysed, but nothing was found.

Stephen will, of course, be pleased when it's all completed and the Queen, or similar, performs a grand opening ceremony in May 2000. He then can live a normal life again. 'I can't quite say I have enjoyed it. All of us know it has been significant, and we'll probably never work on anything as big or as important again in our lifetime, but "enjoy" is not quite the word. It's like travelling down some white-water rapids. If we all get out alive and well at the end, then we'll shout "Wow!" and start punching the air. At the moment, were just concerned about not hitting any rocks . . .'

★ ★ ★

Next to the Lowry Centre will be something called The Digital World Centre, in a separate building but still part of Stephen's orbit. It will have a research and development area, involving the University of Salford, and will also do commercial work.

Stephen took me to another room to show me a video of the sort of modern technological stuff they might be demonstrating there and in the Lowry Centre itself. Not that I was much wiser afterwards.

It was an American video, made by MIT, and it showed a man sitting in a chair, rigged up to computers and making music by simply waving his hands in the air, moving his head, lifting his legs, kicking with his feet. It all seemed miraculous to me, or some trick.

'It's because he is sitting in a sensor chair which detects mass, speed and movement and translates them into sounds.'

Oh yeah, of course.

Stephen then had to go to a marketing meeting, but he handed me over to Duffie White, an American who was looking after the Digital World Centre. It was going to be called the Virtual Reality Centre, but these words were apparently not the cool, trendy, vibrant words they had first appeared some ten years ago. 'That was only ever one small part of a big development in modern information technology. What we are really talking about is the digital world. That's the new revolution which is going to change so many things and have such commercial and economic effects.'

Hmm. I do have a cheapo Amstrad word processor, very basic, which I can vaguely operate, without really understanding it. I scream and shout every time something goes wrong or there's an electricity cut and I can't work, which often happens while we are in Lakeland. That always amuses my wife. She does all her writing with a fountain pen. She can't type, never mind operate a word processor, and has no idea what a computer is. I'm not quite that bad. But, er, tell me, Duffie, what exactly does 'digital' mean?

'It's the on-off switch on a computer, which transfers an instant dot, as opposed to analogue.'

Yeah, but what does 'analogue' mean?

'That refers to sound which depends on the frequency of waves in the air. In the digital world, you are transmitting by a computer code, not by airwaves. The advantages are enormous, not just in speed and definition, but you can store it. The digital revolution will mean companies can interface all over the world. Instantly. It will be like sitting in a chair with the person opposite.'

Yup, it all sounds very exciting, if a bit complicated and confusing. I was quite pleased to get outside into the fresh air at last and have a look at something I could more easily understand – a very big hole in the ground.

★ ★ ★

I was taken around the site by one of the young project managers, Niall Wright, aged 31. First of all we went to get our gear on, which meant big wellies, a fluorescent jacket and a hard hat. The royal family and cabinet ministers get to wear them all the time, and look pretty silly, but it was my first go, and I felt equally silly. I now realise hard hats are so called because they are hard to wear, being heavy and clumsy, and very hard to forget. One can't concentrate on what one is being told for fear of causing one a neck injury or falling and breaking one's legs, don't you know?

Niall was born in Belfast and educated in Leeds, where he took a degree in quantity surveying, followed by a postgraduate course in project management at Heriot-Watt in Edinburgh, which is where he met his wife. 'The quantity survey course was pretty boring, about as exciting as accountancy. But Leeds was one of the few places that did it. Edinburgh was better. I loved the project managing course from the beginning.'

His main job at the Lowry Centre was supervising the flow of information between the design team and the contractor, to make sure construction runs smoothly and to budget. The main services were being provided by different firms, including builders, steel-makers, concrete-makers and glass-makers.

We started at the front door, or what he said would be the front door. He explained how the entrance hall would be wide and open, leaving visitors free to wander off in any direction, right or left or up the escalator, whichever took their fancy. The building is made mainly of steel and glass, with most elements visible from wherever you are, which is meant to entice you on.

They were already up to three levels high that day, and the shape of the main theatre was very clear. I stood on the stage, looking down into the orchestra pit, which will be electronically moveable so that it can be covered over to provide more seats. The space and shape of the smaller theatre will be even more flexible.

As we walked around, various people came up to Niall to tell him things. A girl engineer said some concrete section was two weeks late. A foreman said there was water trouble somewhere or other. Niall nodded sagely and made notes.

There were about 100 workmen on the site that day, which will rise to around 350 in the final stages. I had noted the female engineer, a sign of our enlightened times, but I hadn't noticed one black face anywhere on the site. In London, that would certainly not have been the case.

'Would that coat be pure Donegal now?' said an Irish voice behind me as a workman caked in mud went past, carrying some concrete posts. It was a nasty cold day so I was wearing my herringbone tweed coat, the sort John Cole used to wear. Yes, said Niall, he's one of our Irish workers. One of the many. In fact, he estimated 90 per cent of the workmen on the site that day were Irish or of Irish descent.

That was probably how it was a hundred years ago on this very site, as it was the Irish who helped build our canals, just as they went on to build the railways. It was also near here the world's first passenger railway opened, the Liverpool–Manchester in 1830.

'We have four different building firms on site at the moment – and all of them happen to employ Irish people. They all know each other, which is good for security. A total stranger trespassing on the site would soon be spotted. It does mean they all go off early together if there's anything special on, such as an Irish funeral in Manchester. On St Patrick's Day, we had to shut down for half a day.'

After a childhood in Essex and university at Leeds, Manchester was a bit of a shock. 'My wife wasn't at all keen when I got this job. Not after Edinburgh. Now, that is a beautiful city.'

Not like Manchester, I said. I told him how I hated Manchester when I lived here, though I liked the work.

'I didn't like it either when I first arrived. Manchester hasn't got a heart, hasn't got a decent centre, or many decent buildings, apart from the Town Hall. Leeds is actually more attractive, with wider, nicer streets.

'Manchester hasn't got many parks either, not like London. In fact, I thought it was decidedly scussy when I first came.'

Scussy? Sort of scruffy and dirty, he said. He didn't know where he had picked the word up from. Somewhere between Belfast, Essex, Leeds, Edinburgh and Manchester.

'But Manchester is an excellent cultural centre. Far better than Leeds, which can be a bit sterile. Manchester does feel an exciting place to be in. And the people are very warm. It took me a while, but now I don't want to leave.'

The Lowry Centre will, of course, make it even more culturally exciting, so they hope.

★ ★ ★

Back in downtown Manchester, I bought a copy of the *Manchester Evening News*. For old times' sake. The Danimac rainwear firm was closing, bringing almost to an end Manchester's tradition of textiles. I should think that the dump of a street where I lived, once full of little raincoat factories, is now considered highly desirable.

'280 NW Holidaymakers Stranded,' said another headline about some package firm which had gone bust in Spain. The story said that 280 of the stranded holidaymakers were from the Manchester area. Nothing to do with what I call the *real* NW, where I would soon be heading. But some things don't change.

Chapter Eleven

LIVERPOOL

But first to Liverpool, which also thinks it is in the north-west, with itself as the capital. Defoe loved it in the 1720s, raving and exclaiming about a 'town now become so populous and so rich that it may be called the Bristol of this part of England'. Not, you will note, of north-west England.

'Liverpool is one of the wonders of Britain . . . a large, handsome, well-built and thriving town . . . with an opulent, flourishing and increasing trade to Virginia and the English colonies in America . . . and also sends ships to Norway, to Hamburgh and to the Baltick.'

Priestley, on his 1933 visit, decided to make a tour of the slum quarter down by the docks in the company of a local vicar, and visited a school which was full of mixed-race children.

'Although they had mostly been begotten, born and reared in the most pitifully sordid circumstances, nearly all of them were unusually attractive in appearance, like most people of oddly mixed race. A really first-rate film producer could make a film of rare beauty out of these children. Perhaps we have been given a glimpse of the world in 2433, by which time the various root races may have largely intermarried and interbred.'

Television documentaries do that sort of programme all the time. As for the world becoming mixed race, Priestley was projecting himself 500 years ahead. In reality, for many parts of England it has happened in little over 50 years.

Defoe's reference to Hamburg is interesting, at least to me and anyone who knows the Beatles story, for it was Liverpool's traditional connection with Hamburg which sent them there and helped give them their Liverpool sound. Like James Joyce in Paris writing about Dublin, you often have to go away to find out where you are from.

I spent several months in Liverpool in 1966 and 1967 while working on my Beatles biography, by which time they were household names, probably the best-known four people on the planet, but not everyone expected them to last or to be remembered. Thanks to Paul, who helped me write a letter to Brian Epstein, I had secured a contract for their authorised biography, but several people at my publishers were not wildly impressed. 'The bubble will soon burst,' said one. 'Biographies of pop groups don't sell,' said another. I explained they were more than a mere pop group, they were of sociological and cultural importance. 'Sociology? Who needs sociology? No one buys that . . .'

In Liverpool I visited their old homes, old schools, dug out old schoolfriends and teachers, visited places and people associated with their Liverpool years. The most fascinating experience was going to see their parents. All had recently left their original homes, moving into much posher houses. Three were still in the area, having moved 'across the water' to more salubrious Cheshire, while John's Aunt Mimi, who had brought him up, had moved completely away, down to tropical Bournemouth.

Ringo's parents and George's parents were in brand new luxury bungalows, the plastic still on the sofas, the smell of new paint everywhere, surrounded by the trappings of success – or their sons' success – but in many ways they were trapped. They could hardly go out, worried in case fans would find out their new address, then camp on their front lawns and climb through their back windows, which is what had happened in their previous homes. They were also trapped socially, having little in common with the lawyers, bank managers and garage owners who were now their neighbours. So they stayed inside, cowering.

They knew what I was doing, that it had all been agreed, that their sons had rung to say it was okay to talk to me, but they were still nervous, worried about upsetting them. The sons had become the fathers, masters of their lives, almost monsters, in that the parents could not possibly imagine or comprehend what had happened.

Jim McCartney seemed to be coping best, adjusting well to his new life, but then he had been a member of the white-collar working class, a salesman in the cotton trade, with natural charm and social ease. Instead of a brand new luxury bungalow, he had opted for an attractive Edwardian villa in Heswall, where he had a vine, a conservatory and had become a racehorse owner.

He had also got married again, after many years as a widower bringing up his two sons. I could sense that Paul and his brother

Michael were a bit suspicious of the new wife but they said nothing, as Jim himself appeared very happy. I stayed with him a couple of times while researching in Liverpool. On one evening, Paul had just sent up an advance copy of his new tune, 'When I'm Sixty-Four', which Jim took as an honour to himself.

J.B. Priestley on his trip, despite touring the slums, stayed at the Adelphi, Liverpool's posh hotel, but didn't think much of it, finding it too hot and not very luxurious. He also didn't like the Liverpool accent, saying it grated on his ears. That was a very common reaction at one time, but I wouldn't think it is generally true now. The most acceptable British accent today is probably a Scottish accent, so all surveys of the telesales industry report. The Geordie accent, another one Priestley hated, is also popular. Bottom of the pile is probably Birmingham, with Cockney and Essex estuaries accents being not much liked either, or viewed with suspicion. A Liverpool accent is middling popular, rarely ridiculed these days unless someone is imitating Cilla Black. It was the Beatles, of course, back in the '60s who made Liverpool and things Liverpudlian popular and socially acceptable.

Yet who would ever have thought that Paul McCartney would be knighted, or that the little council house where he was brought up would become a national monument? During my visits in the '60s, I had only stared at it from the outside. Now I was going to get my very own guided tour. Three National Trust officials had recently been to see me in London, wanting to borrow some of my Beatles memorabilia for display in the house.

I was pretty surprised, not to say astonished, when I first heard that the National Trust had bought 20 Forthlin Road, but I shouldn't have been. Over the last 30 years, since I did the book, there have been continual surprises. I remember in the 1970s getting a call from a woman who said she was doing a PhD at London University and her thesis was about the Beatles' lyrics as poetry. I could hardly believe it. Now, of course, it is commonplace. Every university accepts that the Beatles are intellectually worth studying.

Then, in the 1980s, I was astonished by Sotheby's. They had always seemed a pillar of the art establishment, yet they were selling Beatles souvenirs. Today we know that Sotheby's is no grander than anyone else. They'll sell anything. We also know that all Beatles stuff has artistic and commercial value.

So in a way it was a natural development for the National Trust to buy Paul's house, though some of their more traditional members wrote letters of complaint. After all, they only have three other twentieth-century houses, one of them quite near me in London, Erno Goldfinger's house in Willow Road, Hampstead, which is an unusual example of 1930s architecture. Forthlin Road is an example of 1950s mass-produced council housing.

The Trust justified its purchase by describing it as 'the birthplace of the Beatles'. Pushing it a bit, I thought. If asked, I would have said the Cavern, now long gone, was the birthplace. On reflection, though, the house does have a historic place in the Beatles story. The McCartney family lived there from 1955 to 1964 – the vital Beatles years. During the day it was empty, as Paul's father was out at work. I remember him telling me how he would come home in the evening and find all the eggs had gone. Paul would deny it at first, as he wasn't supposed to come home during the day, then would admit he'd made fried egg sandwiches for John and George.

Aunt Mimi was never keen on John's guitar playing, and she was a bit snooty towards Paul and George, with their council-house backgrounds. So when Paul and John started playing together, they did it mainly at Paul's house. It was here that early Beatles songs were created or performed, such as 'Love Me Do' and 'I Saw Her Standing There'.

After the McCartneys left the house in 1964 it was taken over by a Mr and Mrs Jones, still as council tenants. They bought it in 1981 – thanks to Mrs Thatcher's policy of encouraging council house tenants to become owners – but continued to live there until 1995, when Mrs Jones decided to sell.

The person who alerted the National Trust was John Birt, now Sir John, Director General of the BBC, who is a Liverpool lad. He was born in Walton Hospital in 1944, the hospital where Paul had been born two years earlier. (Paul was born in a private ward as his mother, a nurse, had once been a sister on that ward. John was born in a public ward.)

I used to play football with John Birt, many years ago, and did some TV interviewing with him when he was a young producer. When he was working at LWT, he rang me up one day to say that his boss, Michael Grade, was looking for someone to do a biography of his family. John had suggested me. Fascinating to do, especially meeting old Olga Winogradsky, mother of Lew (Lord Grade), Bernie (Lord Delfont) and Leslie, who had escaped from Russia in 1912, clutching two of her little boys by the hand. A piece of social history, as well as the inside story of a showbiz family. A pity it didn't sell.

Anyway, I rang John Birt to ask him how on earth he'd come to tip off the National Trust about Paul's house. 'It was all by chance. I just happened to be on a visit to Liverpool, with my parents and my children. I decided I would take them all on a Magical Mystery Tour around the Beatles sites. I'd been on the tour before, but I thought my family would enjoy it. I've always been a Beatles fan. I went to the Cavern as a boy, though funnily enough I didn't see the Beatles play there, but I saw them play elsewhere.

'On the Mystery Tour you see all the houses, the schools. They even take you to the road where John's mother Julia was killed in a road accident. It lasts about two hours and they play Beatles music all the way. It's very moving. When we got to Forthlin Road, I could see a 'For Sale' sign outside.

'By an amazing coincidence, just the week previously in London I had been visited by Martin Drury, Director General Designate of the National Trust. It was a courtesy visit, the sort of thing people do when they take over national bodies, making contacts. In passing, he happened to say that one of the things he hoped to do was make the National Trust more contemporary, to try and have some twentieth-century houses. So a light bulb started flashing in my head as I stood outside Paul's front gate. On the train back to London from Lime Street, I wrote Martin Drury a letter, telling him how important Paul's house was to our culture. By return he rang me back – saying he thought it was a terrific idea.'

A private deal was arranged in November 1995. The price was not revealed, but I estimate it was about £40,000. Then began the long process of getting planning permission, agreements from neighbours and local authorities, and finding the appropriate funds. They eventually got a Lottery grant of £47,500 to help with the restoration.

I arrived to see it in the early summer of 1998, just before the house was officially opened after almost three years of work. As a Beatles fan, I was keen to see inside. And also as someone who had grown up in a similar council house, during the same period as Paul. So had millions of others, from Michael Parkinson to the Archbishop of Canterbury. Why shouldn't such habitats be preserved and remembered? Their furnishings and way of life are just as important to our national culture as stately homes or twee thatched cottages.

No. 20 Forthlin Road was built by Costains in 1952 for £1,369-9s-1d, part of the Mather Avenue estate of 330 houses. It was technically described as 'Intermediate Type Standard Building 5'. They were seen as superior dwellings for the working classes and the council insisted on good-quality materials, specifying that rosewood had to be used for door knobs and solid brass for other fittings. 'My dear mother Mary,' so

Paul remembers, 'had great aspirations for our family, so she was very proud and pleased to be taking a step up in the world by moving from our old house in Speke.'

Julian Gibbs, a National Trust expert on historic buildings, and Sarah Collins, from their regional office, were there to show me around. And jolly excited they were too. That day, all the original windows of the house had been installed. Not the actual windows, of course, but ones from a similar house of the exact period, dating back to 1952 when the house was new. Next they were going to take down the modern fence in the front garden and put back a privet hedge, with concrete posts and railings, just as it used to be.

They were lucky in that there had only been one occupant for the 30 years after the McCartneys had left, but once the Joneses had become owner-occupiers, they had started making so-called improvements, as many people did, putting in PVC windows, ugh, and a fancy front door, yuck. It could have been worse, as I could see from many of the neighbouring houses. Some have been drastically altered – the whole outside brick work re-rendered, bow windows added, porches built on, internal walls removed. None of that had happened to number 20.

'Yes, we have been fortunate,' said Julian. 'We are now able to show the original architecture.'

Architecture? In a council house? I couldn't quite see it myself, till he pointed out that all the rooms were the original shape and size and the out-houses in the back garden (WC, plus coal shed) had been left untouched. Even the outside drainpipe at the back is the original one, as known to many Beatles fans. Michael McCartney, Paul's younger brother, took a well-known series of photos of the house while they were all living there. One shows Paul climbing up the drainpipe, which is what he and Michael did if they forgot their front-door key. They then got in through the upstairs lavatory window, making sure, of course, the seat was down before clambering in.

Inside, they had successfully uncovered the original fireplace, dating from 1964, put in by Mrs Jones but of a similar design as the one used by the McCartneys. This also can be checked in one of Michael's photos, which shows Paul and John playing their guitars in the front room. These photographs have been invaluable in tracking down and matching furniture and fittings.

They have also installed original 1950s Bakelite light fittings and switches and even managed to acquire some of the original internal doors, which a Beatles dealer had cannily bought some years ago, though they haven't got the original door to Paul's bedroom. That was bought by the Hard Rock Café. But they have one of the exact type.

The wallpaper has proved an awkward problem. In the front room downstairs, on the left as you go in, which was their living-room, there appear to have been three different types of wallpaper, all at the same time. Over the fireplace the restorers had revealed some in an abstract stone design, which is of the right period, but on the left wall they found traces of some rather fancy Chinese-style wallpaper. They have done research, talked with wallpaper experts who have identified it, but been unable to find an old roll of the original. Perhaps when the public are allowed in, someone might eventually recognise it and have an old roll in their attic. Most of the other walls in the house have been painted cream. That was the colour the council used for internal walls when the house was first built.

It was weird, in a way, to think of the care and attention that has gone into the project, almost three years researching what were basically cheap, mass-produced decorations and furnishings. It's not as if it was Chatsworth or Althorp. But then research is research, regardless of how much it originally cost.

'Now look at this,' said Julian, leading me upstairs where there are three bedrooms and a bathroom. In what was Michael's bedroom, under Mrs Jones's carpet, they had found what they hoped was a piece of the original McCartney linoleum. Golly.

It was exactly the same pattern as the stuff I had in my bedroom in Carlisle – and I hated it. All council houses were freezing in the '50s, as, of course, there was no central heating. And all our mothers had a passion for horrible lino, which made it worse. In winter, as both Paul and Michael remember well, you almost froze when you stepped out of bed.

Like most upper-working-class households of the time, even if you were only a council tenant, some sort of decorating was always being done. My mother constantly bought odd pots of cheap, nasty paint from Woolworths and was forever redoing the walls in the kitchen. The houses got very dirty with the open coal fire, but materials were cheap and the space to be covered was small, so it was easily done. It would appear that Mrs Jones totally redecorated about six times in her 30 years, a social phenomenon new to Julian. In his professional life with the National Trust, he has dealt mainly with stately homes or similar, with massive rooms and sometimes massive budgets. The average for totally redecorating amongst the upper classes is more like once in 30 years.

Overall, 20 Forthlin Road is a much nicer, and bigger, house than I expected. It still has almost a rural view from the rear, looking over the grounds of a police training school. You can see why the McCartneys felt they were going up in the world. It also had a telephone, very posh, the only one in the street. This was because Paul's mother Mary had become a midwife and needed to be on call. She died of breast cancer in 1956, just a year after they had moved into Forthlin Road, leaving Jim to bring up their two sons.

Paul's bedroom, the smallest, was at the front upstairs. They had not put much furniture into it, keeping it fairly bare. That has been one of the major concerns for the National Trust – how to furnish the house. Their main aim, said Julian, is to offer a space which can be experienced, where you can stand, breathe in and imagine, yup, this is where those Beatles all began. So they hope National Trust members will not expect a film-set version of a 1950s council house, crammed with dinky period stuff. Nor will Beatles fans find some sort of shrine, though there will be one room with a cabinet of Beatles memorabilia. (The stuff supplied by me. My very best stuff, which includes ten original versions of their songs, some of which I picked up from the floor of Abbey Road to save them being burned by the cleaners, is now in the British Library in London, alongside the Magna Carta and manuscripts by Wordsworth, Keats and others.)

I agreed with Julian that it was probably best to keep Paul's bedroom fairly sparse, but I did think they should provide a decent amount of furniture downstairs. He said the kitchen would be fitted in period style, with the original Belfast sink, a 1950s electric cooker, a dresser, crockery and period items like packets of Fairy Snow and Omo. But he was still trying to decide about the main living-room.

There would be two period armchairs and a settee, complete with antimacassars, and a black and white Pye TV set, but he didn't want to overcrowd the room. No piano? Come on, Julian. You've got to have one. The McCartneys had one, and it can clearly be seen in one of Mike's photos, so a similar one must be pretty easy to find. All visitors will expect to see a piano, even if it's not the one Paul ever tinkled on. It will strike a musical note, ha ha, the moment you walk into the house, and, after all, the importance of the house is musical. Julian said he would think about it, if they could find a suitable piano. But I felt I hadn't managed to persuade him. There has to be a resident custodian, who will have to use the living-room as his living-room, another reason not to overcrowd it. He or she will sleep in the bedroom which Mr and Mrs McCartney used, so that won't be open to the public.

To create as little local disturbance as possible, visiting is being restricted to 127 days a year, with minibuses from Speke Hall, ten minutes' drive away, bringing parties of only 14 at a time.

In Michael's bedroom, there was a painter doing some finishing touches before the opening. He was using a county cream colour which seemed a bit posh to me, compared with the nasty cold, yellowy creams I remember on my council-house walls. This was thicker, richer, more National Trust in fact, but perhaps all modern paints are better these days.

The painter was from Woolton, near the parish church where John and Paul first met at a church fête in 1957 when Paul was invited to join the Quarrymen. Was he a Beatles fan?

'Oh aye. Always liked the Beatles. And the Stones,' he added diplomatically.

I asked about the house, how he'd found it from a professional point of view. Excellent workmanship, he said. No cracks, no damp, all floorboards intact, woodwork terrific, very easy to decorate, really.

'But I have been disappointed we haven't found more. I hoped when I took some of the modern wallpaper off that we'd find something interesting. But there was nothing.'

He had got excited when he'd uncovered some graffiti on one wall, but it was clearly from the Jones era. According to Michael's memory, their father had allowed them to draw and scribble poems and songs and stuff on their bedroom walls and in the upstairs lavatory. All signs of these had been erased by the Joneses.

I noticed how well the painter looked and asked if he'd recently been on his holidays. 'Goa,' he said. That seemed a bit, well, lavish for a working man. J.B. Priestley would have been surprised. So would Jim McCartney. In his day, Butlin's in North Wales was the furthest-flung holiday destination.

'It was a surprise trip, like, booked by my wife for my 60th birthday. I didn't know where we were going till we got there. I knew it was abroad, cos I'd had to have the jabs. But that was all.'

So you've got a nice wife, I said.

'Well, I have been treating her well for 35 years,' he said, returning to his painting.

Opening the house had created five new jobs in all. They had to employ two drivers for the minibus, to ferry people back and forward from Speke Hall. Then they needed two administrators on the telephones, to arrange bookings and issue tickets. And, of course, there had to be a custodian, which sounded the best job of all. In their minds, they were looking for a Liverpool person with at least three years' experience of customer service, dealing with the public in some way. Being a Beatles fan would, of course, be a plus. The salary was going to be £9,760.

'We've had 50 replies to our advert,' said Sarah. 'Now we're down to the shortlist and will be appointing very soon.'

Oh, and where did you advertise? In some National Trust publi-cation?

'No, in the *Big Issue*.'

Not quite how they find staff at Chatsworth or Althorp.

Chapter Twelve

ROCHDALE

I last went to Rochdale about 40 years ago to visit a colleague who worked with me on the *Manchester Evening Chronicle*. Rochdale was his home town, where he lived. In the office, I used to make fun of Rochdale. For no reason, really, as it's not considered a 'funny' town in English mythology, like Wigan or Scunthorpe, towns which have grown up being mocked, the butt of comedians, an excuse for a cheap snigger. All countries have 'funny' towns, for reasons outsiders can never understand, just like countries have national comedians, whose comedy doesn't travel, whose famous faces stare out at you from foreign papers, whose very physog makes the natives smile, yet who are completely incomprehensible.

It was the way Cedric pronounced 'Rochdale', the way he was so proud of it, that made me smile and, of course, that made him defensive, so he invited Margaret and me for Sunday lunch. I can't remember anything about the town except that it was a dump, and very dirty, but Cedric's house was clean and bright, new and modern, and I was impressed that anyone just a few years older than me should have his own house. All through the lunch, his wife kept on saying to him, 'You've no ambition, Cedric.' That phrase, said in a sing-song, Lancashire music-hall accent, has been part of our own family mythology for 40 years. Even our own children say it, though they don't know who Cedric is, or that it all originated in Rochdale.

J.B. Priestley missed it out on his journey. I wonder why. But Daniel Defoe, who went everywhere in the 1720s, arrived in Rochdale one August. 'In some places the harvest was hardly got in, we saw the mountains covered with snow and felt the cold acute and piercing, but even here we found, as in all those northern counties, the people had an extraordinary way of mixing warmth and the cold very happily together.' Defoe said that Rochdale was well known 'for a sort of coarse goods called halfthick'. I wished I'd known that when mocking Cedric all those years ago.

No sign of any mountains as I approached Rochdale, but then a Londoner like Defoe probably thought every pimple on the landscape was a mountain. And I was concentrating hard, head down, eyes focused, trying to make sense of the nightmare of motorways which encircle Rochdale. I used to think the M25 was the nastiest road on the planet, but the M60, M61 and M62 are far worse. To make it even more hellish, one of them changed its number, right before my eyes, as I was driving along. 'M60 – Formerly M61,' so a flashing sign informed me. It was like a faded pop star trying to change his image, assuming a new name in the hope that we'd forget his former nastiness and failures. I was already in a state of confusion, stuck nose-to-tail in miles of belching trucks and lorries and bad-tempered commercial travellers, but now it turned to panic as I tried to consult my maps and work out what the hell they were playing at. I thought I was on the M62, now they tell me it's the M61, sorry, the M60, we've had a name change. Oh no. Can't wait to get to Cumbria and leave all this motorway madness behind.

It was a blessed relief to get off it and roll on to a simple dual carriageway ring road, whirling along towards Rochdale, blindly following signs saying 'Town Centre' with absolutely no idea where I was, just grateful not to be on a motorway. I saw 'P' for Parking, so I drove through an arch, and took a ticket at a barrier, expecting to arrive in an underground car park. Instead I found myself in the open air. I got out, looked round and thought, oh, bugger it, that motorway has so scrambled my brain that I've driven straight onto someone's roof. The police will arrive, convinced I'm a suicide bomber, tow my car away across the Pennines and blow it up in a controlled explosion.

An Indian gentlemen was walking slowly towards me, so I said excuse me, do you know where I am, but he walked straight past, as if I wasn't there, disappearing over the edge of the roof. I could see other people, arriving from different angles, then they too disappeared. Well, that's one way of keeping the population down. Overspill, I think it's called.

Then I saw a sign saying 'Pay in the Mall Before Leaving'. So it was a proper parking place, even though it was on the roof of some building, but where was the mall? I stopped an elderly woman and asked if she could tell me the way to the, er, to the, you know, er. I have this problem with the word mall. Is it a short 'a' or a long 'a'? Forty years of living in London, and I still hesitate whenever the name Pall Mall looms up. Is it

Pal, as in friend, or Paul, as in McCartney? And is the second word Mal, as in Malcolm, or Maul, as in what lions do to you?

I pronounced it Mal and then Maul, muttered and mutilated it, did a lot of hand gestures and pointing at the sign, till eventually she said follow me. She took me down some steps which I hadn't seen, leading down from the edge of the roof into, yes, a massive shopping mall, and there was a little ticket machine, 70p for two hours, what a bargain, cheaper than Pall Mall, er, that street near Buck Pal.

It was a most impressive mall, bright and new, clean and warm, much better and smarter than Derby's, almost up to the standard of Milton Keynes's. I hadn't intended to go on a mall-inspecting tour of the provinces, but yes, this was my third so far. Well, I had done three stately homes as well – counting Paul McCartney's. I must make sure I also do three walks.

My first sight of Rochdalians for 40 years was quite reassuring. No halfthicks. No buskers. No beggars. The natives looked pretty affluent, till my eyes slowly adjusted and I could see, floating and flitting sideways amongst them, the usual hollow-eyed, close-cropped, thin-bodied 14-year-old urban lads in trainers and T-shirts, hanging around, looking hard, looking for trouble, looking for dope, a stick of glue or just looking for a laugh. You see them in every mall, modern versions of the Smikes and Artful Dodgers observed by Dickens. Watching them were the inevitable security guards, the modern versions of Bow Street Runners.

No sign of any mobile phones. I was now definitely in the Far North. Nor, alas, any sign of a cappuccino, or any fancy coffee shops with fancy foreign names. I tried another shopping mall nearby, the Wheatsheaf. No decent-looking coffee there either, so I sat down in Russell's Café and Piano Bar, chic name, chic place – at least for anyone whose notion of chic has not moved on since tea in Binns in 1950s Carlisle.

I ordered a cup of coffee, even though I could see it was that stewed stuff kept in a glass goldfish bowl. As she served me, the waitress behind the counter slopped it all over the saucer. 'Eee, I do that all the time,' she said cheerfully.

I burst out laughing, wanting her to say it again. Eee, I just love your accent. Rochdale these days is little more than a northern suburb of Manchester, but while the Manchester accent is harsh and unattractive, Rochdale's is old-fashioned, music-hall Lancashire. Think of Victoria Wood in her 'Can you see it on the trolley?' sketch. Or Jane Horrocks playing Bubbles in *Ab Fab*.

I sat down beside a grand piano, which I thought would be merely a prop, perhaps even made of plastic, to justify the café's name. I was slurping my saucer when an elderly man arrived, sat down and started playing, ever so casually, informally, as if he had just been passing and fancied a tinkle. I asked a girl who appeared to be the head waitress, tottering past alarmingly in some monstrous high heels, her short skirt almost up to her neck, if this was the regular pianist.

'Oh aye, every day from 11.30, except Sundays. He's reet good, i'n't 'e?'

She looked about 13, very pretty, very thin, incredibly chirpy and cheerful. Just outside the café's entrance I could see some of the Hard Lads, the hangers-about, looking in, looking sullen, pathetic and deprived, beaten up by life already, when their life has hardly begun. Yet the two teenage girls, one behind the counter, the other tottering about on her high heels, glowed with life and optimism, energy and enthusiasm, even though they were in dead-end jobs earning about £2 an hour. I could hardly take my eyes off them, speculating on their life to come. Would they be let down, used and beaten by some brute, or would they flower and flourish?

The pianist, eyes shut, countenance closed, was giving nothing away about his life or feelings and might as well not have been there, not in the flesh, except for his fingers, which were playing his own variation on the theme of 'A Hard Day's Night'. I hadn't spotted it at first, as he approached from such an acute angle, wandering off, coming back, all very clever, very amusing. Two middle-aged women on the other side in tweed hats and scarves were totally ignoring him, their heads almost touching, talking non-stop through every note. When the pianist finished I gave a small lone clap, then walked out to explore Rochdale.

Rochdale is famous for Gracie Fields, born over a fish and chip shop in 1898. She ended up in Capri. Quite a wise move. Today in Rochdale they have the Gracie Fields Theatre. It's famous also for Cyril Smith, the heavyweight Liberal MP. Right, that's enough about famous folk from Rochdale. Apart, of course from the Rochdale Pioneers.

Who? That's what my wife had said when I departed for Rochdale that morning. Toad Lane, I said, you must have heard of Toad Lane. You did O and A level history and a history degree. Yes, but she never did modern history. Modern history, in her day at Oxford, was basically the Tudors.

I went to find the local tourist office to see if the Pioneers were remembered in Rochdale today. It's situated in the Town Hall, an astounding building, how could I never have heard of it, grey and Gothic, about the size and grandeur of a cathedral, out of all proportion for such a little town. Well, not as little as I had imagined. Rochdale itself has 94,000 inhabitants but the figure usually given is now 200,000, since it has grown into the Metropolitan Borough of Rochdale, incorporating Middleton and Heywood. Big enough to have a Premier League football team. Instead it does no better than Carlisle, languishing in Division Three.

I bought some postcards of Our Gracie and picked up a leaflet about the Corgi Heritage Centre. That museum in Tring was surprising enough, with all the dead dogs, but a museum devoted to just one species sounded most unusual. Then I realised it was to do with die-cast models. Another exhibition described itself as the Home of the World's Largest Working Steam Mill Engine. That was a relief. I knew they'd have a world's first, best, greatest if I looked hard enough.

And yes, there was stuff on the Rochdale Pioneers, with a map showing me how to get to the Pioneers Museum. I set off, clutching the map, but none of it made sense. Like provincial town centres everywhere, Rochdale has been relandscaped, redrawn, with new malls and walkways, and pedestrian passages. Streets which appear big on the map, and were once big in local lives, turn out to be dead ends.

I eventually worked my way to the exact spot on the map, in Hunters Lane, finding myself back behind the Market Shopping Mall block where I had parked my car. No sign of the Pioneers Museum. I asked a middle-aged woman and she stared at me as if I'd come from outer space. A young man in a smart suit had no idea either. Perhaps I was using the wrong name. The locals might know it as something else. Then I spotted a traffic warden, and yes, he knew where I wanted. I was only 50 yards away. But not in Hunters Lane – as on the map. It's in Toad Lane, which runs off Hunters Lane – but, ah ha, not for very far. Toad Lane is a dead lane, cut off in its prime and now contains only two buildings, an attractive-looking public house and, next door, the museum.

I went inside but could see no one. I peered around, but still no sign of life – and came to some stairs. 'Shop!' I shouted up the stairs. It had used to be a shop. Shouting 'Museum' would have sounded rather strange.

Down the stairs bounded a very fit-looking, handsome, square-jawed man of around 60, a bit like Jack Hawkins coming off the bridge to greet some of his new chaps. His strong Welsh accent didn't quite fit the English officer part but, close up, he was still remarkably clean cut. He said he was Malcolm Price, the warden, not curator, but yes, he would show me around.

He led me to a display on the life of Robert Owen, not one of the Rochdale Pioneers, he said, and I said yes, yes, I know, I did do modern history in my degree. (Nineteenth-century social, the soft option.) Owen was a Welshman, with Scottish connections. How come he's mixed up with the Pioneers? 'It's true he never came to Rochdale, but the Pioneers were greatly influenced by him. I always like to begin the tour with him.'

There were 28 Pioneers, all local textile workers, all men, who created a little shop in Rochdale in 1844 – and the Co-operative movement was born, growing into one of the greatest social, economic and political movements of the nineteenth century.

Workers in Rochdale, and elsewhere, were being exploited by the Industrial Revolution. Trade Unions attempted to help them in the workplace. The Co-op aimed to reduce another form of exploitation – by ruthless shopkeepers and merchants who mixed sand with oatmeal, plaster of Paris with flour, fiddled their weighing scales and generally ripped off poor customers. The Co-op insisted not only on high-quality goods, but on total equality.

'There were other co-operative societies in existence long before the Rochdale Pioneers,' said Mr Price, 'but they were the first to start a proper movement. They said from the beginning that the customers would actually own the shop and all members would share equally in any surplus – the famous divi. The first cash dividend in 1845 was 3d in the pound. Look, here's all the original books and ledgers.

'They opened their first shop here, on 21 December 1844, at eight in the evening. They all had other jobs, you see, during the day. When I show parties around, I always say we were the first "late late shop" in Rochdale. That amuses them. You see these signs everywhere now, don't you, saying Late Late Shopping.'

The building dates back to 1792 and was originally a woollen merchant's. The Co-op had it from 1844 to 1870, after which it passed through several hands. It was a pet shop for a while, then in 1930 the Co-op bought it back and opened it as their own museum. Each year, they get about 8,000 visitors.

Not many from Rochdale, I suggested, judging by my experience so far. I told him about all the people who had no idea where it was. 'Yes, Rochdalians are the least of our visitors, though we do get quite a few local schools and Women's Institutes.

'Most visitors, when they look around, say isn't it a shame what's happened to the Co-op? They say this because so many local Co-ops have gone, which is, of course, a shame. They were an important part of every local community in Britain at one time. Oh yes. Important. Do you remember the Co-op Women's Guilds? Well, they were important.'

No, don't remember them, but I do remember our local Co-op in Carlisle in the 1950s. My mother shopped nowhere else and I can still remember our number, 16923. My wife can also remember her mother's Co-op number, 360. She often boasts about it. It proves her family had lived longer in Carlisle than ours.

'In 1931, there were 50 different Co-op societies within ten miles of Rochdale. Now there are only 48 in the whole country.'

What happened was the arrival of the supermarket chains, able to compete in power and price, size and range, which quickly made the Co-ops seem very old-fashioned, especially the smaller societies.

'But what people don't realise is that the Co-op today is even bigger and more successful than ever. Not perhaps in retail shops, but in other fields, most of which were there from the beginning. There's the Co-op Bank for a start. Now that's huge. Co-op travel, Co-op insurance, Co-op farming, they're all doing well. And did you know we're about the biggest funeral operators in the land?'

I picked up some leaflets and was most impressed to find that the Co-op today has a turnover of £15 billion. But hasn't there been talk of some takeover bids? Didn't I read about some chancer trying to get hold of the shares and strip the assets?

Mr Price looked pained and disbelieving at the very idea. 'Oh, I don't think that will happen. Look again at our rules, over there on the wall. We have democratic control – one member, one vote. So no, I don't see it could happen.'

But there is usually some clever City slicker who can get around most rules if there's a killing to be made, whether it's taking over a football club or a motoring organisation.

Mr Price then led me up the stairs, pointing out displays of all the foreign Co-ops based on the English system. 'There are over a hundred around the world with 750 million members. Guess where the biggest is? Didn't think you could. Japan. I knew that would surprise you. Look at this photo. They've built their own reproduction of this Toad Lane shop in Kobe. That's a little bit of a fact for you . . .'

I stood for a long time examining a photograph of 13 of the original Pioneers taken by a local Manchester photographer in 1865. The definition and detail is amazing, their waistcoats and chains fascinating, their jaws remarkable, their mutton-chop whiskers and hairstyles hilarious. A good example of the technology of the past being just as good as that today. In fact, I don't think you could get a modern black-and-white photograph as clear and as sharp.

So, Mr Price, with your square jaw, any little facts you can tell me about yourself, such as how you, a Welshman, came to be here, in charge of a museum in the heart of Lancashire? 'Rugby, that's what brought me here,' he replied.

I might have known he'd played a bit, though in my experience blokes who play a lot in their twenties and thirties are often crippled by arthritis by the age of 60. Perhaps he hadn't played much, after all. Park rugby, was it?

'I was first capped for Wales in 1958, then I went on to play for the British Lions against Australia and New Zealand.'

Hold on. We have a superstar here. Malcolm Price? I'd begun to think his name was vaguely familiar, though rugby stars in 1958 didn't quite have the profile, or the money, of those today.

'When I was first picked for Wales, I had to get the bus to Cardiff from my home village, Talywain, which is near Pontypool. No one had cars in those days. My mother, God bless her, was a clippie on the buses for almost 40 years. I always hoped to God she was on the bus, so I could travel free. Then I could charge the bus fare and make myself a few pennies.

'My first match was against England. We beat them 6–5 but I can't remember much about it. We had to walk across a duckboard to get on to the pitch. It was a very muddy day, so they'd put this duckboard down. Now, I had new boots on that day, which my mother had bought me, paying them up each week on the never-never. I felt ten foot tall, walking out for Wales for my first international, in front of a crowd of 70,000. Then I fell off the duckboard. I could feel the mud and water oozing over my new boots. That's still my clearest memory of the day. Though I did give Dewi Bebb the pass which put him through for our try . . .

'I got my first cap for the British Lions in 1959. In 1962, I left rugby union for rugby league.'

Why?

'For the money, of course. What else? I went to Oldham for a very large fee.'

How large?

'It was £9,000. I got it all, as I was an amateur. I went into digs when I first came up here, then I bought my own house, paying in cash, a detached bungalow which cost £2,100. Very nice it was. While with Oldham, I got capped for the Great Britain rugby league team, so I've been capped in both codes.'

He ended his league career with Rochdale Hornets. When he

172

eventually retired from rugby, he had his own business, then joined the Co-op, becoming a manager and finally an area controller for the Norwest Co-op Society.

'I was one of those people in the '70s, alas, who had to go around closing local Co-ops. It was very sad.'

He retired from work in 1993, aged 55, and took a part-time job at the Pioneers Museum. When the warden left, he took over full time. He still lives locally, but alone. He was married, with four children, now grown up, but is divorced. He keeps fit by doing circuit running and playing lots of badminton.

No, he didn't envy modern rugby players. Their fame and salaries are not quite on the scale of our soccer stars, but they are still enormous, compared with his day.

'The best money when I played was when you turned out for your country. You got £25 for a win, £9 if you lost. When I played for Great Britain at Swinton against Australia, we got beaten, 9–3. I scored, but all I got was £9. I still thought that was good.

'In ordinary rugby league games, you got between £9 and £12 for a win and only £3 for defeat.'

Today, a top rugby player – union or league, for they are all professional now – can earn up to £2,000 a week, with transfer values up to half a million pounds. 'You've got to hand it to Mr Murdoch, for bringing in all this television money, but that doesn't bother me, really. I considered I was well paid, thanks to getting my transfer fee. I was comfortable, thank you very much.

'What I do envy is the style of the game today. It's much faster and more athletic than it used to be, which is why it's a more entertaining sport to watch. In my day, it was slower and more physical. The game was dominated by what we used to call the "steam pigs" – the big blokes in the scrum. I was a centre three-quarters. In some games, I'd only touch the ball two or three times.

'So I think I would have done well today. It would have suited my style, being faster, more open. That's what I envy, not the money. I'm content with what I got.'

And content to live in Lancashire? 'I like it here, but I still feel Welsh. When I went to my mother's funeral, back to Talywain, I cried my eyes out. I drove there in a dream. I can't remember anything of the journey. I came back and apologised to my next-door neighbour about rushing off without telling him – and he said you did tell me. When you got the call about your mother, you came in and told me you were off. Do you know, I don't remember a thing about that either. Funny, isn't it?'

He always goes back to Wales for the rugby internationals. 'I'll be there for the '99 World Cup. Can't miss that. Not just because I get a free ticket, but I want to cheer on Wales.'

A free ticket? 'Oh yes. If you play for Wales, you get a free ticket for all their home games. As long as you are alive . . .'

That is a help. Not much use turning up in your coffin, even if it is a Co-operative funeral.

* * *

When I attended that Downing Street bash given by the Prime Minister, I was quite disappointed that none of the Blair Babes was there – not, of course, that I would have used such a term, certainly not. But the success of so many women was a major feature of that May 1997 general election triumph. A total of 102 female Labour MPs were returned, some of them remarkably young, if not quite babelike, and most of them remarkably inexperienced in national politics.

One of them was Lorna Fitzsimons, MP for Rochdale, just 29 when she was elected. I set off to see her, clutching a street map which the tourist office at the Town Hall had given me, with their MP's office marked in Oldham Road.

It turned out to be a run-down, scruffy road, with pounding traffic and nowhere to park, but I found a backstreet car park and put enough money in a meter for two hours. I banged on the front door of the address I'd been given. There were Labour Party posters all over their front wall, so that was a good sign, but no sign of life. I went into a sandwich bar next door and they said there's hardly ever anyone there. It's just a club room the Labour Party uses. The MP doesn't have her office there. Oh no. And I'd wasted a whole 60p in the meter.

I got totally lost looking for the correct address, which was further down Oldham Road, then into some light industrial estate. Her office was in an equally rundown building – but this was temporary, before moving to newer, swisher offices. Lorna was on the phone. She stared at me suspiciously as I entered. Reddish hair, spectacles, about five foot tall, neat and efficient looking, wearing trousers and what looked like a cream woollen cardigan. I said I'd made an appointment through her research assistant, Mark, in the House of Commons. He had answered the phone when I'd rung and been very helpful, partly because he'd read one of my books. She said she didn't know anything about that.

'I'm not sure I want to talk to you. It was Mark who booked you in. Not me. What's it about, anyway?'

Not a lot, really, just me wandering through England, end of the millennium, J.B. Priestley book, that sort of stuff, no angles, not trying to prove anything. She looked at me even more suspiciously. 'Would you like some coffee?'

I started to follow her into a back room, which is what I always do in someone's house or office, using it as an excuse to have a gape, observe their little rituals. Lorna said she didn't want me to see it, as it was untidy. Only one year in the House of Commons, but she had clearly become wise to some of the ways of the prying world.

She was born in Rochdale in 1967. Her father, now dead, was a textile worker, a spinner in a local mill, but he managed to buy his own stone cottage in a cobbled street in Wardle village, just on the edge of Rochdale. Lorna still lives in the same cottage, with her mother. The cottage cost £500 when her father bought it in 1960. Now it's probably worth around £200,000.

She has a twin sister, Liz, not identical, born two and a half hours later, and a younger brother, Dave, who is a chemical engineer with ICI. Liz is now a lawyer. 'We're chalk and cheese. We couldn't be more different.'

In what way?

Well, she's tall and brown-haired and I'm small and red-headed. She's introverted and I'm an extrovert.

Was she more intelligent at school than you?

'I can't believe you said that. How invidious!' She sat glaring at me, supping her coffee. I'd thought I'd start on some harmless stuff, such as her childhood, but now I'd mucked up. I apologised.

'I actually got better grades than she did at art and music, but not so good at other things. I'm dyslexic. I didn't know that for a long time. People still think it's a middle-class-mum's excuse for a lazy child.'

The phone rang and she immediately picked it up. 'Yes, go on. Well, who are they? Why is it they want to meet me? What is it they want from me?'

She spoke briskly, bossily, but whoever it was did get given an appointment. The minute she put the phone down, it rang again. This time the conversation went on for ages as she took someone through the interview technique for getting some job in local government.

I groaned inwardly. Mark had obviously booked me in during some sort of telephone surgery time. I'd never get to grips with her, or have a decent chat, if she was going to be on the bloody phone all the time, though now and again she put her hand over the receiver and made a face, indicating she wouldn't be long. I stared around the room, running my eye down the filing cabinets, noting they ran alphabetically, from Abortion through Unemployment to Women.

She hung up – and it rang again. This time there were loud shrieks and roars of laughter, an enormously dirty and loud laugh for such a small body, then she fell silent as the person on the line took her through some trauma.

'She's a woman who's been mugged,' she said, hanging up. 'She has four young children, and four already grown up. She's had a very bad experience . . .'

I sympathised and then said, er, do you always answer all your own calls? 'I don't normally at the House of Commons, but I do when I'm here. People are always surprised. They don't expect to actually talk to their MP.'

At 15, she had left school and gone to the local art college, where she had her first experience of being an activist. 'We had a visiting art lecturer who made some of the nude models go into bondage, you know, getting them all tied up. Well, this was disgusting. The models felt they had to do it or they'd lose the work, but I said no, put your robes on. I went to see the Principal and told him what was happening. I knew what the college would worry about was it getting into the local paper: sex and drugs and rock 'n' roll at the art college. But I made my point. That lecturer was not invited back.'

She went on to Loughborough College of Art, to do a degree in textile design, and it was there she got into more political agitation, fighting a move to close the college. Her campaign was successful. She found herself taking part in more student politics, locally and then nationally, becoming President of the NUS in 1992. She was the first non-university student to hold the post, as she had been at art school, not a university.

She was nominated for the Rochdale seat in 1996, her first attempt at Parliament. 'It was other people who suggested it. I would only have tried in Rochdale. I wouldn't have become a carpetbagger.'

For 25 years, Rochdale had been in the hands of the Liberals, notably with Cyril Smith, and then the Lib Dems. Liz Lynne was the sitting MP with a slim majority, but Lorna wasn't at all confident of victory. 'What we didn't know was how the Tories would vote – would they switch to Labour or not? It could have gone either way.'

She got in with a majority of 4,545, which represented a 4.85 per cent swing to Labour. She didn't quite believe it till her first day at Westminster. 'When I got my pass, that's when it seemed real, that my existence had been acknowledged. I just stood there with a childishly large grin. What was nice was not just the large Labour majority but that so many of my friends had also got in, like Stephen Twigg, who had beaten Portillo, winning what everyone had thought was an unwinnable seat. Also Phil Woolas in the neighbouring constituency of Oldham East. It meant I had friends to share the experience with me.'

She started off sharing a room, as most new MPs do. 'We were told if we behaved well, were good children, turned up for late votes, then we might get our own room. After six weeks it hadn't happened, so I complained. I did a bit of wheeling and dealing and got my own room.'

Lorna was one of five new women MPs still in their twenties, the youngest being Claire Ward, aged 24, MP for Watford. (While passing near Watford, which also happened to be on the route of my journey from London, I rang Ms Ward's office three times, then sent two faxes and two letters – but never heard a cheep. Not a sausage. Ah well, I'm sure she was awfully busy.)

Labour's women MPs were immediately christened 'Blair's Babes', so I wondered how she felt about it. The phrase, which I thought I had put in quotation marks, was hardly out of my mouth when she roared at me, practically blasting me out of the room. I promised not to use it again.

'And I hope you won't. It degrades women and detracts totally from what they do. It suggests we are just a gaggle of silly women with no skills who are brain-dead. Well, excuse me. We were New Labour before New Labour was created. We were practising New Labour thoughts and ideals before Tony Blair became leader. We were not created by him. We created the sort of party he went on to lead. So, excuse me . . .'

But there had been suggestions, in some quarters, by some political commentators, that Labour's women hadn't actually achieved a great deal in their first year. I didn't quite finish the question, moving my seat back just in case she exploded.

'That is rubbish! We have played a very important role in legislation. What about the single parents benefits, welfare to work, family tax credits, childcare strategy, working . . .' She reeled off a long list, not all of which I got down, and then a long list of brilliantly clever and talented women MPs such as Yvette Cooper and Patricia Hewitt.

After she had calmed down a bit, I asked what she considered her own personal achievements in her first year. 'Getting Rochdale a new hospital. Tony Blair and I personally promised it to the people of Rochdale before the election. It was one of my pre-election games, getting him interviewed by the local paper and making sure he said it. Having done that, he had to deliver, didn't he? After all, we'd waited 25 years for it. The first sod will be cut in July. Three years later it will open at a cost of £28 million. And it's all government finance, not private money, which is happening elsewhere. I don't think it's really sunk in around here how phenomenal that is. We've also managed an extra £9 million for local schools.'

How about speaking in the House of Commons? Had she done much of that? 'Oh, lots, but I don't keep tabs.'

Like most new MPs, especially the women, she has been pretty appalled by the long hours and conditions of work in the House of Commons. 'The Commons is in need of a reality check. No wonder there are so many broken marriages and alcoholics. You often have to wait around for hours and hours for a late vote. And if you're diligent, you've already done a full working day of engagements. It's like being stuck in a very expensive prison. You feel not in control of your own working life. It gives a very destabilising feeling. It's hard to know if you have any power at all.

'If you get on the wrong side of the Speaker, then you'll never get called to speak. I know one MP whose life was made hell for five years because he'd fallen foul of the Speaker. But no names . . .' Meaning no name for the MP. We all know the Speaker is a woman, Betty Boothroyd, so that surprised me. Lorna made a face, but would not elaborate further.

So what's to be done about the House of Commons? 'You can't just ignore the history, even if it is stifling reality. You have to work with it, work with the system in order to change it. I now know it's like any office, any organisation. You have to suss out who's who, who you can trust and not trust, who's a friend and who's a foe. My eyes have been opened to all the vested interests. The object of politics is to make sure the people will gain, but, alas, not everyone has the same object. It's all very erratic, and very exhausting.

'The Commons took a long time to build. The men have been running it for several hundred years. You can't expect women to change the whole thing in just a year. I'm amazed that you or anyone should even think it.

'People anyway are very scared of change. You have to learn the system, be able to speak from knowledge of the system, otherwise you get ridiculed and laughed at.'

Have you been ridiculed? 'I'm not going into that sort of thing. I'm not getting into personalities.'

Well, then, do you worry that you'll be institutionalised, get sucked in, become part of the establishment and end up like the rest, unable or unwilling to bring about change?

'You mean go native? No chance. But I just have to bide my time, to keep remembering you can't be wrong all of the time. On the other hand, you have a career to think about. There's no point in crucifying yourself.'

There was one incident during her first year which made most of the national newspapers and is probably all that anyone outside Rochdale knows about her. In an interview with the *News of the World*, she was quoted as saying that if she wants to go to bed with a bloke, she tells him. She was also quoted as saying that as she looks around the House of Commons at some of the men, she often thinks, 'Cor, I could give him one.' Not that she would, of course. Being an MP meant that 'her chance of having three-in-a-bed romps are now over'.

I never saw the original article, only bits quoted elsewhere and out of context, but I remember thinking she was being funny, sending up the *News of the World* interviewer. All the same, I said, it would have been a bit safer to have given that sort of stuff to the *Independent* or the *Guardian* . . .

She stared at me hard, moving not a muscle.

'So that's what you've really come to talk about,' she said at last, coldly furious.

No, not really, I said. I just wanted to talk to a new MP, preferably a woman, after their first year. That just happens to be the only time I read about you.

She continued to glare at me, saying nothing. We were interrupted by a postman lumbering up the stairs to deliver a package. She signed for it. Then a Labour Party activist arrived to confirm some arrangements for the forthcoming party conference. This was followed by two phone calls.

When there seemed at last to be a pause, I said that all I wanted to know was had she been joking, or not?

'I was totally let down,' she said, giving a long sigh. 'There was no proper interview as such, but I was told I would be able to read and vet anything about me which might appear. That was a verbal promise, not a written one, alas.'

So you could have alerted the editor, told him about the promise, and demanded to see the copy?

'I did, but I was told the story's all harmless, nothing to worry about, you've said nothing that will harm your political career . . .'

And did it? She was now looking sad rather than furious. 'I am basically very shy. When I was little, I worried all the time about my dyslexia. I was paranoid and self-conscious. So since about the age of 11 I have tried hard to weigh things carefully, not to do anything embarrassing which would make me ridiculed. And then that happened. I was let down, in public . . .'

There was a long pause. She looked even sadder, and vulnerable.

'What I have to do is learn from it. You are judged more by how you handle a mistake, how you deal with it afterwards, than by the original mistake. It's how you take the knocks in politics that matters, whether you can keep level-headed after something goes wrong.

'So, that's the last time I'll have a laugh with anyone in the media. One mistake. But I've learned my lesson. That's why I was so suspicious of you arriving here. I wondered what you were really after.

'I want to be seen as a dynamic young woman who is doing her best for Rochdale, who has worked hard in the House of Commons, who has achieved a lot, who serves on various committees and has been made chair of the Labour Party Women's Group.'

Yes, I've got the list on your CV. Very impressive, for one so young and so new. Given all that, and forgetting that one mistake, would she say she was enjoying it?

'Enjoyment isn't the word I would use for my working life. I've never been in a job which is so unregulated. There is no way to evaluate your performance. Am I a good MP or not? How does anyone know? If I get re-elected, does that prove it? Of course not.

'Personally, I think we should have fewer MPs but with more power. For example, at the moment I'm furious that I can't send out a letter to all the people of Rochdale, all my constituents, giving them an annual report on their MP. That would seem reasonable, wouldn't it, a useful service? But I'm not allowed to – not if I use House of Commons notepaper and postage. Yet I couldn't afford to do it personally. The system is so arcane.'

But surely you can report your progress in other ways, take an advert in the local paper, or give an interview?

'I couldn't afford an ad, but I have leaned on the local paper and taken them through my pledges to the people of Rochdale, detailing how, one year on, I have kept them.'

And how about her personal life, one year on?

'I haven't got one. I work every day, and at the weekend. I have no private life. I live at home, with my mother. In London, I have a room in someone's place. I can drive, but I haven't got a car. I don't go to many places, not for personal pleasure. The only thing I've done recently to try and relax is join a gym. But I've hardly been.'

Any boyfriends? 'None. And being aged 30, it's hard to meet many people of my own age at the place where I happen to work. If I do meet any men outside work, they're all taken.'

What if she did meet someone and fall in love? Would she give up politics?

'I'd like to think I'd say "Love me, love my job" and be able to carry on. But it would depend on how much I loved him. I might not be able to make compromises, then I'd have to think seriously about politics . . .'

The phone rang again. A long conversation was clearly about to begin, so I mouthed my thanks for all her time. She put her hand over the phone, said she would be finished soon, I could come and see her at home, no hurry, she could spare me any time I needed.

I waved goodbye and went quietly down the stairs. A dynamic, committed, hard-working, successful woman. I'm sure a load of fun when you get to know her, warm and entertaining, but somehow I couldn't help feeling sorry for her . . .

Chapter Thirteen

MORECAMBE BAY

Before the coming of the railways, one of the routes from Lancashire to the Lake District was across Morecambe Bay. If you look at the map, you can see the reasons why. The Lake District appears to be a peninsula, with various dangling bits hanging down like a cow's udder. Going round by road to get on to this peninsula, or any of the dangling bits, could take days, but going straight across the water provides a short cut that can be done on foot in a few hours. Yes, on foot. Not by boat, or even by walking on the water, but by walking on the sands.

One of nature's many tricks is that every eight hours, since nature began, Morecambe Bay, which is normally a wide expanse of open sea some 20 miles across at its widest, becomes a massive expanse of open sand. Daniel Defoe, when setting out from Lancaster, remarked elliptically that it was 'a sea without ships'. He could see ships further out, battling away, taking coals between Whitehaven and Ireland, but in the Bay itself, there appeared to be 'no sea port or place of trade'. Nothing much to interest merchants, or himself, or his masters, so he hurried on, without waiting for the tide to turn to discover that the Bay was a place of transport, not of trade. Short-cutters, people in a hurry, people wanting to save time and money, adventurers and romantics, they have all set out to dash across the Bay. You can tell today how some of them got on by looking at the local gravestones, especially at Cartmel Priory. There you will read the sad tales of those who didn't quite make it.

A writer in the *Lonsdale Magazine* of 1820 describes how he was wakened at five o'clock in the morning in his Lancaster hotel by the coach driver bursting into his bedroom. 'For God's sake, make haste! The tide is down . . . if you delay, we shall all be drowned.'

The sands might look flat, dry and empty when the tide is out, but, of course, they are not. The Bay has two main estuaries, where the River Kent and River Leven run into the sea, and even at the lowest tides they are still trickling away, ready to trap the foolhardy. There are also channels and gulleys to trip you up and banks of sand that appear dry and safe but can suddenly collapse on the unwary. Nastiest of all are the quicksands. They can suck you in, squeeze you in, and never throw you out again.

All the same, for hundreds of years there were regular coach trips across the Bay. The first stage was from Hest Bank, just north of Morecambe, across to Kents Bank, near Grange-over-Sands. After a short stretch of permanent dry land, it was back on the Bay again for the second stage, over the Leven estuary, to the thriving little market town of Ulverston. Travellers going from Lancaster to Ulverston and Furness regularly used this route, saving themselves about a day going north up the main turnpike to Kendal, then west through Lakeland.

Poets such as Thomas Gray and William Wordsworth did the trip and never forgot it, considering it one of the most exhilarating moments in their lives. Turner, the artist, did it at least four times, doing sketches as he went along. He produced two watercolours each entitled 'Lancaster Sands'. The earlier one, done in 1816, shows a stagecoach in the middle of the sands, battling against the wind and rain. In the second one, from 1825, a coach and some walkers are arriving on shore, looking tired and exhausted, the incoming tide behind them about to overtake the stragglers.

During his 1816 tour, Turner spent about two months in the north of England. He had a commission from Longman's to provide 120 watercolours for a series of books. His fee was £3,000, his biggest ever commission. Still seems an enormous amount. No book publisher would offer an illustrator a comparable sum today, but then I am always surprised by how much artists and hacks could make in the nineteenth century. In 1809, Southey was getting £100 an article from the *Quarterly Review*. You don't have to multiply by 100 to get today's equivalent – because it is today's equivalent, at least if you contribute to the so-called literary end of the market. As I write, my wife is sending off a review to Auberon Waugh's *Literary Review* for a fee of £50. I have contributed a column to the *New Statesman* for the last two years for which I get £160 a column. It used to be £150, but I moaned and groaned. (On the other hand, I would expect £1,000 when I write a 1,000-word piece for the *Daily Mail*. So it goes.)

It was the railway which finished off coach trips across the Bay. In 1857, Lancaster was linked to Ulverston by a series of dramatic railway viaducts and coastal embankments, cutting the journey time to a mere 17 minutes. End of ancient route, end of an era, end of romance. Ah, but not quite. Today it is again one of the most exhilarating, romantic journeys in Britain, and each year some 10,000 people do the crossing, all thanks to the energy and enterprise and knowledge of one man.

For something like 20 years, I have been longing to do this trip. I don't know why I've never managed it, right on my Lakeland doorstep, when over the years I have somehow managed to fit in other exciting-sounding routes and journeys. Such as the Orient Express from London to Venice. That was excellent, though once was enough, thank you.

But now, at last, coming from Lancashire and heading for Lakeland, I had the excuse to walk the sands, along with my dear wife – a true Cumbrian, as she is always telling me, for she was born in Carlisle, whereas I only arrived there aged four, sneaking in across the border from Scotland. She had never done the walk either, but then she is a North Cumbrian. Going to South Lakeland is like going to a foreign country.

We went first to Grange-over-Sands, in what is known as Cumbria's Riviera, where the sky was blue and the sun was shining. When I first visited Grange, it did seem like the South of France, lush and affluent, healthier and more colourful than our grittier, greyer North and West Cumbrian towns. They do have a palm tree, of sorts, the shops have hanging baskets and there are pretty promenades where you are expected to promenade as opposed to huddle and shelter, which is my memory of childhood trips to Silloth, the traditional seaside resort for folks in Northern Cumbria.

Grange is favoured by invalids and the recuperating, the retired and the dying. My father, who spent all my childhood as an invalid suffering from multiple sclerosis, had his one and only holiday at Grange-over-Sands, allowing my mother her first break in some 20 years of looking after him. In those days, in the '50s, there was little in the way of disability benefits, rehabilitation or respite care, but somehow the local health authority had got him into a nursing home at Grange for a whole week. He hated it.

We drove through Grange along the coast to Kents Bank, the little railway station where we planned to leave the car. The walk starts on the other side of the Bay but ends up at Kents Bank. Walkers who arrive by car – which, alas, most Lakeland walkers do, therefore creating endless problems and annoyances for permanent residents – have the option of leaving their vehicle at the beginning or end of the walk, then taking the railway in between, the little but spectacular line which runs all around the West Cumbrian coast, from Carnforth up to Carlisle.

About a hundred people had had the same idea. I could hardly believe it. They were crowded on to the little platform in the early-morning sunshine, all glowing and excited, in shorts and trainers, carrying little rucksacks, holding hands, chattering and joking. Most were in family groups, some with quite young children, plus there was a smattering of wizened walkers. The accents sounded mainly Lancashire or Yorkshire. Most of the people had presumably zoomed up the motorways in the early hours from industrial Merseyside, Manchester or Leeds.

Out of a little railway cottage at the end of the platform came scuttering a rather agitated elderly man in shorts, carpet slippers and apron. Poor bloke, I thought, you come to live in this isolated place and you get woken up by what sounds like a football crowd outside your front window. Or is he some sort of railway worker? Over his shoulders he was wearing a battered British Railways fluorescent bib, the sort railway workers wear when working on the line. I followed him up the platform, hoping to find out what he was doing.

'No, I'm not the stationmaster, or the guard,' he said. 'I just don't want folks standing on me plants. I put them all in, you know. Nobody paid me, nobody looks after them, just me, 300 yards of them. Heh you, don't stand on them bloomin' plants . . .'

He shouted at some kids who were pushing each other into his plants. The garden was terrific, all the way along the platform and on the other side as well, the shore side, where it must be hell to grow anything with the salt winds and rain. I complimented him on his excellent work. 'Well, a few local people have given me some of the plants, but I do all the gardening.'

I asked his name, and he stopped, peering at me. 'Why do you want to know?'

It was a bit presumptuous, to ask a total stranger his name. The answer, I suppose, was habit. In my mind, I still fear a bollocking from the news editor of the *Manchester Evening Chronicle* for not coming back with the correct name and age of everyone met. 'Even if they say Smith, you still bloody ask them to spell it, as there's more than one way to spell Smith.' I explained I was working on a book.

'Right, then, I'll try and think of a daft name to give you.' He closed his eyes and thought. 'Brian Robinson. There, will that do you?'

Originally from Cheshire, he said, where he worked as a joiner and bookkeeper, he retired to Kents Bank five years ago. 'I've got to wear the bib when I'm gardening, see? Safety. Have you looked in the waiting-room yet? You should. There's some swallows there, just arrived from South Africa. You can see their nests. Only problem is, I can't get in there to paint the walls. No, I don't get paid to paint the walls. I just like to keep the station neat and tidy . . .

'PLEASE STAND BACK! PLEASE STAND BACK!'

I almost jumped in the air as he let out a bellow. He had seen the little train in the far distance and was now rushing up and down the platform, shushing children and pushing them clear of the track. I was wrong about him being annoyed by this football crowd outside his bedroom window. He was clearly loving it.

We all piled on to the train, filling the two coaches completely. I grabbed a window seat on the right so I could look out across the Bay and see where we were going to walk. The train hugged the coast and then glided out over the estuary itself, across the viaduct to Arnside, where we all got out. No guard selling tickets had appeared on the train, so thank you Virgin, or North-West Trains, or Northern Spirit, or whatever fancy name they now use. Not often you get a free train ride.

Arnside, a little 1930s leftover seaside town, was already up and awake, even though it was a Sunday morning. A baker's shop was selling bread and buns but the biggest surprise, as we trooped in a crocodile from the station, was when we reached the promenade to find an even larger crowd of people already there, waiting for the walk to begin. I estimated we were now a horde of some 300, all of us terribly expectant, terribly excited, Israelites about to cross the Red Sea, or similar, but not quite sure what was going to happen next, when, or how, or with whom.

All I knew was that our guide was going to be Cedric Robinson. I had spoken to his wife on the phone, who had given me the time and meeting place, but that was all. My wife was moaning about the crowds. She'd expected only a handful, that we would be in a small and intimate party of discerning walkers, not this rather noisy football crowd which was growing all the time as kids rushed around, shouting, yelling and being told off.

I looked around, trying to work out if Cedric was already amongst us. If so, which one? Must be getting on a bit, with a name like that. Old gadgies from my youth were often called Cedric, or Reg, or Stanley, or Cecil. I don't think I've met a Cedric in the flesh for 40 years, not since my Rochdale friend.

A whistle suddenly sounded and off on to the shore strode a very fit-looking man in jeans and short-sleeved shirt, carrying a rucksack and a stick. No words had been spoken, no commands given, no stewardess had given out safety instructions, no pilot had welcomed us aboard and said we would be flying across the sands at three miles an hour. Cedric, if it was he, had arrived out of the sky, or out of the sands, and was now off, leaving us like 300 startled and chattering starlings to work out what had happened, then scurry after him. Very Cumbrian. None of that messing around and mollycoddling, being bossy and self-important, charming or patronising, which you might expect on a southern guided walk.

We followed him obediently along the shore for over a mile, through some fields and a camp site, before coming out again on to the sands, where he blew his whistle, allowing the stragglers to catch up. He told us all to sit on a bank beside the shore and wait there while he went ahead on to the wet sand, just to check. When he came back, we all set off after him, heading at last across Morecambe Bay.

Cedric had been wearing trainers with no socks but had now taken them off and was walking in his bare feet with his jeans rolled up. Most people did the same. I was in my walking sandals, thinking the sand might either get soft or rutted and it would be less tiring on the ankles. My wife had bare feet and kept on saying I should do the same, it was lovely, take your stupid sandals off and carry them.

The seawater puddles were warm and clear, the sand only gently rutted, the various channels and pools quite shallow, so our progress was easy, though very quickly we had spread out into a long line stretching half a mile back. In the front were some older kids and teenagers, yelling and shouting, splashing and pushing, deliberately getting muddy and wet.

Ahead, looking towards the north, I could make out the hotels and houses of Grange-over-Sands, but we were walking west, as if going out to sea, following the line of the Lancashire shore, keeping parallel with the River Kent. It was impossible to see from a distance how wide or deep the river was. The light plays tricks on wet sand and you can't tell what is sea, what is sand and what is just wet, nor, of course, what is treacherous and what is safe. Cedric had still not given us any specific warnings or advice, apart from telling us to follow him. He seemed quietly confident, almost casual, but whenever we came to a deeper-looking channel he did go ahead and poke the water with a stout stick, and if people strayed too much, he rounded them up.

I managed to walk beside him at last and saw he was older than he'd first looked, aged about 60, but with almost a young country girl's complexion, ruddy yet rosy, with a barrel of a chest and surprisingly thin legs. His thick, greying hair was blowing back in the breeze.

'Look at his feet,' hissed my wife. 'Such beautiful feet. I have never seen such nice feet on a man. He's like a ballet dancer.' How come she's an expert on naked male feet? How many ballet dancers has she met? But I did agree Cedric had fine feet.

I asked about the route we were going to take and he pointed ahead to what appeared to be a line of little branches I'd not noticed so far, stuck in the sand, spread out at about quarter-mile gaps.

'I did the whole route yesterday. Always do, before a walk. The sand is never quite the same two days running, but mostly I take roughly the same route from Arnside. At the beginning of every season, I mark the main way with laurel, sticking bits into the sand. On the higher, dryer banks, the laurel will stay all season, but I usually have to replace the others.'

Laurel has traditionally been used, going back hundreds of years, to mark a route across the sands. The advantage is that laurel leaves do not fall off as the branches die, even when they have turned from green to brown, so they can still be seen from a distance.

'Turner spotted them,' said Cedric. 'You'll see them in his paintings. Not that I've got one . . .'

Later, I looked again at the Turner paintings – and he was right. Little twigs of laurel can clearly be seen, stuck in the sand.

We were still following the line of the River Kent, as if heading out to sea, but at last Cedric stopped and said we had come to a stretch where it was safe to cross. He sent a helper ahead, whom I had not realised was with us, a friend of his who lived locally, who stood further up the river at a point which we had not to go beyond. Then Cedric told us to follow him, as he waded into the river. We all felt tremendously daring and excited. The Red Sea crossing at last, or at least a religious pilgrimage, holding hands, humming hymns, feeling exhalted, putting our trust in Cedric, the good sea shepherd.

There were many dogs, held tightly on leads, and they were immediately swimming. Some of the younger children were also soon swimming as the depth grew to about three feet. There was no obvious current, which was reassuring, nor did the water get above any adult's thighs. Mostly it lapped gently around the knees, but looking around at the solemn, silent faces, steadily ploughing through the water, some moving slower and slower till we were stretched out in a long line, I could sense a few of us had mentally turned into Scott of the Antarctic or David Livingstone, battling through the snow or up the Zambezi.

Once most of us were across, Cedric blew his little whistle and told us to stop and wait, allowing the stragglers to catch up.

I caught up with him again and asked what he carried in his rucksack. Not much, he said. Just a pullover, a bottle of water and a two-way radio. The radio was a coastguard's radio, as Cedric was also a coastguard, with a range which stretched as far as Liverpool. 'I usually have a mobile phone as well, but it's on the blink.' What a shame. That would have been my northernmost sighting so far.

I could see in the distance what looked like a stagecoach coming across the sands towards us. Could it be Turner, wanting me not to print details of his Longman's commission as the tax man would be after him? Or was it a mirage and there was actually nothing there? As we got nearer, I could see that it was a wheeled vehicle – a tractor. It had now stopped and the driver had got out and was standing beside a twig of laurel, waiting for us.

'It's me nephew,' said Cedric as we got near. 'A good lad. He brings my tractor out to meet us here, in case anyone can't carry on. Oh, they all start off rushing and running, then they run out of steam when they get across the river.'

One little girl, aged about six, was being carried by her father, who himself looked pretty knackered. Cedric suggested she rode home on the tractor. But no one else took a lift, all determined to do it on their own feet, though some were clearly flagging.

I chatted to two young women in their twenties from Blackpool, both hairdressers. They had started off in their swimming clothes and were now shivering, but said they loved it. A surveyor from Halifax said he was doing the walk for the third time. A family from Blackburn were shouting for their little girl called Caitlin, so I went over and asked if they used to read *Punch*. They had no idea what I was talking about. I did a column in *Punch* for many years about my children, one of whom is called Caitlin, and people often wrote to say they had called a daughter after her. How embarrassing you can be, said my wife, refusing to walk with me any further.

So I walked beside Cedric. He still looked completely relaxed, despite being in charge of 300 people, some of whom had been a bit too boisterous at times. It was only slowly I'd realised how prepared he had been, how ready for any emergencies. Which can easily happen. He then launched into some scary tales of folks drowning or getting lost, or tractors totally disappearing. One recent saga, which took him ages to tell, was about a bloke coming out of Carnforth station, slightly the worse for drink, and deciding to walk on the sands. He was soon stuck in quicksand up to his waist, unable to get out. He shouted for help, but no one heard him, so he was there all night. Being a bit tipsy probably helped, in that he didn't struggle or panic too much, and he dozed off. In the morning he was spotted by someone who called the coastguards. It took them ages to free him.

How do they do that, Cedric? That was another long story. They use a sort of mud sledge to get alongside the trapped body, then a high-pressure hose pumps water into the quicksand to liquefy the mud until the person's feet can be freed.

In Cedric's 35 years so far of guiding people across the sands, he has personally encountered only one fatality.

'This gentleman, aged about 80, comes to our house one day, saying it's his life's ambition to cross the sands. He wants to do it before he dies. My wife Olive advises him to wait for a real good spell of weather, as it can be very cold and windy out there. A few weeks later he comes back – on a really horrible day, but he insists on going. He's on his own, but his family is waiting for him at the other end. Well, we'd just crossed the river – and he collapsed with a heart attack. We did get the emergency services, but he'd died by then. It wasn't really the walk that did it. The doctor said his heart would have given out that day anyway.'

Apart from that, there have been no accidents, though the previous week one of the walkers had lost her dog. They searched everywhere, then decided the dog had drowned, so they carried on with the walk. Several hours later the dog turned up, back at Arnside, having managed to find his own way to where they had started. Cedric often worries that some daft humans might try the same thing, or attempt to repeat the walk on their own, because he has made it all look so safe and easy.

'You just have to watch the tide coming in to realise the dangers. It comes in at the speed of a galloping horse. You can't beat it. And, unlike a galloping horse, it never runs out of energy.'

One minor problem Cedric often has is with unruly children and teenagers. 'Discipline is not what it used to be. I had a school party once and this kid was being very stupid, running ahead when he'd been warned not to. His teacher eventually told him off – and he came up and hit her! She was knocked to the ground. Other folks rushed to pull the boy off her. The boy then sulked, sat on the sand and refused to carry on. "Just leave him be," I told the teacher. I made them all walk on. Just when we were almost out of his sight, I could see him slowly getting up. He then hurried after us – and was as right as rain after that. No problems.'

We were now in sight of Kents Bank and I could see people waiting on the shore, ready to greet the heroes, welcome back the pilgrims. A few boys, those with a bit of energy left, wanted to race each other to the shore, which we could all clearly see. Cedric wouldn't let them, not until he said the way ahead was totally safe.

Waiting for us on shore was a motor car with its boot open. From it, a woman who turned out to be Olive, Cedric's wife, was selling parchment certificates, £1 each, as proof that we had walked the sands. Naturally I bought one, being keen on all memorabilia. And, after all, Cedric had not charged us a penny for the walk. That seemed remarkable in this day and age, when even the most minor service and humble facility has to be paid for. So who pays him, how does he live, how does he manage? I did notice, however, that one of the groups on our walk, the Kirkby Lonsdale Rugby Club, were organising their own little whipround and shoved a few quid into Cedric's pocket.

Olive was also selling some paperback books, *Sand Pilot of Morecambe Bay*. It was only when I bought one I saw that the author was Cedric Robinson. We all know that anyone can write a book. No qualifications needed, no licence required, no tests to pass. But, all the same, I was surprised. So I asked Cedric if he could spare some time for a chat, when he had a moment.

He was being photographed by various of our walkers, his autograph sought, his hand shaken. All were thanking him for one of the experiences of their lifetime. People actually used those words, which Cedric humbly and casually accepted without any vainglory or conceit, smiling and chatting.

Some of the people seemed to know all about him, treating him almost like a famous pop star. I had, of course, not been in Lakeland for the last six months, or read the local papers, or seen the local TV, so I wasn't aware till someone told me that Cedric had recently been acclaimed Cumbrian Personality of the Year by the Cumbria Tourist Board. Wow. He had even been interviewed on Border TV's *Lookaround*. Living in London, you see, you are cut off from the real world, from real people.

Cedric waited for everyone to finish with him, and for those going back on the train to Arnside to depart, and then said I should come back to his house with him, not stand in this deserted little railway station. He got into my car, I followed Olive in her car and we drove half a mile to his house, Guide's Farm. I thought at first it must be local usage, but no, it's the official name for Cedric's official residence.

The house itself, right on the shore, dates back 700 years and Oliver Cromwell is supposed to have stayed there, but Cedric has never found the proof. With it goes four fields totalling 12 acres, making it a smallholding rather than a farm. Inside, it was all low beams and handmade rugs. On the wall above the fireplace was a photo of Cedric in full academic gear, with mortar board, gown and hood, taken in 1989 when he received an honorary degree from Preston University. He's also got one from Lancaster University.

Cedric was born at Flookburgh, two miles away, where his father was a fisherman. He left school at 14 to join his father fishing on the sands, not by boat but by horse and cart, the traditional way of catching cockles, mussels, shrimps and fluke on the sands. (Fluke is a form of plaice, hence the name Flookburgh.) That could explain why Defoe didn't see any fishing boats out in the Bay. He should have been looking for fishing carts.

Fishing by horse and cart meant dragging nets behind the cart, over the sands, through any puddles, hoping to pick up any fish. When they hit deep water, the horse would start swimming, still able to pull the cart but not the nets behind, especially if they were full. One of Cedric's jobs when young was to let out the ropes pulling the nets till the horse had reached a point where it could stand up.

The fishing season began in the spring and lasted until autumn. In the winter, they did some farm work, or anything else they could find. It was always a precarious living, what with the tides and quicksands and horses who might bolt and panic, and also economically unreliable. Prices rose and fell and over the years fish got fewer.

By the 1950s, they had moved on from horsepower to tractors, though Cedric never found them as reliable. A good horse can feel the depth of the water, can respond to the slightest command, can sense a change in conditions, but a tractor is basically stupid – it just bashes on, till it sinks. Oh, the stories Cedric could tell about tractors sinking without trace.

It also became very competitive. Fishermen would tear across the sands in their tractors when a good catch was expected and end up almost fighting each other. Cedric never liked that aspect of the work.

Gradually, there was little work left for any of them. The cockles got fewer, or polluted. Was Sellafield to blame, just further up the coast? Cedric would not be drawn on that, on who or what was to blame. All he knows is that when he began, in the 1940s, there were 20 full-time fishermen on the sands. By the 1960s there were only five or six fishermen, all of them part time.

In 1961, Cedric got married to Olive. She was originally from Yorkshire, but had moved locally with her first husband. She had been left a widow after 13 years of marriage, with four young children. She went on to have a daughter, Jean, by Cedric.

By 1963, Cedric was no longer able to feed his family of seven by fishing and so looked around for another job. 'I had a pal at a factory in Barrow and he got me in there, but I only lasted a week. I hated it. I only knew about life on the sands. I couldn't stand it, couldn't fit in.'

He then worked as a navvy, digging trenches at Heysham, Lancs, for a nuclear power station. That at least was in the open air. He did it for one winter, hoping that in the spring he could do some fishing again. This was when he heard there was a vacancy as a guide and was encouraged to apply. He got the job and was officially appointed Queen's Guide to Sands on 17 October 1963.

There are two Queen's Guides, one who looks after the Kent estuary, which is Cedric's patch, and the other across on the Ulverston side. They come under the Duchy of Lancaster, hence the royal connection. Guide's Farm comes with the position and there is a salary of £15 a year, which has not changed since 1882. At one time, the 12 acres of land was more than enough for a guide to live on by farming, making up for the token salary. In theory, the guide was meant to be available at all times to guide travellers across the sands, but often these duties were ignored or neglected.

'The guide before me only organised crossings about once a season. He was a right character, chewed tobacco all the time and swore like a trooper. He got the job at 63 and lasted 13 years. I used to swear a lot myself, when I was a fisherman. I stopped all that once I started dealing with the public. Now I never swear.'

When he and Olive first moved into Guide's Farm in 1963, there was no electricity and the house was dark and very damp. The Trustees of the Duchy of Lancaster wouldn't make improvements at first, so Cedric had to pay to have electricity installed, though he was later reimbursed.

He kept cattle in his four fields, as well as some pigs, goats and ponies. They grew their own vegetables, and in the early years they were self-sufficient. Then came the slump in farming. 'You can't make a living on such a small plot today. I usually have three or four Limousin calves, which I buy young and feed on my own hay to fatten them up, but when I sell them these days, it's not worth it. I'll be buying some more soon, but it's really just a hobby. There's no real profit in it.'

But right from the beginning he was determined to make being a guide, even on only £15 a year, into a proper activity. 'I just felt so grateful to have this position and be able to live here, on the sands. That's all I have ever known, the only thing I really know about.'

In the first few years, he organised six crossings a season. Even after placing advertisements in the local press, there were rarely more than 20 walkers at a time. But gradually people heard about the crossings and his local fame grew. The local media came to interview him and found he was a good storyteller, natural and at ease. He has since appeared on countless radio and TV programmes, the names of which he now can't remember, though Olive has a record of them somewhere.

Today, he no longer has to advertise. The problem now is keeping the numbers down, not up. He averages 30 walks a season, which runs from May to October. At one time, they tried to limit it to a maximum of 150 per walk — until it was found that another 150 were tagging on behind, not subject to his guidance, who might do something silly. So the usual number is now nearer 300. His record has been 800, but that was with a special party. He also does occasional shorter walks, taking handicapped people in wheelchairs — as long as they have at least five strong men to help in deep water — or the elderly, whom he takes on his tractor, sitting them on specially constructed seats.

One reason for the enormous popularity of his walks is the present passion for sponsored walks. People get their family, friends or colleagues to promise so many pounds per mile if they complete a certain task, with all proceeds going to charity. It began with children, but now adults of all ages are doing it. Schools, churches, clubs, charities and groups from every part of the country bombard Cedric with requests. Olive takes the bookings by phone. For a group of any size you have to book up a season ahead. Individual walkers might get a date just a few weeks ahead, if they are lucky. 'I love every walk,' says Cedric. 'I am thrilled to be doing it, and thrilled when people so clearly enjoy it. I must get about a thousand letters a year from people thanking me, wonderful letters, some from disabled people who never thought they'd ever do such a journey.'

The idea of a book first came up about 20 years ago. A local man, aged 90 at the time, suggested Cedric should jot down his memoirs, and he would help knock them into shape. 'I'd never thought of writing anything till then. At school, mind you, I had been very good at spelling.'

He got started, with pencil and paper, but unfortunately the old man died before Cedric had finished, so he gave up. A few years later he went back to it, completed a rough draft and sent it off to a publisher, David and Charles. To his surprise, it was accepted. 'Even better — I got paid £600! Wasn't that amazing? I've been told since that it was too little, but I was very pleased, and still am.'

The book sold out, but is now back in print. Meanwhile Cedric has written another three, all about his life on the Sands. The new edition of his first book, the one I bought, has drawings by Olive, a foreword by Lord Cavendish of Holker Hall, a Trustee of the Duchy of Lancaster, and an introduction by Hannah Hauxwell, who also came to writing late in life.

All the same, I still found it hard to understand how he makes a living. The books can't sell in great numbers, and his share of them, even those sold from the back of Olive's car, can't come to much. The 'Crossing the Sands' certificates do help, but they are a recent innovation. In the early days, someone else not connected with Cedric produced the certificates, till it was pointed out that he should do it himself.

'Under the Trustees' rules, I am not allowed to charge for guiding. I don't mind that. I consider it a privilege to do the work. We have had hard times, when we didn't know where the next penny was coming from, but we've managed. I still do a bit fishing, just for the family, like, putting them in the deep freeze when we have a good catch. So we do eat a lot of fish.'

Three years ago, Cedric had a heart attack, much to the alarm of Olive. That was how her first husband had died.

'Cedric was carrying this load of hay and he suddenly said he felt a pain in his shoulder. He wouldn't do anything about it, of course. Said it was just muscular. It would soon go. Then he took to his bed, said he felt sick. He was eventually rushed to hospital – and later had heart by-pass surgery.

Cedric says he is now as fit as a fiddle. He could easily go out now and do that same walk all over again, no bother. But he does have trouble with his eyes, due to a detached retina, and a slipped disc. He minimises these problems, though, doesn't want to talk about them, and takes comfort from the example of his father, who had a heart attack at 63 – and is still going strong at 94.

'There was a bit in the *Westmorland Gazette* last week about me being Cumbrian Personality of the Year. They mentioned my father – and said he had died. So I rang him up, to warn him what was in the paper. And do you know what he said? "It should have one good effect. It'll mean the milkman might not come for his money next week!"

'Oh, he's a right joker, my dad. I'll tell you one of his jokes, one that always makes him laugh. There's this old man who rings his local paper to ask what the advertising rates are. He wants to sell something, you see. He's told the rate is £3 an inch. "Oh, that's far too much," he says. "I can't afford £3 an inch. I'm wanting to sell an 18-foot ladder . . ."'

Cedric laughed loudly at this, though he must have heard it, and told it, umpteen times. Ah, the simple pleasures.

He has never been abroad in his life. Doesn't want to. Even when he did National Service, he served in England. Nor has he ever been in a plane.

'I was offered a ride in a helicopter once. There was this walker I'd taken across the sands who asked me if I'd ever seen the sands from the air. He said how marvellous it was, how I'd love it. Turned out he had his own private helicopter and he'd come back in a few weeks and give me a ride. Well, I didn't know what to say. Out of politeness I said thanks, that would be very nice. I came back and told Olive that if that fellow ever rings, I'm not in. Anyway, he never did come back, which was just as well. No, I really didn't fancy it. I don't want to go anywhere.'

He doesn't know the Lake District either, despite living so near, and has never been to Carlisle. Or even Keswick. But he has been to London, twice, on quick trips. The first was when he was a lad, playing trombone in the Flookburgh Band and they got to a brass band final at the Albert Hall. The other time was when he and Olive and Jean, their daughter, decided to go to Crufts to show their dogs.

'We set off in the van at four in the afternoon, not knowing how long it would take to get to London. Shows how ignorant we are. We got to London in the middle of the night – and got lost.

'We saw this dark person – am I allowed to say that? Should you say black person, or does that upset them? I never know. Anyways, he was very obliging, put us on the right road. We gets to Crufts and find we're first in the car park, as it is only five in the morning, four hours before opening. We had a grand day, but no, we didn't see anything of London. We stayed at the show all day, then drove straight home in the evening.'

While he may not have seen much of the country himself, many of the country's personalities have come to him. In 1985 he led Prince Philip over the sands, sitting beside him on a carriage and four as they drove across. Just like ye olden days. He has also had the pleasure of conducting Melvyn Bragg across the sands and many other well-known people, most of whom he can't remember. 'Now who was that historian? A.J.P. Taylor, that's it. I had to give him a piggy back.'

One of the reasons why Cedric minimised his various operations, and also asked me not to mention his exact age, is a worry about the future. There is no retirement age for a guide. You go on till you can't go on. But, unlike recent guides, Cedric has created a large workload for himself, with 10,000 people a year wanting to be guided by him, people he doesn't want to let down. He doesn't have a work pension. He will be out of a job and a house, when he does retire. So what will happen? Where will he go?

'No idea. Perhaps I'll have to look for a tent. Unless I get some sort of council house. I suppose you could say I've helped the council a bit, bringing in these tourists all these years.

'All I hope is they can find me a little place round here. I never want to leave the sands. It's all I know . . .'

Chapter Fourteen

WINDERMERE

J.B. Priestley didn't get into Lakeland on his 1933 journey. The furthest north-west he got – using the term in the broadest possible sense, as spoken in Lancashire – was Blackpool. But almost every other traveller of note over these last 300 years did manage to make Lakeland. Accounts and guidebooks about journeys to or inside Lakeland have been published regularly since the 1770s, when tourism as we know it began. They were also being written at least a hundred years before that, but were not always published, as with Celia Fiennes. She did her main journeys through England in 1697–8, but they were not published until 1888.

Priestley's object was to write a book. That's why he did his journey. And nothing wrong with that. Defoe was a spy, amongst other things, reporting back to the government on what was happening out there. He had also been a travelling merchant, before going bankrupt. Then he became a journalist and knockabout satirist, which got him into prison. His journeys were therefore done for a variety of reasons, some of them still mysterious. As he was himself. He was born Daniel Foe in London in 1660, son of a tallow chandler. It was only around 1695, after he'd got himself a couple of little government jobs, one of them managing the royal lottery, that he added the 'De' to his name, making himself sound a bit more aristocratic.

Celia Fiennes went on her journeys simply for her own pleasure and amusement. She was a well-bred woman, granddaughter of Lord Sayle and Sele. Priestley had his chauffeur-driven Daimler. Defoe took coaches. Ms Fiennes carried out her journeys on horseback, riding side-saddle, travelling on her own apart from a couple of servants. She occasionally took her greyhound along as well. She stayed with friends or family or at wayside inns and pubs and was fascinated by the new, be it houses or trades, noting how mines were dug, how farms were run, how merchants operated. She referred to her journals as a book, not because she expected them to be published, but because she hoped they would be read by her friends and family in the future. 'Especially my own sex,' she added. Presumably to encourage women and girls to get out and about, to explore and expand the mind, as she had done.

She was very keen on prices, always mentioning them, a trait which most travellers find hard to resist. I have tried to avoid them, apart from that of the odd cappuccino, as prices so quickly become meaningless. In Chesterfield she bought two 'very good fatt white chickens for six pence the pair. I am sure they were as large and good as would have cost 18 pence if not two shillings a piece in London.' Well done, Celia. What a bargain.

In Carlisle she got herself ripped off, so she alleged. 'My Landlady ran me up the largest reckoning for almost nothing. It was the dearest lodging I met with and she pretended she could get me nothing else. So for two joints of mutton and a pint of wine and bread and beer I had a 12 shillings reckoning.' But she did get her own back on the said landlady, suggesting the real reason why she, a woman in her late thirties, travelling on her own, was not quite getting the sort of treatment and attention she thought she deserved. The landlady was 'young and giddy' and 'could only dress fine and entertain the soldiers'.

Celia Fiennes, like Defoe and Priestley, was not much concerned with people. Overheard remarks, perhaps, or a couple of lines describing landlords or people she met, but nothing in the way of proper conversations or interviews. Yet how people live, how they came to be here, what they are currently worrying about, is to me one of the fascinations of any sort of travelling. Celia had the chance, being well connected and sometimes staying with the quality, but she didn't do much about it. While in Lakeland, she managed to get herself into Lowther Castle, where Lady Lonsdale kindly gave her a meal – but, alas, they never met. 'Lady Lonsdale sent and treated me with a breakfast, cold things and sweetmeats all serv'd in plait, but it was so early in the morning that she being indisposed was not up.' Or was she avoiding her?

Other travellers to Lakeland over the years have managed a few first-hand observations on Lakeland's famous. John Ruskin, when he was only 11 years old, kept a diary of a coach journey in 1830 through the Lakes with his parents (which wasn't published until 1990). While in Keswick, they went to Crosthwaite Church, where young John spotted the Poet Laureate.

'We were put in a seat that would have been a disgrace to any church, it was so dirty, but we easily put up with that as in the seat directly opposite Mr Southey sat. We saw him very nicely. He seemed extremely attentive and what we saw of him we should think him very pious. He has a very keen eye and looks extremely like – a poet.'

Very witty, for an 11-year-old. When they got to Ambleside, they went to Rydal Church, hoping to have a gape at Willy Wordsworth. 'We were lucky in procuring a seat very near that of Mr Wordsworth. We were rather disappointed in the gentleman's appearance, especially as he appeared asleep the greatest part of the time. He seemed about 60. This gentleman possesses a long face and a large nose with a moderate assortment of grey hairs and two small grey eyes, with a mouth of moderate dimensions that is large enough to let in sufficient quantity of beef and mutton and to let out a sufficient quantity of poetry.'

A good description, though Wordsworth would not have liked the suggestion that he stuffed himself with mutton. He prided himself on existing on fresh air, fresh water and porridge, but young Ruskin was not to know that. Wordsworth went on to become a Lakeland tourist attraction himself, with people coming to his gate to catch a glimpse, or, if they were really lucky, a lock of his hair which his gardener would let the fans have, for a consideration.

Most Lakeland travellers in the early days were coming for the scenery and were pretty horrified when they reached the mountainous part of Lakeland. It was the people's houses that particularly horrified Celia Fiennes in 1698. 'Sadd little hutts made of drye walls, with no mortar or plaister, within or without.' They had no proper chimneys and were always freezing, which she thought was partly their own fault. 'It shews something of the lazyness of the people.'

But mostly it was the landscape that horrified. Defoe in the 1720s described it as 'the wildest, most barren of any that I have passed over in England'. John Brown in 1753, in a letter to his friend Lord Lyttelton, wrote that 'the full perfection of Keswick consists of three circumstances: BEAUTY, HORROR and IMMENSITY'.

William Wilberforce, while a Cambridge undergraduate aged 19 made a journey from Cambridge to Lakeland in 1779. He too kept a diary, which again was not published until many years later, in 1983. 'The lake of Buttermere is one of the most savage ones I saw.' Not something most visitors would claim today, unless they were referring to the problems of getting into the car park. Wilberforce also noted that there were piles of stones at the tops of mountains on which people had written their names. That still goes on. And so does petty vandalism. Coleridge in 1799, on a Lakeland walk with Wordsworth, found that when they got to the famous Castlerigg ancient stones near Keswick, someone had got there first and defaced them with white paint.

Some travellers, alas, never kept a diary, so little or nothing has remained of their journeys. In a Lakeland newspaper called the *Derwentwater Record* dated 4 August 1856, there is an obituary of a woman called Mary Messenger who had just died aged 93. In her lifetime, so it said, she made several journeys between Keswick and London – on foot. On one trip, coming back from London, 'she brought a stand table over her shoulder, an achievement which she frequently spoke of in her later years when speaking in disparagement of the effeminacy of modern manners and fashions'. I don't know how big a stand table was, but carrying any sort of table from London to Lakeland was pretty remarkable. Today, of course, she would get herself sponsored.

There is another more recent journey to Lakeland I would like to know more about, but the people concerned did not keep a record, or so they say, yet it happened relatively recently. The journey was undertaken in 1974 by William Clinton and Hillary Rodham, two young Americans who had just finished law school at Harvard. They came to England and worked their way north to Lakeland. After walking around Ennerdale Water, Bill proposed to Hillary.

Mrs Clinton herself confirmed this important event when I met her at the American Embassy in London in 1997. That's near where we live in Lakeland, I said. So where did you stay? She couldn't remember. A guest house, a farm, or what? She couldn't remember. Did you then go on to Carlisle, or what? No idea. All she could remember was that it was definitely Ennerdale where Bill had proposed. And did you accept at once? She shook her head and smiled. No, it took her about a week to say yes, then she did. I've often wondered why she hesitated.

* * *

Most visitors head for Windermere when they first arrive in Lakeland, which both Celia Fiennes and Daniel Defoe did, and each commented about the same local speciality.

'Winander Meer is famous for char fish,' wrote Defoe, 'found here and hereabouts, and no where else in England. It is a curious fish and, as a dainty, is potted and sent far and near as presents to best friends.' Celia Fiennes made a special trip to the lake itself to see the char being caught, but, alas, she had timed it badly. It was not the season. Bad planning there, Celia. But she did describe what they looked like – a sort of cross between a trout and a salmon, with reddish spots around the tail and fins.

There were professional char fishermen in Windermere up until the last war, but they have now given up, as the char has almost died out, though not quite. Last year in Buttermere I had fresh char for dinner at the Fish Inn – just a little one, caught by the landlord's son in Crummock Water.

Windermere the town, as opposed to Windermere the lake, did not exist when Celia Fiennes and Daniel Defoe were there, not till 1848 and the arrival of the railway. Wordsworth tried to fight the railway, fearing that the great unwashed from Lancashire, the 'advance of the ten thousand', would soon start flooding in. Today, Windermere, the slightly newer little town, is linked to Bowness, which is an ancient village, and together they make the biggest settlement in the Lake District National Park, with a population of some 8,500. So not at all that big. But Wordsworth was right. On a bank holiday there are around another 10,000 walking up and down the streets, six abreast, in fluorescent kagoules and baggy shorts, eating chips or drinking, waiting for their guest houses to open and their landladies to start the evening fry-up – unless, of course, she is entertaining soldiers.

Keswick, Ambleside and Grasmere are little better, but then only a first-time visitor would be foolish enough to want to visit any of them in the height of the season. Even so, it is still possible in just one hour to get away from any of these honey-pot centres, as they are now called by the Tourist Board, and be up on the fells, on your own, communing with nature, as lonely as a daffodil.

Apart from the masses, the railway also brought the well-off into Windermere. You can still see the splendid holiday mansions which the Lancashire merchants built for themselves. Most of them are no longer private homes, but the splendour lingers on, as at Brockhole, now the National Park Visitor Centre, and Belsfield, now a hotel.

Belsfield was built by H.W. Schneider, who owned ironworks in Barrow. He had his own little pier on Bowness Bay and each morning he would walk down to the pier followed by his butler, who would carry his master's breakfast on a silver tray. He would get on his own motor launch, *Esperance* (which can still be seen at the Windermere Steamboat Museum), and eat his breakfast while steaming down the lake to Lakeside. There he would get off and board a special coach on the Furness Railway, which he also owned. On the train would be his secretary, who had already picked up the morning's post, which he would have dealt with by the time he had got to his office in Barrow. Ah, those were the days. Who needs faxes or e-mail?

I don't actually care much for Windermere, apart from gazing at those Gothic fantasies and Italianate villas, wondering about the lives of the industrialists who built them, and also staring into the front rooms of the guest houses at the paper napkins all laid out, the sauce bottles lined up, the little bossy notices and at the twee front gardens. But that amusement doesn't last long. Then I start wishing I was in Cockermouth. Not just because Windermere is a totally tourist town, which Cockermouth is not, but because Windermere feels foreign. The voices sound Lancashire, not Cumbrian. I never feel I am truly at home until I have crossed Dunmail Raise. This, of course, has always been a geographic, economic and social division, with the natives to the north considering themselves a different breed.

So I quickly left the town and headed for Lake Windermere. Winander Meer, as Defoe and most ancients called it, is supposed to have been named after Winand or Vinandre, a Norse hero. All of the 16 Lakeland lakes except one have the name 'mere' or 'water' already attached, so you should never have to add the word 'lake' as well. With Windermere, I usually do, otherwise it gets very confusing. (Bassenthwaite is the only lake which strictly needs the word 'lake' as 'thwaite' refers to a clearing.)

Windermere is England's biggest lake, some ten miles long, and always seems so vast and so busy, with thousands of boats of all descriptions stretching as far as the eye can see, like an inland ocean. I can quite understand why first-time visitors ask what time high tide is, or when the next boat goes to the Isle of Man. Oh they do, they do.

At one time, there were flying boats buzzing around Windermere. Beatrix Potter in 1912 became so upset by their noise that she went public and protested, something she rarely did. She normally kept her head down and guarded her privacy, preferring to talk to sheep than meet her fans. But when she heard that a flying-boat factory might be built on Windermere, she wrote a letter to *Country Life*, even signing it Beatrix Potter, as opposed to Beatrix Heelis, her married name, which she usually hid behind. The factory was never built. But during the Second World War, just after she had died, Short Brothers built a factory outside Bowness to make Sunderland Flying Boats. Remains of it are still visible, but there are no flying boats on Windermere today.

The three ancient steamers are still there, *Swan*, *Teal* and *Tern*, which ply up and down the lake all day long, now even in wintertime, though with a reduced timetable. I took the first one, which was *Tern*, and sailed down the lake to Lakeside, following the route which Mr Schneider used to take. The railway station is still there, and they still use steam engines on three miles of track to Haverthwaite, but the Furness line is gone, so you can't get a train to Barrow any more.

When I got off the boat, I noticed two curious things which had not been there the last time I was at Lakeside. Celia Fiennes was always going on about 'Curiositys' and went out of her way to find them. In Manchester, while visiting a college, she 'saw the skinn of a Rattle Snake six foote long, with many other Curiositys, an anatomy of a man wired together, a jaw of a shark and alsoe a whispering trumpet'.

I'm not sure what a whispering trumpet was, nor was I sure about an Aquatarium, which was the name of a new building I could see beside the pier at Lakeside. Some sort of superstore selling posh rainwear? It turned out to be a giant aquarium, boasting 'Britain's biggest collection of freshwater fish'. I gave a small clap. I was almost at the end of my journey, but it was nice to see people still trying to excite us, even if it wasn't quite a world's first or world's biggest.

The building was purpose-built at a cost of £1.7 million and tells the story of Lakeland's water and its inhabitants, from mountain streams to Morecambe Bay. In one display I saw some small sharks. Pushing it a bit, I thought, though they do have sharks in the Atlantic. The best thing was a glass tunnel going under an artificial lake so you can look up and see ducks diving. Diving ducks are not an unusual sight, but what was curious, and fascinating, was watching them from below the water as they did their diving, seeing them tucking their heads in to dive down, turning almost into fish, then bobbing back up again at incredible speed.

The guide who took me around, aged about 30, used to be a schoolteacher, but he got fed up with the national curriculum, all the paperwork, all the meetings. He decided to do something completely different, anything which would get him to Lakeland, even though the pay is a lot less. Instead of wasting time looking for mobile phones, I should have been looking for more people who trained for one life then changed to another. That is a feature of our times as we end the millennium.

It was when I got out and was hanging around the pierside that my eye caught the second Curiosity – a notice which seemed to be offering submarines. A new fast-food outlet? Surely the Lake District National Park wouldn't allow that on the shore of Windermere? The notice directed me to a makeshift office in a portacabin where a man in a nautical pullover explained that they were doing submarine dives, three times a day, each trip lasting about one hour, price only £39.50, hurry,

hurry. Seemed a lot of money, but he said no, it was a bargain, compared with, well, what else can you compare a submarine dive with? A hot-air balloon, perhaps? I did that a year ago, also in Lakeland, and it cost at least twice as much. So I booked for the next dive. Then went to have a coffee. If I never returned, would my wife know what had happened to me? Or why? I'd said I was going to wander around Windermere and spend the night at the Lakeside Hotel in Newby Bridge.

The submarine, when it appeared, looked very weird, crawling along the surface behind the pier where the steamers dock – and incredibly small. It didn't look at all like a real submarine, but then I've never seen one, not in the flesh, though I have two model Yellow Submarines. Which I'm keeping. You wouldn't believe the price of a Beatles Yellow Submarine. In good condition, of course. Neither of mine has got its conning tower.

Five other people had also booked tickets and we were taken out in a little launch to where the submarine had tied up, towards the middle of the lake. The submarine captain turned out to be the same man who had sold me the ticket, name of Alan Whitfield, a real submarine pilot, he said, who had sailed submarines all over the world, diving for treasure, searching for missing bodies or exploring for commercial purposes, mainly in the Caribbean and the Pacific.

His submarine was called the *Mergo* and had been built in Finland in 1990 at a cost of $1.2 million. About the size of a German U-boat, said Alan. This was a trial season on Windermere, to see if there would be enough demand for submarine trips into an English lake. So you are a pilot doing a pilot, I said. I don't think he quite got that, as he was busy checking his instruments and stuff.

Business wasn't too bad so far, apparently, but it wasn't proving the attraction it would be in the Caribbean. I took that as a bit of an insult, being a Lake District lover. What have they got we haven't? Bloomin' cheek.

We all got into the submarine, with difficulty, lowering ourselves down a little hole, like Alice in Wonderland, going into another world, gingerly, fearfully, wondering if we had made a terrible mistake. Inside, it was shaped like a cigar, long and thin, arranged like a little bus, with seats for ten people plus the pilot. It had appeared very cramped, but once we had sat down and got our knees comfy, it felt quite airy and spacious.

Most people were middle-aged to elderly. One had even hobbled aboard on sticks. The man beside me, from Essex, boasted that he had spent ten years in the merchant navy, been everywhere, seen every sea, but had never actually been in a submarine. He was really looking forward to it.

It was pretty scary as we slowly began to submerge, imagining what might go wrong. Would water flood in? Would we get caught up in old ropes or cables? What if the pilot had a heart attack? Who would know what to do? Not to worry, said Alan, as if he had heard our worries. He pointed to a sonic screen in front of him which he said would give warnings of any obstacles in front of us. I peered forwards, but all I could see were a lot of dots. And if anything did go wrong, continued Alan, there was enough emergency air and water on board for four days. 'But it will mean crossing your legs,' he added cheerfully. 'There's no WC on board.'

We were down to about ten feet when water started dripping on my head. 'Oh my Gawd,' said the man beside me, the one who had boasted about being a merchant seaman. 'What's going wrong?'

'Just condensation,' said Alan, handing us a towel to mop up the water. 'It will soon stop.' Which it did.

After that, it felt fine. No sense of claustrophobia, which I had expected, or of speed or movement or depth. Or of anything, really. There was nothing to see out of the little portholes, just a sort of thick, fuzzy-looking dark-greenish water. No sign of any char, or fish of any sort. Not even tiddlers. Were they all hiding?

'Lots of plankton,' said the pilot, indicating bugger all, just more of the same soupy nothingness. In a hot-air balloon, the views all around are marvellous and exciting. Being in a submarine is about as exciting as sitting in an automatic car wash.

I then discovered why diving in the Caribbean or the Pacific has the edge on Windermere. In the Pacific, said Alan, you can have clear visibility down to 1,000 feet. In our lakes, it becomes pitch black at about 100 feet. No contest, really.

Once we got down to about 80 feet, we then started moving forward – at least, the pilot said we were moving forward. Even with his underwater lights on, it was hard to tell.

I eventually got the hang of the sonar screen and all the bleeps and could tell when there were shapes or objects ahead. We were on the trail of a submerged wreck, so the pilot explained. Gosh. We all strained forward, hoping something might become visible or understandable, apart from thicker soup or louder bleeps.

There are lots of wrecks of old boats and launches on the bed of Windermere, so the pilot said. What about bodies? Oh, quite a few of them as well. The Lakes have always been a popular place for dumping unwanted females. People drive up from Lancashire in the night, with the wife or girlfriend in a sack in the boot of the car. They take a boat out into the middle of a handy lake, then whoosh, over she goes, down to the bottom. A spot of cement is advisable, if you want to get back to Lancashire and pretend it never happened.

There was a recent case in Coniston where a bag of female bones, dropped some 21 years earlier, was found by some amateur divers. If the murderer had studied the lake charts properly beforehand, said Alan, he would have gone on for another 20 yards, then dropped the body. It would have landed in an underwater valley some 180 feet deep, where no ordinary diver would ever have found her. Instead she was dumped on a shelf.

The floor of every lake is as hilly as the surrounding landscape, with valleys and peaks, highs and lows. The highest range of mountains in the whole world, so the pilot told us, is not the Himalayas but the bed of the Pacific. A price of £39.50 didn't seem so expensive after all, not with all this information thrown in.

Wreck ahead, announced the pilot. We all immediately got really excited, straining to see through the pea soup. Suddenly we were right beside the body of Jenny. Not some unfortunate woman but the wreck of a pleasure launch which had gone down 55 years ago, after a collision. The searchlight picked out some damage to the hull. We could clearly see the polished wooden seats inside, and make out the name of the boat, but there were surprisingly few signs of rust or decay, almost as if it had gone down yesterday.

It was then time to head up to the surface again. Just before we emerged, we could see on the screen the surface of the lake around us, boats in the distance, hills beyond. It was slightly disorientating, like spying, because we ourselves were still unseen by anyone on the lake. Our periscope, or similar, was presumably sticking out of the water, giving us a sneak view of what was ahead. What a surprise someone in a rowing boat would get if we bobbed up beside them. We in fact bobbed up near the little launch which had taken us out.

As we glided along the surface towards it, I asked the pilot how his bookings were going. Only adequate, he said. He had expected more younger people to be interested, but it had been mostly the middle-aged so far. They, of course, are more likely to have £39.50.

The oldest so far had been a woman of 87 who celebrated her birthday on the bottom of the lake by opening a bottle of champagne. The youngest had been a couple in their early twenties. They had each looked nervous on entering the submarine, holding hands very tightly, but once they hit the bed of the lake, the boy turned to the girl and said, 'Wendy, will you marry me?' She said yes. Out of his pocket he took a ring.

I wanted to talk further with the pilot, but he had to take the sub back to its base while we boarded the little launch to Lakeside. I wished him luck with his venture, but he didn't seem optimistic. Overall, it was an interesting experience. Something I was pleased to have done, without wanting to do it again. But I'd like to see it continue. I'm all for Curiositys in Lakeland.

Chapter Fifteen

LOWESWATER

Loweswater is in the north-west of the north-west, the far bit of Lakeland, away from the main tourist spots. There is a lake called Loweswater, a little one just over a mile long, and a settlement called Loweswater, also very little, more of a huddle of houses than a village. There are two other lakes nearby, Crummock Water, which is two and a half miles long, and Buttermere, about the same size as Loweswater, making three pearls on the same string. There is also a beautiful valley called the Lorton Valley, much admired by Wordsworth. He was born in Cockermouth in 1770, the local town.

On 7 May 1987 I came up for the day from London for an auction at the Globe Hotel in Cockermouth, an ancient hotel on Main Street, at the other end of the street from Wordsworth's house. Outside the Globe is a plaque which says that Robert Louis Stevenson once stayed there, a piece of historical licence which drove me mad when I was doing a biography of RLS. He did do some Lakeland walks when young and wrote some little essays, but I could never find proof that he actually stayed at the Globe.

There was only one object being sold at the auction, a house in Loweswater, and I had promised my wife I would bid no higher than £80,000. If I got it, I would stay the night. If I failed, I would be back that evening. In those days, long gone, you could easily get up by train from London to Lakeland, take a taxi to lunch at Sharrow Bay, have a walk along Ullswater, then back in the evening. No chance now, with the lousy train service.

For the previous ten years we had had a country cottage near Caldbeck, John Peel Farm, which was very old, eighteenth century, and did have John Peel connections. We loved it dearly and spent about 13 weeks a year on holiday there when the children were young, but it was very small, rather damp and not very comfortable. And also very dark, which you have to expect in an old Cumbrian farmhouse, in bad weather or in winter. Wordsworth and his wife and children used to go to bed in the middle of the afternoon when it was really miserable.

What we wanted was a house with more light, so there would not be that feeling of skulking and crouching on dismal days, and more space, so we could each have a room to work in. While we were at it, we thought we'd like to be in Lakeland proper, not the outer, wilder Caldbeck fells, within sight of a lake, perhaps. Oh, and height, that was the fourth priority, so that we would have views and vistas. And fifth, we wanted to be part of some community, not as isolated and remote as we were at Caldbeck.

Most of us go through life with such fantasies, a list of essential elements we'd like when we eventually meet Mr Right or Mrs Right, or find the perfect job, the ideal holiday, the ultimate home. Most of us are lucky if we end up achieving half of one fantasy list. With the Loweswater house, almost everything was present – only a lake view was missing, though I had glimpsed a hint of some lake through the trees by leaning out of a top window. All the other elements were there, which was why there was such a good turnout for the auction. I was furious when the auctioneer said it was the best situation of any Lakeland house he had sold. I found myself bidding above my promised limit, but I got it for £92,000.

It seemed a fortune at the time, but it was going to be our home for the future, in which we would live and have our being. Only holidays for the first two years, as our youngest was still at school. Then we would move up full time. Maybe. Probably.

For the last eight years, it's been half and half, coming up in May and staying till October. This year it was the usual joy, seeing the familiar fells, rushing down to the lake, being welcomed home by our neighbours – except that there was less than a welcome from some councillor elsewhere in Lakeland. According to the local newspapers, he and others were being horrible to second-homers, turning them into hate figures who contribute nothing, push prices up, take homes away from poor locals and leave villages dead and empty in the winter.

Naturally, I don't look upon myself as a second-homer, or an off-comer, as we both originally come from Carlisle – okay, I was born in Scotland, don't go on about it. I like to think I am part of the community, do contribute, employ local people to help me with my guidebook to Lakeland, which I have always printed in Lakeland, never by firms abroad or foreigners in Lancashire. And haven't I just chaired the annual general meeting of the Cumbria Wildlife Trust and helped judge the Lakeland Book of the Year awards, not to mention all those talks to women's institutes, some of which attracted audiences of double figures? Anyway, I work up here.

I have what I call my office in both London and Loweswater (study always sounds too grand), which means I have two cheapo Amstrads, two printers, two phones, two fax machines, two sets of filing cabinets. My dear wife, in her office, uses only a fountain pen for her work so needs but one, as pens are portable – and does she laugh when we have an electricity cut at Loweswater, which we often do. She carries on merrily while I scream and shout and moan about all the pages suddenly wiped out, the work that can't be done. We also have two sets of clothes, two sets of trainers and wellies. Best of all, we have two sets of routines, two sets of walks, two lots of eating-out places, two sets of friends.

In theory, we could live anywhere in the world, as our children are now grown-up. With modern communications, distance is now dead. We did live abroad once, many years ago, when our children were pre-school age, trying out a fantasy which many people have, from beginner writers to Lottery players. You hear them saying it in the Lottery queues on Saturdays. 'When I win, you won't see me for dust, I'll be living on a beach in the West Indies or the South of France.' But they never actually do it, not once they've won. They realise they don't want to change their lives, apart from having a better house. Writers very often do flee, telling themselves they are voyeurs anyway, observers of the world, they can live anywhere.

We didn't go to the South of France or the Caribbean, alas. For reasons I can't quite remember we spent the first six months in Malta. After six weeks I was waking up and groaning oh no, not another perfect day. We then spent six months in Portugal, which was much better, but even then we were soon longing to be home. As a foreigner, you can never truly be part of the native life, so you end up with the ex-pats, who seem appalling at first, right wing and colonial, or drunks and bores, then you find some who are interesting and amusing. One year was quite enough. Thank goodness we got it out of our system when we were young.

In London or Loweswater, we don't feel foreign in either place, cut off in any way, either from local or mainstream national life. I quickly become a person living in London, or a person living in Loweswater. Now I am here, I become irritated when there are acres in the morning paper devoted to London people or topics. They're at it again, I groan, convinced that London is Britain, that only London matters, that what concerns folks in London must concern folks elsewhere. How wrong they are, how condescending. I turn over quickly when I see stories about spin doctors or yet another piece about Tina Brown. Doesn't matter who she is. The point is, only six people sitting in the Groucho Club are interested anyway.

We long to get away to Loweswater as each spring approaches, ticking off the days. The moment we arrive, I pick up the reins at once, feel settled, in the swim, at ease, at home, as if I have never been away. A six-month gap, in the country, is no gap at all. Many folks think we have been here all the time.

When autumn comes and it's time to return to London, we never actively look forward to it. It hangs over us rather than excites us. Then, when we do get back, it takes weeks to readjust, feel settled, become Londoners again.

It is, of course, a very privileged, self-indulgent, unusual sort of life, or lives, being able to combine the two. That's the first thing most people point out. The second is to ask a question. You do go on about Loweswater all the time, how you love it and that, till we're all pretty sick, so are you going to live there full time, as you said you would? Good question. I'm thinking.

★ ★ ★

Meanwhile, it's time for the Loweswater Show, one of the joys of Loweswater life. There are rural shows and games, agricultural and sporting events, held all over Lakeland every year, from early summer to autumn, have been for centuries, ever since the earliest Celts, Romans or possibly Norse settlers boasted they had the best sheep, the fastest hound or could run up the nearest fell quicker than anyone else.

Loweswater Show is always held on the third Thursday of September and is about the biggest of the smaller shows. Grasmere Show and Ambleside Show are big shows, with big arenas, but Loweswater is a mere hamlet. In our immediate Loweswater Neighbourhood Watch area, there are only 20 houses, with a population of no more than 50, though we do have a church and a pub, the Kirkstile Inn. The nearest village proper is Lorton, some three miles away, which has a church, a pub, a school and a shop. Then there is Buttermere, about five miles away, which has a very small church but two biggish inns.

Together, the three places form a combined parish with a total population, spread over ten miles, of some 800. But come Loweswater Show day, we increase one hundredfold, becoming a hubbub, a metropolis, a sea of people and animals, trucks and trailers, filling the little roads and fields for miles.

The moment I always look forward to is three days before, taking my evening walk, when the valley is still empty, still calm, then suddenly, in the distance, I spot the hint of a flag, the flash of a white sheet, and realise that the first of the massive tents is going up in the showfield. I get near and see that a small platoon has already arrived, soldiers preparing for Agincourt, arms and equipment laid out, ready for the main army to march in and do battle.

When I first arrived in 1987 and didn't know much about Loweswater Show, I rather mocked when I got my first schedule from Joan White, our neighbour, widow of a former vicar of Loweswater, who is chairman of the Ladies' Committee which runs the Industrial Section. The terms, for a start, seemed funny. 'Schedule' doesn't mean timetable of events, as I imagined, but a printed list of categories which can be entered. As for 'Industrial', this has nothing to do with industry in the machinery or manufacturing sense. It refers to making things in the old-fashioned sense, such as tea bread, brown cobs, plain scones, orange cake, apple plate cakes, three squares of gingerbread. That's just some of the 99 different categories in the Industrial section of the 1998 schedule.

If you don't know precisely what these terms mean, you haven't a chance of winning. I entered a brown loaf one year, as I was into home baking at the time. I thought it was brilliant, best I'd ever baked, but it was disqualified for not being the right size and right shape for a brown cob. There is a specific definition of a brown cob going back into local history, which I had failed to find out. If you are going to enter the Hand-Knitted Rugs category, which also comes under Industrial, then you have to know the difference between Hookey and Prodded.

Industrial is only one part of the whole. Animals of all sorts are in the majority, divided into endless subsections, followed by humans doing things such as running and riding. Altogether in 1998, which was billed as the 126th Loweswater Show, with the strap line on all the little posters boasting 'held in the most beautiful setting of the Lake District', there were some 184 different categories representing about 2,500 entries. Bigger on paper than the World Cup or the Olympics. Amazing how one little place can organise so much for so many, with not a computer or a paid organiser between them.

And for so little. If, for example, my little brown loaf had been deemed a brown cob and, oh joy, it had been considered better and tastier than all the others, I would have won £2. That's the standard prize money for a first in the Industrial section. Followed by £1.50 for a second and £1 for a third. In the Animal section, for something like a prize bull, the money is a bit bigger – £15 for first, £10 for second, £5 for third. Ah, but in all sections you also get a little rosette – yellow for a third, blue for a second and red for a first. That is the ultimate, what it is all about, what people plan for and prepare for and dream about all year, to have a red rosette which says FIRST PRIZE LOWESWATER SHOW. What bliss. My wife did it one year with a flowering hibiscus.

Before the 1998 show I went to see Jeannie Hope, general secretary of the show, a formidable woman who stands no nonsense. She lives alone in a small cottage in the middle of Lorton. When I entered she was sitting at a little table by her fire, writing out lists by hand and addressing envelopes. Beside her was a red telephone on a long lead which she had stretched across the room, over the Hookey rugs, by the look of them, ready to answer urgent calls, urgent moans, urgent queries.

I got off to a bad start by asking how long she had been the secretary and how old she was. 'You can whistle,' she said. 'That's what my grandmother used to say when people asked her age. But you shouldn't ask anyway. It's personal.'

Very Cumbrian, or at least very rural, both of which Jeannie clearly is, despite the fact that she was born in the USA, on a ranch in a remote part of Montana. Her parents were both from Cumbria and had emigrated to the USA.

'My father went first to find a job, then, a year later, my mother joined him. She went out carrying her wedding dress and got married out there.'

They had four daughters. Jeannie was the youngest. Two days after she was born, her mother died. The father struggled for a year to bring them up on his own, then an aunt came out from Cumbria and brought all four girls home to be brought up by their grandmother in Gosforth, near Seascale.

As a young girl Jeannie was in the Young Farmers Club and it was through that organisation that she met and married William Hope from Loweswater. For many years they farmed at High Nook, at the end of Loweswater lake. William died of lung cancer in 1975, leaving Jeannie with two sons but not much else. He had been a tenant farmer, not an owner, but she managed to find a little place to rent in Lorton.

'In 1976, a year after he died, I was asked if I'd like to be show secretary, as the man who had done it was retiring. I suppose they thought it would be something for me to do. I said no, I can't do that, I haven't got the knowledge. They came back later and said why didn't I give it a go, until they found someone else. So I agreed. Here I am, 22 years later, still doing it.'

As with most people who are active in the show, there are family connections going back many years. On her wall she has a clock given to her husband's grandfather in 1891, when he had been show secretary. But Jeannie had to pick up knowledge of administration as she went along, writing letters, dealing with officials, making arrangements. Organising the show is almost a year-round activity, with the first meetings taking place just a few months after the last show. That week there had been some drama because the printer who for many years had produced the Catalogue – which is what the programme is called – had gone bust. Jeannie had had to find a new one at the last moment.

What makes Loweswater the best of the smaller shows is that they have almost every sort of event and activity which is normally associated with the big shows, such as sheepdog trials, showjumping, fell running, hound trailing and now, in the last couple of years, Cumberland and Westmorland wrestling. Since Jeannie became secretary, Poultry has also arrived and is now one of the biggest sections, with a whole tent to itself. Other newcomers include Shetland Ponies, new last year, and Jacobs Sheep, a new category in 1998.

'Goats are a bit poorer this year. Not as many entries as usual. Our show is always late in the year and it doesn't tie in with the goats getting sheared. But every other category is going well. The Beef Cattle is better than it's ever been.'

What Loweswater doesn't have is any gimmicks, any fancy stunts or showbusiness attractions. At many county shows you now get funfairs, roundabouts, bouncy castles, T-shirt stalls and paid appearances by minor soap opera stars. Loweswater does not believe in such things. Everything, even the trade stalls, must have a genuine rural or agricultural connection.

Jeannie wasn't sure precisely when it all began in its present form – 1860s or perhaps 1870, she thought. They did miss a few of the war years. She wasn't sure either how many people they get every year. It's hard to estimate, she said, because some folks get free tickets, like the judges, and people go in and out during the day. 'It's not how many people come that's important. It's whether they enjoy themselves. That's what matters.'

Her biggest worry every year is always the same: the weather. The rain and wind have been so bad on some occasions that the secretary's tent has been completely blown away.

One of the entrants and judges in the past was Beatrix Potter, an expert breeder of Herdwick sheep. I have some letters written by her between 1930 and 1935 in which she writes about the Loweswater Show. In one she is thanking them for her five guineas prize for her sheep. 'And also for the Fell Dale prize which they obligingly supplied in brown grease.'

I was a judge myself one year, in the homemade-wine category. I was stotting long before the show had opened, having made the mistake of taking a sip out of each bottle, not realising there were 100 entries in all, and not realising that homemade wine is so much stronger than bought wine.

This time, the day dawned fine and it looked like being a good turnout. My wife was a judge, in the Children's Handwriting competition. She got a very impressive-looking red badge to wear saying JUDGE and walked in looking very important. I was only a humble entrant – not, of course, in her category. I had entered the limerick competition – subject: The Herdwick Sheep – and the photography competition – subject: Wildlife – hoping to do well for once.

The Industrial tent always looks bigger empty than full when the judges are doing their judging. They stand alone at each display on the massed ranks of the overladen tables, lost in deliberation, while the helpers keep quiet, knowing their place, keeping a record of the deliberations and then finally, when their judge has judged, pinning on the red, yellow and blue rosettes. They get placed on every prize-winning entrant, whether a sheet of a child's handwriting, a soft-feather bantam cock or a massive Limousin bull.

The animals are mostly outdoors, or under half-tents, lying around in their temporary pens or stalls, side by side, with fresh straw and very fresh-looking farm hands got up in their best, or what presumably must be their best. Some of the younger farm hands are dressed as if going to the disco, others simply have on their cleanest overalls and newest wellies. The animals look either bored or proud, especially those with a coloured rosette stuck on their bum. Close up, the bulls and the Clydesdale horses look absolutely enormous, yet for some reason they are not at all belligerent, intrigued rather than alarmed by all the attention and inspections. They know they are on show, expected to turn on a performance, so they loll or lounge around, stare at the people staring at them, or preen themselves like a Miss World entrant. The handlers seem oblivious to all the attention, even the ones wearing disco clothes, as they fuss over their charges, brushing and cleaning, making sure that coats are shining, hair gleaming, teeth glistening, tails teased.

The Herdwicks, a breed of sheep native to Lakeland, are the only animals where a degree of artifice is allowed. On show day, they get dusted with a reddy powder, haematite, which is brushed into their coats, turning them a deep ruddy brown. Rudded, it's called, a tradition which goes back centuries, used to bring out their highlights, accentuate their finer points.

The poultry is all inside, in a large tent all to itself, arranged in layers of little open cages containing about 400 hens of all varieties, colours and sizes, most of them crowing and gabbling away. The winners do a lot of strutting, looking decidedly superior. The handlers seem a different breed from the cattle handlers outside, wearing bulkier, untidier clothes, drinking from enormous flasks.

The most exciting events are the races, for hounds and for humans. There are three fell races, one for boys and girls, one for boys, and one for men, up the nearby Low Fell, then down the steepest side, which I have never attempted, even walking slowly. Then there are three hound trails. Crowds rush to a far field to watch them set off, and even more gather to watch the finish. Hound trailing is fox hunting without the fox, done in the summer off season when there is no real hunting. Two men drag an aniseed-soaked cloth over the fellside for several miles which the hounds then have to follow. There is keen betting on the results, with bookies from all over Cumbria and the north setting up their stalls, chalking up the odds, taking in the money.

I used to take my father-in-law to hound trails and he knew all the dogs and understood all the odds, which I never did, but I always loved the end of each race. The owners, using binoculars, catch a glimpse miles away of the leadings dogs and start yelling and whistling encouragement. As they draw into sight, the owners are hoarse and practically demented, willing on their hounds, waving fillet steaks, prime cuts of beef on tin plates, anything to tempt their hound to one final effort to be first over the finishing line. The dogs, as they approach, have such funny lolloping, galloping strides, yet they are moving like the wind, gliding over walls and thorn hedges, across becks and bogs. Then they, and their owners, collapse in a heap, all passion spent.

That day, I estimated more than 5,000 had turned up, an average to good number, and I'm sure they all enjoyed themselves. Even the losers, such as me. It's the entering that matters, taking part, having a crack, meeting old friends, keeping the traditions going.

After every Loweswater Show, I always think how wonderful, how natural – real country people enjoying real country activities, salt of the earth. Not like football, where money is now the motivator. Nor has sponsorship or marketing arrived. It is still the Loweswater Show. Not yet the Eddie Stobart Loweswater Show or the Jiffy Condom Loweswater Show. That could come, in another 126 years, but I doubt it.

It's not like a London gathering, with people showing off, moving in cliques, spotting the famous, taking social sides, making contacts. There are no mobile phones, no city slickers, no PRs or spin doctors. It would be hard to think of a gathering more different from that party a year ago at Number Ten Downing Street.

So why, then, now that the show is over, am I thinking once again about packing up and moving back to London? Have I not learned anything, by travelling slowly up through England?

★ ★ ★

J.B. Priestley, at the end of his *English Journey*, did a sort of summing up, pronouncing that there were now three Englands. There was Tourist England, which was Old England, the country of churches, inns, stately homes, places like the Cotswolds and Durham Cathedral, places the guidebooks sent American visitors to. Then there was Nineteenth-Century England, a land of mills and factories, railways and town halls, docks and slag heaps, dirty, sooty towns, most of them in the Midlands and the north. Thirdly there was New England, the modern England, a land of bypass roads, petrol stations, dance halls, wireless, Woolworths, cigarette coupons and factory girls dressed up like actresses. He didn't care for this New England. Its birth, he said, was in America. He found it 'lacking in character, zest, gusto, flavour, bite, drive, originality'.

He much preferred Old England and even sooty Industrial England, though he felt ashamed of all the people on the dole. At least all English people were free, there was no secret police, most English people were naturally kind and courteous – except for Londoners. 'I have noticed more downright rudeness and selfishness in one night in the stalls of the West End theatre than I have observed for days in the streets of some dirty little manufacturing town where you would have thought everybody would have been hopelessly brutalised.'

His main conclusion was that, despite everything, he loved England. 'I would rather spend a holiday in Tuscany than in the Black Country, but if I were compelled to choose between living in West Bromwich or Florence, I should make straight for West Bromwich.'

Priestley was living in London, in his posh Highgate house, when writing that book. But when eventually he tired of London, he didn't move to West Bromwich, or back to his native Yorkshire. I interviewed him in 1966, towards the end of his life (he died in 1984), and he was living near Stratford-upon-Avon, very definitely Tourist England, in what appeared to be a small manor house.

Neither Daniel Defoe nor Celia Fiennes attempted any summing up at the end of their journeys, but it is clear they both adored London, considering it the finest, noblest, grandest, most important, most exciting place to be – not just in England, but anywhere on the planet. Defoe described London as 'the most glorious sight without exception that the whole world at present can show'. I don't think many people would claim that for London today, least of all Londoners, who have grown more self-aware and cynical with the decades, knowing full well that there are many cities which are now bigger, richer, cleaner, better run and definitely with better public transport.

As for England today, I find it hard to categorise in the way Priestley did. Olde Worlde England is still there, growing all the time, bringing in the tourists, whether to stately homes like Chatsworth or to the Lake District. This area is booming, providing more jobs than all manufacturing put together – which isn't difficult. Industrial England has now long gone. Even in Rochdale or Salford, I didn't see it.

The New or Modern England is run on information technology, not steam and smoke, but its birth pains were mostly felt first in the USA, just as in Priestley's day. Unlike then, you can now find traces of it everywhere, not just in the soft south. Mobile phones, as a common sight, might at present peter out somewhere in the Midlands, but they will soon be in every High Street, as ubiquitous as computers, videos, camcorders.

Drugs are also everywhere, even the so-called hard drugs, and local papers in Cumbria regularly report heroin abuse in the smallest village, the most peaceful countryside, amongst both the deprived and the affluent. In Modern England, you are also just as liable to be robbed or mugged in the country as in the town. London no longer has the monopoly on nasty things. Few people leave their doors open in Loweswater any more.

Townies used to consider country folks backward, superstitious, simple, slow. Country people saw townies as degenerate, corrupt, adulterous, slaves to fashion, lacking moral standards. These long-held myths, which we believed about each other, or half-believed, or liked to believe, have all gone. Morally, we are all much the same today. Marriages collapse and children get abused or abandoned just as frequently in towns as in the countryside.

Ethnic England, which Priestley did not comment on except in those Liverpool docks, because it did not exist on any national scale then, is now part of our culture, accepted by all – but it is far from everywhere. Moving up through England, there are whole towns and cities, in the Midlands and Lancashire, where black or brown faces are totally the norm, yet elsewhere, such as Cumbria, even in the bigger towns, you can see none. The countryside, everywhere, is still white. I didn't see one black face at the Loweswater Show.

Then there is a Lottery England, which is spread fairly evenly across the country, an abstract concept in some ways, but we will be seeing some of the physical results soon in towns and villages up and down the land, at least in those places where they have been quick or smart enough to work the system and grab some of the various Lottery awards. Villages will have spanking new halls and playgroups, towns will have million-pound theatres or new bridges, urban areas will have multi-million-pound arts complexes, space-age centres, heritage developments, millennium monuments and other excitements. They might not, of course, all be quite ready for a grand opening in the year 2000, but they represent billions of pounds currently swishing around, the biggest creation of capital projects since the war.

On my journey, I only paused to consider two, the Lowry Centre and the Sustrans people, but there were others all along the way I could have investigated.

There is also a Rich and Poor England, but then there always has been, with the rich getting richer, as it always was – though not necessarily the same rich. Economically these divisions can be seen everywhere, in town and country, north and south.

If you have to divide or categorise England along the lines that Priestley did, then the easiest way is London and the Rest. The differences are not as obvious and enormous as in the days of Celia Fiennes and Daniel Defoe, or of Samuel Johnson, when London dwarfed the nation, but they are still there.

London is young. People are leaving, according to those figures quoted in the first chapter, except for one significant section – those aged between 20 and 30. They move to London as an escape, from parents, to have a fun time, a wild time. London has young fashions, young music, young markets, young entertainment. If you are tired of London, one of the things it means is that you have grown up.

London is liberal. Gays escape to London knowing they won't have to pretend. Others come to forget their social or religious background and conventions. London is more tolerant, more classless, more fluid than the rest of the country. London in turn gives a lead to the rest of the country, politically and socially, making it freer, more liberal than it might otherwise be.

London is cosmopolitan. It is blacker, browner, more Chinese, more Japanese, more West Indian, more Irish, more Australian, more Jewish, more ethnic than any other British city. For size of population, economic power, grandeur and allure, London might not be what it was when Defoe was a boy, but it is probably the most successfully multi-cultured city on the planet.

London is exciting. This is more arguable. After all, one person's excitement is another person's headache. While most people today would agree that London is liberal and London is cosmopolitan, though not necessarily seeing these as wholly good things, there are those who maintain that Manchester, Leeds and Newcastle are just as exciting: vibrant regional capitals, with their own media, own theatre, own cultures. True, but the scale and influence is not quite the same. In almost all the arts, the professions, finance, the law, politics, the media, London still leads. The national newspapers, the main publishing houses, the BBC – they are all there. The West End theatre, always on its last legs, still dominates the theatre world.

What has Lakeland got? What lots of unspoiled countryside has got – peace and tranquillity, beauty and majesty. I am truly stunned every morning when I walk down to Crummock Water and see the reflections of Melbreck and of the sky radiating on the surface of the lake, taking me with it, making me one with nature. Can't get that in Kentish Town High Road.

People have time, not just beauty, in the countryside. Time to talk, to stare, to wait, to commune. A conversation with a local farmer is a proper conversation, without point-scoring, without an agreed end. In shops in Cockermouth, you are treated like a person, not a check-out number, with real service, real courtesy, real interest. You can get jobs done, craftsmen will arrive, do their job, not rip you off. Very often the problem is paying them, as they are slow to send in their bills.

I'd rather eat out in Lakeland than in London, where the prices, the service and the food can be appalling. Driving in Lakeland – okay, you shouldn't do it – is still a pleasure compared with the horrors of London. Lakeland life is slow, but why not, as we are all going to the same place anyway. Lakeland life is traditional, with some things, some values never changing. And yet Lakeland is not out of touch. No one is, not if they don't want to be, not in this IT age.

So why am I going back to London for the next six months, not living here full time? It's not the obvious excitement I am going back for, as I don't go to West End theatre, have no interest or connection with the City. One visit to Canary Wharf was horrible and frightening enough for one lifetime. One party at Downing Street was quite sufficient, thank you very much.

In a word, I am going back for the stimulation. Not the stimulation of the famous excitements associated with London, but that of ordinary London life. Camden Town High Street, however scruffy and dirty, is stimulating to the eye and the mind, seeing all the faces, the colours, the shapes, the displays, the clothes, the postures. Walking a hundred yards to our local post office in London, I can have five brief conversations with people I know, people I have known for many years, some of them toilers in the same vineyard, but not all, and can come back with enough thoughts, enough fodder to keep me going for hours. In Lakeland, I can walk for hours and meet no one, see only lovely things, enjoy every lovely second, then come back with little new to think about.

Lakeland might be stunning and uplifting, but it's not stimulating. At least, I don't find it so. Wordsworth did, but then nature was his subject matter. I don't find that nature nurtures. It soothes and pleases, calms and eases. I need a fix of London, regular injections to stimulate the mind which I can hug to myself, then bring back to Lakeland and recollect in tranquillity, grateful that I don't have to live there all the time, suffer the dirt and squalor. In a way, I need the horrors of London to make me appreciate Lakeland even more. But I don't think I could stand it here full time, all the year round, living wholly in the country, living wholly in a country mind set. I love both lives equally. One is not better than the other. I am fortunate, at present, to be able to cram both of them in. I like to think it's like living twice.

But what might happen in the future, when I can't have both, when health or whatever might force me to choose one, and only one? What agonies. It would probably have to be London, alas.

Right, it's late October. The nights are drawing in. The clocks are going back – or is it forward? I can never remember. I know that in the morning I am going back to London. In order to return to Loweswater . . .